NEBRASKA GOVERNMENT AND POLITICS

EDITED BY

ROBERT D. MIEWALD

Nebraska Government & Politics

UNIVERSITY OF NEBRASKA PRESS

LINCOLN AND LONDON

The paper in this book meets the
guidelines for permanence
and durability of the Committee on
Production Guidelines for
Book Longevity of the Council on
Library Resources.

Library of Congress Cataloging
in Publication Data

Main entry under title:

Nebraska government and politics.

Bibliography: p.
Includes index.

1. Nebraska – Politics and
government.
I. Miewald, Robert D.
JK6616.N43 1984
320.9782   83-3684
ISBN 0-8032-3078-8
ISBN 0-8032-8113-7 (pbk.)

TO ADAM C. BRECKENRIDGE

SCHOLAR, TEACHER, ADMINISTRATOR AT THE

UNIVERSITY OF NEBRASKA—LINCOLN

1946–81

CONTENTS

Preface

It is easy for people, including natives, to jump to conclusions about the Nebraska political experience. This was brought home to us political scientists at the University of Nebraska–Lincoln when we were visited by the leader of a European socialist party. He observed that he had added Nebraska to his tour because of the public ownership of electric utilities: he wanted to learn more about this island of radicalism. But he was not the first to find that things in Nebraska are not always what they seem, and we suspect that rabid reactionaries in the state have also been frustrated in their attempts to gain converts to their crusades. Nebraska's politics, we may all be thankful, is not as extreme or as violent as its weather. The state's foundation of common sense and quiet moderation, however, can be misinterpreted as something else.

We have to admit at the beginning, then, that we are unable to report on the high drama of glamorous political dynasties, or the intricacies of ethnic politics, or the outrages of world-class scoundrels, or the colorful antics of public buffoons. Perhaps the lack of these leaves us with the politics of dullness. But before making that judgment, we should consider the possibility that mainstream politics in the United States has degenerated into a branch of the entertainment industry. Nebraska's way, although superficially unspectacular, is probably closer to the way that self-government is supposed to work.

In any event, we are not convinced that the topic is unexciting. If comparisons are to be made, Nebraska's politics is much closer to its topography. For travelers on Interstate 80, the state is an endless stretch, devoid of many landmarks, to be gotten across on the way to someplace more interesting. But those who spend a little time on the backroads will discover subtle difference in an everchanging landscape. So it is with the political system. Political scientists from other states note the Unicameral and then move on. They overlook other peculiar features of the state's government. The ways in which Nebraskans elect their legislators, impeach their officials, manage their natural resources, and set their tax rates, among other items, can be added to the list of governmental oddities.

We hope that this guidebook will do justice to the rich texture of the state's government and politics. If it does, then the reader may be a little more hesitant in making easy generalizations about Nebraska.

In this venture, we also hope that we are continuing the tradition established by the dean of Nebraska political scientists and the man to whom this book is dedicated: Professor Adam Carlyle Breckenridge. "Breck," as he is known to people throughout the state, came to the University of Nebraska in 1946, after earning a Ph.D. at Princeton and serving during the war in the U.S. Navy. Until his retirement in 1981, he devoted a productive career to serving the best interests of the university, the state, and his profession. He became an institution within the institution, holding at various times the positions of chairman of the department, dean of faculties, director of international programs, acting dean of libraries, vice chancellor for academic affairs, and interim chancellor. But despite all these important administrative duties, his proudest title was still that of professor of political science, and when his stints in the Administration Building were over, he always returned to the classroom and to his research.

At major universities, when so distinguished a member as Professor Breckenridge retires, an elegant collection of scholarly essays, known as a Festschrift, is often prepared by friends, colleagues, and former students. Such volumes look impressive, but they frequently remain unread, even by the recipients of the honor. We knew that Breck, with his intense dislike of pomposity and academic gamesmanship, would disapprove of a project intended only for his glorification. We proposed, instead, this volume, which we hope will be read and will help to carry on Breck's mission of thirty-five years—to teach the people of Nebraska about their government.

Finally, we must express our great appreciation to several people who read all or part of the manuscript and shared with us their knowledge about state government and Nebraska. Russell W. Maddox, Don Pieper, Joseph Steele, Patrick O'Donnell, Andy Cunningham, and Don Leuenberger provided many comments and criticisms that prevented us from making errors in fact and emphasis. And as always, we are grateful to Velma Schroeder, Lori Davison, and Jackie Leger for their typing of several versions of the manuscript. Naturally, the responsibility for the final text is entirely our own.

NEBRASKA GOVERNMENT AND POLITICS

ADAM C. BRECKENRIDGE

ONE

Nebraska State Government: An Introduction

A rational reader probably needs some reassurance that the investment of time in a book on state government, even one's own state government, is worthwhile. There was a time, not too long ago, when scholarly authorities told us that the states were obsolete, that the national government and the cities were the only units that mattered. An intermediate level, if needed, should be freed from the boundaries created by historical accident and turned into an administrative link between Washington and the local communities. More conservative critics, alarmed by federal involvement in a variety of state and local activities, were inclined to believe that the virtual elimination of the states, as independent political forces, had already occurred.

Even friends of the states must be somewhat disappointed by the rather lackluster record of performance compiled by those governments. The idea that the several laboratories of democracy would lead to constant improvements in the art of government has not been realized. Few states, until recently, have been particularly venturesome and many of them were content to carry out a limited number of traditional functions pertaining to the protection of persons and property. Even if the state has now taken on a greater variety of governmental assignments, these additions have not always been enthusiastically accepted.

State governments may not have much to say about the great issues that shake and shape our times—war or peace, prosperity or economic collapse—nor do they play an immediate role in many matters that intrude on our daily lives, be it unleashed dogs or unfilled chuckholes. But the state is all around us. It is state government that takes official notice of our birth and authorizes the means for disposing of our mortal remains. In between, the state channels our behavior in a hundred different ways. Although the state's policy makers may often seem to be an unexciting lot and the issues they wrestle with appear rather mundane, it is because of their actions that we are educated, that we can safely drive the highways, that convicted criminals are locked away. Moreover, these leaders must be sensitive to the cost of all the many services. So while the subject matter of state government may strike some as being fairly commonplace, the work it does is essential to our well-being.

Whatever the present function of the states, they also continue to figure prominently in the plans of both liberal and conservative political leaders. The Reagan administration's "New Federalism" could more accurately be called the "newest federalism," since it is only the latest in a line of proposals for revitalizing the state and farming out functions now dominated by Washington. The unanswered question is whether states are willing and able to assume a larger part or whether they are still, as one writer once put it, the "fallen arches" of the federal system.

What then is the future of state government? In the view of some writers, the words *states* and *future* do not go together. One of the sharpest indictments of state government by a reputable scholar was written in 1965 by Professor Roscoe Martin:

Rural orientation, provincial outlook, commitment to a strict moral code, a philosophy of individualism—these are the components of the state mind. If they evoke memories of the oil lamp and the covered bridge, why this very spirit of nostalgia is also characteristic of the state mind. One of the most unhappy features of the state (and its leaders and institutions) is the intermittent and imperfect contact with the realities of the modern world.

The rural-oriented, anachronistic nature of states, Martin felt, has incapacitated the leadership: "State leaders are by confession cautious and tradition-bound, which ill equips them for the tasks of modern government."[1]

A superficial observer might argue that Martin had said all there was to say about Nebraska government. However, in the following pages, my colleagues from the political science department at the University of Nebraska, in a brief but comprehensive survey of developments in the years since the World War II, lend little support to Martin's criticisms. Nebraska is certainly rural, and probably conservative, too, by most people's definition. But Nebraskans are not guilty of blind and stubborn resistence to the twentieth century. Within the brief period under discussion, readers will note a pattern of constant change within a basically stable system. Motion and stability are the fundamental themes of Nebraska government. Has the state changed too little and too late and is it moving in the right direction—these are questions the readers will have to answer for themselves.

Perhaps the best way to get some handle on such questions is to view Nebraska comparatively. To what extent is it like and unlike other states? The remainder of this opening chapter will be devoted to reviewing the several chapters with an eye to the similarities and dissimilarities of Nebraska institutions and political behavior in comparison with the rest of the nation.

* * *

In his remarks on the state constitution, Bruce Winter carefully examines the cherished foundation of all governments in the United States: the written constitution. Nebraska's is one of the older documents; despite several amendments, it is still the constitution of 1875. Although Americans are keen on celebrating anniversaries, Nebraskans will not remember any public ceremonies during the centennial of their constitution. This is probably because state constitutions are hard to become emotionally involved with. They tend to be long-winded limitations on what government can do rather than positive grants of power. Although not the wordiest of constitutions, Nebraska's is still fairly detailed and written in legalistic language not likely to stir the souls of the citizens.

1. Roscoe C. Martin, *The Cities and the Federal System* (New York: Atherton, 1965), pp. 77–79.

Government reformers have advised Americans over the years of the need to modernize state constitutions if those units of government are to compete effectively within the federal system. Although conventions are provided for in most of the states, their convening has been a rare event. At Nebraska's last constitutional convention in 1919–20, the result was not a "new" document, but only a series of amendments. We can probably conclude that state constitutions, whatever their defects, have accumulated around their various provisions a number of special interests with a stake in the status quo and so inertia is the dominant principle. Piecemeal adjustments, proposed by the legislature, have been the tradition in most states, although Nebraska tried something different in 1970 with the creation of a constitutional revision commission.

* * *

The overwhelming influence of the federal model can be seen in the traditional three branches. The states went a step further in preventing the centralization of governmental power by requiring the election of a number of executive officers. From the beginning, the office of governor was perceived as the most important of these, but the common perception did not necessarily translate into effective control of the executive branch of state government. There has been a long-term trend towards strengthening the office of governor and, by most objective measures, Nebraska has gone as far or further in this direction than a majority of states. As Susan Welch shows in her chapter on the executives of state government, formal power is only part of the story. A governor must also want to play the role of a strong executive. In this broader area, firm measures of executive power are lacking, but Welch suggests that the political climate of the state has not encouraged a tradition of forceful gubernatorial leadership.

The relationship between the governor and the legislature in Nebraska has some unusual features because of nonpartisanship. The absence of a formal party organization in the legislature, as is found at the national level and in all other states, has created a novel set of problems in executive-legislative relations. The matter has become an even more intriguing research question with the rise of tacit partisanship within the legislature. That is, party affiliations are no secret;

yet it is not always clear how such attachments translate into support for the programs of the governor.

* * *

It is rare for someone interested in state government who meets a Nebraskan to not inquire about the "one-house legislature." Unique among the states, Nebraska has had, since 1937, a unicameral structure instead of the traditional bicameral model. Although contemporary critics believed this bold experiment would be a failure, time has proved them wrong. The legislature, popularly known as the "Unicameral," rates quite well within the state and elsewhere in the nation. Appraisals done independently give it generally good marks in comparison with other state legislatures. At the same time, the advocates of unicameralism were mistaken in their belief that their innovation would be widely copied. Although states have occasionally sent delegations to Lincoln to observe unicameralism in action, other Americans apparently remain unconvinced of the value of such a change.

Dr. Jack Rodgers, the long-time director of research for the legislature, and Professors Robert Sittig and Susan Welch point out many of the special features resulting from a unicameral system. The main point of their chapter, however, is that the major factor in legislative behavior and policy outcomes is not unicameralism but nonpartisanship. The absence of party labels, as just mentioned, colors the interaction of the legislature with the executive; it also affects the connection between the citizens and their elected representatives. Such an effect, of course, was the intention of the early advocates of nonpartisanship, but the actual results have not been in the anticipated direction. Parties, whatever their faults, do give voters some guidance in making electoral decisions, and that is missing from the Nebraska system. Furthermore, those good government reformers of a generation or more ago would be appalled by the steady decrease in voter participation that is associated in Nebraska with nonpartisanship. Thus, while the unicameral feature of the legislature is no longer controversial, the nonpartisan aspect certainly deserves further scrutiny by scholars, officials, and citizens.

* * *

Like most states, Nebraska has had to move toward improving its judicial system. The traditional patchwork structure, combining both statewide and local elements, yet without a single source of direction, has been thoroughly overhauled by a series of reforms beginning in the 1970s. This has resulted in a ''unified court system'' under the general direction of the supreme court. That quaint but questionable relic of frontier life, the justice of the peace, was eliminated at the same time.

Under the auspices of the legal profession, court reform has been something of a national project, with innovations passing among the states. As Robert Sittig points out, Nebraska has borrowed from the Missouri Plan for selecting judges and the California Plan for policing the qualifications of sitting jurists. Still, no two state court systems are identical and Nebraska retains some special features. Especially noteworthy is the involvement of the courts in the process of impeachment of public officials.

It is a safe prediction that Nebraska's courts will, in the next few decades, undergo more change than the other branches. This is not only because of the rapidly increasing load of criminal and civil cases. A growing role for all courts is that of umpire among contending groups for a share of shrinking public resources. In Nebraska, as described in the chapter on intergovernmental relations, this is illustrated by the agonies involved in finding a suitable formula for the distribution of state aid to local government; the supreme court has been at least as important as the governor and legislature in this ongoing drama.

* * *

Nebraskans share in the typical American ambivalence about their public service. Bureaucrats and bureaucracy are no good, while more and more public services are being demanded. And who else but the dreaded bureaucrats can deliver the desired goods? In the period under discussion, government has become a growth area, both in terms of financial resources and personnel, yet few candidates have run on a platform of ''big government.'' Nebraska, it must be admitted, was never in the forefront in the expansion of public services, but officials could not ignore the national mood of the times, when there was a general feeling that government could make a positive difference in the lives of its people. Even if state policy makers did not gladly initiate programs, they found themselves under great pressure from the federal government to participate in a wide variety of aid programs.

Political scientists have concluded that, in terms of overall government activity, the specific features of state government have little bearing on policy outputs. Therefore, an inventory of state activity in Nebraska will show most of the bureaus are doing the same work in the same way as those in other states. By the early 1980s, government growth was slowing, perhaps temporarily, for a number of reasons— taxpayer resistance, the resurgence of the conservative movement in American politics, a realization that there are limits to what government can do, even a general sense of pessimism about whether any human organization can accomplish much in solving some apparently intractable problems. But this does not mean that the battle with bureaucracy is over, for governors and their allies are more interested than ever in finding the mechanisms for making sense out of and asserting control over the complexity of public administration.

In this quest, as Michael Steinman argues, Nebraskans are in the American grain, for they are probably not completely serious in their expressions of desire for a streamlined, thoroughly efficient administrative machine. No less than the federal government, the states have become beneficient dispensers of dollars to a wide spectrum of recipients. Since we are all getting some of these payoffs, few of us can afford too drastic a change in the existing pattern of distribution.

Nebraska has had periodic fits of enthusiasm for government reorganization, and the state record is as good, or as bad, as that in the rest of the country. State government remains a patchwork of over a hundred bureaus, commissions and quasi-independent units orbiting around those who put the budget together each year. Their continued existence and the whys and wherefores of their interrelationships are more functions of political power and historical accident than prescriptions of a rational blueprint. So it was in the beginning and so it shall probably remain.

* * *

In theory, democracy is based on broad popular participation so that the citizens can determine what government does or does not do. In our reveries about the beauties of "grassroots" government, we Americans like to claim that such participation is most effective at the state and local levels. Theory aside, however, effective participation depends on two major ingredients. First, government must be structured in such a way that avenues of participation exist. Second, and more important, the citizens themselves must know about their rights and feel that participation, which is not without some cost, makes a difference. The way in which people view their political system and their role within it is what political scientists call the political culture of a society.

In his chapter, John Comer reviews the empirical evidence, compared to folksy speculation, about the political culture of Nebraska. Survey data indicate that citizens may be moving toward a more assertive posture vis-à-vis their government, although in the most important area, voting turnout, Nebraskans have compiled a less than exemplary record, especially since statewide executive elections were changed to nonpresidential years. In another aspect of political culture, Comer concludes that even though Nebraska is often classified as one of the staunchest Republican states, party affiliation is not deeply rooted.

The discussion of political culture in Nebraska is greatly aided by our access to the Nebraska Annual Social Indicators Survey (NASIS), a yearly telephone poll of a stratified sample of Nebraskans. This service allows social scientists to keep their fingers on the pulse of the state. The major drawback is that comparable data for other states are not readily available. If we had similar statistics for all states, we would be able to have a clearer picture of the mysteries of political life in the United States.

* * *

Nebraskans share with other Americans a growing sense of frustration with the structure for financing state and local services. At one time, all states, cities, counties, and school districts relied heavily on the property tax, both personal and real. Nebraska resisted change in this area longer than most states and when tax reform could no longer be avoided, in the 1960s, the result was a turbulent time that is still not over. In fact, as John Peters shows, the state is still heavily dependent on property taxes as a component of total state-local revenue. Recent sessions of the legislature have been preoccupied with lessening the local property tax load while coming up with an acceptable formula for the distribution of replacement aid from the state to local governments.

Peters also describes Nebraska's contribution to the "science" of public finance in the form of the Board of Equalization and Assessment. This body, composed of the governor and four other state officers, had until 1984 the authority to set the state's income and sales tax rates. Criticism of this mechanism reached new heights during a period of fiscal exigencies in the early 1980s, and in 1983 the legislature reassumed the job of setting taxes. The experiment illustrated, if we needed the proof, that there is no happy way for politicians to raise taxes.

* * *

As much as any state, Nebraska has stressed the local element of state government. Robert Miewald, in a chapter on local government, and Keith Mueller, with his description of problems in intergovernmental relations, speculate on the strengths and weaknesses of the complex arrangements of the political units at the substate level. There can be no doubt that Nebraska has quantity at this level. The quality of the service provided by a large number of independent units, however, has become a significant political issue.

By most measures, Nebraska ranks as a highly decentralized state. That is, units of local government still bear a heavy responsibility for providing essential services with relatively little state supervision. But this attitude of localism is being challenged and consolidation or other forms of interlocal cooperation are being adopted, following varying degrees of coercion from the state and federal governments. The creation of natural resources districts, which consolidated many (but far from all) water-related special districts, is one example of this trend. School district reorganization provides a more controversial case. As Mueller argues, local governments are going through a period of considerable stress and some of the weaker units will not survive.

* * *

It has become increasingly popular to prepare lists of states and cities according to their good or bad features, such as the enumerations of the "most liveable" communities. We political scientists are generally suspicious of such lists because they are hopelessly subjective. Moreover, we may have learned a lesson from the past, when, as a profession, we were ready to lecture Americans about their political deficiencies and, indeed, to flunk whole jurisdictions because they did not live up to our lofty expectations and preconceived notions of "good government." We contributors to this overview of Nebraska government do not presume to grade the state, at least not on a strict curve. Most of the writers, I am sure, would be willing to give the state a passing grade in the specific area they considered. But we leave it to the reader, whether or not a Nebraskan, to make the ultimate evaluation.

TWO

The State Constitution

Americans have always placed a great deal of emphasis on a single written document as a foundation of all governmental action. This no doubt stems from the unhappy experiences with the British Constitution, which led to the Revolutionary War. That constitution was not a single document; then as now, it was a rather loosely defined collection of common law court decisions and practices, certain acts of Parliament, ancient documents such as the Magna Carta, and an accretion of sundry customs and usages. It was too vast in scope, subject to too much latitude in interpretation, and too indefinite in application.

The founding fathers wanted a constitution that would avoid all those deficiencies. They chose to write a comprehensive, integrated document that stated specifically the rights of citizens, the limitations on governmental power, the creation of governmental offices, and the authorization of governmental functions. All this was spelled out clearly and concisely so that it could be read and understood by anyone who might be concerned. As a result of this historical experience, when average Americans today speak of the constitution, they are usually referring to the document written in 1787, approved in 1788, and amended twenty-six times since then. Likewise, a similar image of a single document comes to mind when the phrase "state constitution" is used.

That single document is the core—admittedly, the essential core—
of a constitutional system, but any blueprint of government has to be
made to "work" and to be open to change. The words of an eigh-
teenth-century English statesman are still relevant here: "By constitution, we mean . . . that assemblage of laws, institutions and customs,
derived from certain fixed principles of reason, directed to certain
fixed objects of public good, that compose the general system, according to which the community hath agreed to be governed."[1]

This statement brings us closer to reality, for it recognizes a comprehensive operating system; it includes the practice as well as the
written word as determinative. The phrase "to which the community
hath agreed to be governed" introduces the necessary political ingredient. Using the same comprehensive sense to describe the Nebraska
Constitution, we can then say, "It is: the written Constitution of 1875,
as amended and as interpreted by the courts; the aggregation of
legislative acts, ordinances, and resolutions, plus executive rules and
regulations issued in pursuance of legislative acts; customs and usages
evolving from constitutional, governmental, and political experiences; the established agencies of Nebraska state and local government and their interrelationships; all pursuing what seem to be beneficial goals towards what is perceived to be in the public interest,
according to the political desires and aspirations, and the accepted
political practices of the citizens of the state."

Perhaps it might be helpful to think of the constitutional system this
way: the written constitution of Nebraska sets up a legal framework of
governmental institutions, limitations on the powers of these institutions, and a bill of rights, which guarantees for citizens protection
against arbitrary and capricious governmental actions. The courts
interpret and enlarge the scope of the constitutional text and thus
create the operating rules of the written constitution. But the citizens
of the state have the ultimate power to describe how the legal, written
document will work and develop. They do so as they express their will
through the political process—through their exercise of the freedom
of communication and assembly, political campaigns, the electoral

---

1. Lord Bolingbroke, quoted in C. Herman Pritchett, *The American Constitution,* 3d
ed. (New York: McGraw-Hill, 1977), p. 1.

process, the news media, and a number of other ways. In short, the citizens in this representative democracy are always contributing to the development of their own "political constitution," and, in the long run, the political constitution continually shapes, affects, and adjusts the form and operational features of the written document.

It must always be remembered, therefore, that the constitution is not a hallowed text, floating above the political fray. Instead—and especially in a representative democracy—the constitution is a function of politics at the same time that it attempts to shape the political process. This fascinating reciprocity must be kept in mind as we turn to a discussion of the growth and development of Nebraska's written constitution.

The Federal and State Constitutions

One of the least understood features of American constitutional law is the difference between the federal and state constitutions. The confusion probably arises because of superficial similarities. All state constitutions share many features with the federal document: they all have a bill of rights, they all have articles establishing the three branches of government, they all have one or more articles on raising revenue and other financial matters, and they all have an article prescribing procedures for amendments and the convening of constitutional conventions. It is plain to see that, for the most part, the states, including Nebraska, fashioned their constitutions on the federal model. Yet the resemblances are an intellectual trap, for the state constitutions have a purpose fundamentally different from that of the national government.

An elementary principle of American constitutional law is that the constitution controls the law made by the legislature. However, there is a major difference in the way this control is exercised at the federal and at the state level. The U.S. Constitution confers or delegates specific powers to Congress, while a state constitution places limitations on the legislature. Thus, the federal government is forbidden from doing anything except that which is constitutionally authorized, whereas state governments are allowed to do anything that is not constitutionally forbidden. For example, the federal constitution states, "Congress shall have the power . . . to establish Post Offices and post Roads.'' From these words, one can clearly understand that Congress is given authority to legislate on the subject. But if we follow the same logic and conclude that, because Nebraska has laws against speeding, there must be something in the constitution authorizing the regulation of traffic, we are misled. In the words of the U.S. Supreme Court (incidentally, involving a case originating in Nebraska), ''A state constitution is not a grant but a limitation on legislative power, so that the Legislature may enact any law not expressly or inferentially prohibited by the constitution of the state or nation.''[2] As to federal powers, the court has said, ''The federal union is a government of delegated powers. It has only such as are expressly conferred upon it and such as are reasonably to be implied from those granted.''[3]

The reader may protest that the image of a limited federal government and powerful states is not terribly realistic. The federal government has, especially in the last fifty years, expanded its control over matters formerly considered purely of state concern. Such expansion of federal power, however, does not necessarily reflect violations of constitutional restrictions; rather it has come about largely through liberalized interpretations of the powers delegated to Congress, such as the clauses concerning commerce or taxation. Moreover, the far superior financial ''extractive capacity'' of the federal government has given it the dominant role in public finance in the United States. As federal rules and regulations follow federal funds, the recipients of federal monies come under more control. It is very often the effect of these regulations which makes federal power so visible.

Even considering federal power expansion in the aggregate, essentially none of the states' legislative powers have been constitutionally diminished. It has simply happened that since the 1930s, the American people have looked to Washington instead of to their state legislatures for social and economic services. So the general impression has developed that the federal government has gained while the states have lost power. The states have simply been less active in launching social and economic experiments. Whatever the reason for

2. *Chicago Burlington and Quincy R.R. Co.* v. *Otoe County,* 16 Wallace 667 (1872).

3. *U.S.* v. *Butler,* 297 U.S. 1 (1936).

such hesitancy, it is not because of constitutional restrictions on the states.

Just how do these differences affect the governing process in Nebraska? Assume that a state senator and a group of interested Nebraskans wished to build a state-supported railroad system. What changes in the Nebraska Constitution would be needed to allow that action? In terms of authorizing such a project, none would be required. It would take only the passage of a regular legislative act, for there are neither federal nor state limitations that would prevent such an undertaking. But financing the project might be a problem. Although there is no federal barrier, the Nebraska Constitution has a debt limit of $100,000 with exceptions made for financing highway construction and certain physical facilities at state universities and colleges. Therefore, the project could not move forward unless Article XIII, which contains these debt limits, were amended to authorize the issuance of bonds for railroad construction. Constitutionally, nothing else would be required. To sum up: a state may do anything except what is forbidden by its own or the national constitution.

Compared to the lean federal constitution, the Nebraska document is rather bulky and readers may assume that, based on what was said above, this is because it contains many limitations and prohibitions. Actually, most state constitutions are longer than they need to be, with many amendments authorizing what is already permitted. This has occurred because most people in the United States assume that amendments are necessary because of the influence of the federal analogy; even state legislators, when they initiate proposed amendments, are often unaware of the differences in the purposes of the two sorts of constitutions. State constitutions also become bloated because special interests prefer to see their favored legislation embedded in the basic law rather than in the statutes; the addition to the Nebraska Constitution of several paragraphs of convoluted prose with the passage of the "family-farm" amendment in 1982 can partially be attributed to this facet of the politics of constitution writing.

However, Nebraska's constitutional text is relatively brief. By actual count, it contained only 18,802 words in 1980. Thirty other states, headed by Alabama (129,000 words), Oklahoma (68,500 words), and Texas (61,000 words), have constitutions with longer texts.[4] It remains now to see how Nebraskans came up with so many words and how the political actors, especially the courts, find out what all those words mean.

The Development of the Nebraska Constitution

While other chapters in this book concentrate on the years since 1945, no such relatively recent date is feasible in a discussion of the Nebraska Constitution. The constitution of 1875, although much changed, is still the basic law of the state. And that document was a revision of even earlier constitutions. Therefore, in this chapter at least, one must begin at the very beginning.

The Kansas-Nebraska Act

Nebraska's first basic law, the territorial "constitution," consisted of Sections 1–18 of the Kansas-Nebraska Act of 1854.[5] According to the act, the Nebraska Territory included what is now the state itself, the eastern portions of what are now Colorado and Wyoming, and the territories of both the Dakotas. The act provided for presidential appointment—with senatorial approval—of the governor, secretary, chief and associate justices of the supreme court, territorial attorney, and a marshal. The legislative power, which extended "to all rightful subjects of legislation consistent with the constitution of the United States and provisions of this act," was conferred on the governor and a bicameral legislature composed of a thirteen-member council and a twenty-six-member house of representatives. House and council members were to be popularly elected for one- and two-year terms, respectively. Voters and legislators were both required to be free white male territorial inhabitants above the age of twenty-one years. Suffrage and office-holding rights were extended to both United States citizens and to those persons who had declared their intention to become citizens. The territorial "constitution" also provided for a

4. *Book of the States, 1980–81,* Vol. 23. (Lexington, Ky.: Council of State Governments, 1980), p. 16.
5. 10 Stat. 277 (1854).

court system and the establishment of local governments, but it did not include a bill of rights. In due course, a territorial government was set up in compliance with the basic law that remained in effect until statehood in 1867.

Statehood and the Constitution of 1866

Nebraskans began to campaign for statehood during the unsettled year of 1860. At this point, Democrats and Republicans alike saw the advantages of abandoning territorial status because they felt that statehood would increase immigration, encourage the influx of capital, and make available the financial yield from public lands for the support of education instead of allowing this money to serve as a bonanza for the benefit of land speculators. However, the first statehood referendum was defeated by a vote of 2,732 to 2,094 on March 5, 1860.

Nebraska's entrance into the Union had strong partisan overtones. In 1864, the Republican-dominated territorial legislature asked Congress to begin the steps leading to statehood. Accordingly, that same year, the Nebraska Enabling Act was passed, thereby laying the groundwork for drafting a constitution for the new state. That action, however, provoked Democratic fears about Nebraska's role in the reelection of President Lincoln, and the party conducted a campaign to seat antistatehood delegates in the scheduled constitutional convention. The "antis" elected a wide majority so that the convention, instead of drafting the constitution, voted to adjourn indefinitely. The justification given for the action was "the inability of the people to sustain the increased cost of state government."[6]

Further action to achieve statehood was deferred until 1866, when the territorial legislature appointed a nine-member committee to draft a constitution. The committee draft was modeled on the Kansas–Nebraska Act. The resulting document "provided for the barest framework of government, the fewest possible officers, the lowest salaries and the most meager functions for the new state in order to

6. Bruce Raymond, *Nebraska's Constitutions* (Ph.D. diss., University of Nebraska, 1937), p. 6n.

forestall objections to the increased expense."[7] As a sop to potential Democratic opposition, the draft constitution limited the franchise to white males.

The constitution of 1866 was approved by a vote of 3,938 to 3,838, but the act admitting Nebraska as a state was vetoed by President Andrew Johnson. Moreover, some members of Congress objected to the limited franchise of the proposed constitution. As a consequence, the admissions act passed in 1867 contained a provision that required Nebraska to amend the new constitution to eliminate the denial of voting rights because of race or color. President Johnson again vetoed the act but it was passed over his veto. Nebraska was proclaimed a state on March 1, 1867.

There are few favorable comments to be found concerning the state's 1866 constitution. In general, it was seen as "hurriedly patched together . . . to meet the exegencies of post-bellum politics and 'counted in' by not too scrupulous methods."[8] Specifically, the constitution was notable for its organizational arrangement of the judiciary and its low salaries for state office holders.

The Constitutional Conventions of 1871 and 1875

After a short trial period, the 1866 constitution was "weighed and found wanting." It could not serve satisfactorily as the state's basic law. It was not surprising that the 1869 legislature passed and submitted to the voters a proposal to call another constitutional convention. Citizen response was very favorable and the call for a convention was approved by a vote of 3,968 to 979.

The convention, sitting in Lincoln, took as a model the Illinois Constitution of 1870. In the debates, the convention covered a vast number of relevant and irrelevant topics in great detail. Apparently, however, the members were not sufficiently in touch with the political sentiments of the state, for not a single convention proposal was accepted by the voters; in the election of 1871, the work of the convention was rejected by a vote of 8,627 to 7,986. Among the more

7. *Nebraska Blue Book, 1976–1977*, p. 40.
8. Victor Rosewater, "A Curious Chapter in Constitution-Changing," *Political Science Quarterly* 36 (1921): 409.

objectionable propositions in the 1871 draft were a section that would have required that unused railroad rights-of-way revert to original owners and a provision for taxing certain church property.

Dissatisfaction with the 1866 constitution increased as the state's population grew and shifted westward. In 1873, the legislature passed another joint resolution that put to the voters again the question of holding a constitutional convention. Once more, in the October 1874 election, voter approval was given by a thumping majority of 18,067 to 3,880.

The 1875 convention sat again in Lincoln. There were sixty-nine delegates who deliberated for thirty days. The Illinois Constitution of 1870 was still used as a model. But in contrast to the 1871 session, the convention successfully labored to eliminate those "radical features" that had led to the rejection of the 1871 draft. In its final form, it provided for enlarged legislative, executive, and judicial branches; larger salaries for state officers; a ban on most types of special legislation; regulation of private corporations; limitations on the taxing power; relief for supreme court judges from the odious task of performing district court duties; and a ban on personal appropriation of fees by state officers. In addition, the convention designed an amending process that, in practice, made constitutional change nearly impossible—a result that was surely not anticipated by the delegates. The draft was referred to the voters on October 12, 1875, and approved by a vote of 30,202 to 5,474.

Selected Constitutional Developments: 1875–1920

Many of the highlights of constitutional change during the forty-five-year interval from 1875 to 1920 revolved around the difficulties inherent in the amending process. Problems arose because an amendment had to be approved by a majority of electors *voting* at the next election of state senators and representatives. Many voters were not inclined to participate in the constitutional referendum even though they voted for a legislator; even if they had no strong opinions on the issue, their nonvote was, in essence, counted as a no vote. Thus, from 1875 until 1906, only one out of twenty-three proposed amendments received enough votes. This barrier to constitutional development became so exasperating that a Nebraska supreme court judge concluded, "Taking the past as a criterion by which to foretell the future, it would seem that under the construction adopted, it will be almost, if not quite, impossible to change the present constitution, however meritorious may be the amendment proposal."[9]

The legislature showed some ingenuity in 1901, when, in the process of revising the election code, it authorized state political party conventions to register a vote for or against any pending constitutional amendments. The convention vote would then be filed with the secretary of state, who would authorize its inclusion on all state ballots as an integral part of a party's ticket. The same section of the statute also changed the form of the ballots so as to make it possible for a party voter to place one X in the circle provided and by so doing to express a choice, not only in support of all partisan candidates but also for any constitutional amendments that had been approved at the state party convention. This legislative innovation was called the Party Circle Law and was said to have been based on an Ohio statute. The state supreme court found the law to be constitutional.

The Party Circle Law brought a much-needed change in the amending procedure, and in the period from 1906 to 1918, nine out of fifteen proposed amendments were approved—most of them by substantial majorities. The most important amendment was the one introducing the elements of "direct democracy." These were the initative procedure, "whereby laws may be enacted and constitutional amendments adopted by the people independently of the Legislature" (Article III, Section 2), and the referendum, by which the people may vote on acts passed by the legislature after presenting the proper petition.

Despite the success of the Party Circle Law and the advent of direct democracy, many Nebraskans were not content with the constitutional and governmental status quo. The early 1900s saw the rise of Progressivism and a new surge toward reform. Politically, Progressives were a strong force in Nebraska, and they saw one peculiar clause of the 1875 text as especially troublesome. The clause prohibited expansion of the executive branch beyond its 1875 limits; and rising demands for new functions and services could only be met by indirection and

9. *Tecumseh National Bank* v. *Saunders,* 51 Neb. 801, 71 N.W. 779 (1897).

subterfuge, which tended to place unreasonable burdens on the eight established constitutional executives. Lines of authority and degrees of responsibility were also becoming muddled.

To meet what seemed to be an obvious need for constitutional change, a fairly low-key movement for calling a convention began in 1903. But at that time, Nebraska voters felt little enthusiasm and so the movement lagged for about a decade. Finally, in 1915, a group of prominent citizens met to organize the Nebraska Popular Government League. This action was the direct result of the refusal of the state senate to join with the house in calling a convention. Because it appeared that the legislature was not inclined to support a convention, the League decided to formulate plans that would circumvent legislative foot-dragging. Since popular support for a convention seemed to be growing, the League came up with a scheme that was believed to satisfy tests of constitutionality while avoiding the need for a legislative call for a convention. In 1917, the League presented a plan that, as an amendment to Article XV of the constitution, would have specified the details of a convention, including the time and place of the meeting.

It appears that the plan might have passed muster constitutionally, but by the time it was ready to be launched, so much popular sentiment had been generated in favor of holding a convention that the legislature decided to take the initiative again and, in 1918, submitted the question to the voters. The call for a convention was approved by a vote of 121,830 to 44, 491. In response to this approval, the 1919 legislature fixed the convention date for December 2, 1919, and arranged for a special election to be held for selecting delegates.

The Convention of 1919–20

Popular approval did not mean the struggle for a new constitution was over. World War I had ended, but the emotional hangover from the nationally sponsored anti-German campaign seemed to follow an irresistible urge to convert itself into a crusade to eliminate all foreign "influences" throughout the nation. Moreover, because it became known that certain prominent members of the Nebraska Popular Government League were foreign born or politically radical or liberal, conservative forces campaigned vigorously against some League members and supported the selection of compatible candidates in a bid to elect a large enough delegation to dominate the convention. However, when the election was over, the one hundred members seemed to represent a fairly middle-of-the road position. The occupations of the members probably indicate a generally conservative orientation. There were fifty-two lawyers; thirty members with agricultural interests; five bankers; five in real estate, insurance, and mercantile businesses; five associated with organized labor; three clergymen; three teachers; and several journalists.[10]

The prelude to the 1919–20 convention was much more exciting than the convention itself. The delegates did pay attention to the constitutional problems of the past. They revised the amending process to reduce the majority needed for ratification; they raised the salary for legislators and certain other state officers; they eliminated the barrier against setting up new executive state offices. Additionally, they reduced the signature percentage needed to launch initiative and referendum proposals, created an industrial commission to handle labor disputes, and proposed enfranchisement of women and military personnel. Eventually, forty-one separate amendments to the 1875 text were proposed and, surprisingly, every one was accepted by the voters. Such an outcome indicates that the delegates were in tune with the sentiments of the state.

Box Score: 1875–1920

Voters between 1875 and 1920 approved fifty-two constitutional amendments out of the eighty proposals submitted to them, including the product of 1919–20 convention. Even if the 1919–20 proposals were included, however, most of the changes made were routine, incremental, and unexciting. The most significant preconvention work was done in 1912, when the initiative and referendum as well as municipal home rule measures were passed. To the antiliquor forces, 1916 would probably be counted as a gala year because of the passage

10. See John G. W. Lewis, "The Nebraska Constitutional Convention of 1919–1920" (Ph.D. diss., University of Illinois, 1924).

of the popularly initiated prohibition amendment. The convention itself, operating almost as an extraordinary legislature, concentrated on solutions to specific problems.

Modernization of the Constitution of 1875

Although not many amendments were proposed from 1920 until the post–World War II era, from the 1950s to the present Nebraskans have done an extensive amount of tinkering with their constitution. Since 1920, 192 measures have been offered for approval to the electorate, and 127 have been passed. In contrast to the pre-1920 record, a number of significant and fundamental changes have been made. However, before commenting on the record, let us review briefly the current provisions available for amending the basic law.

Current Means for Constitutional Change

The *legislative "piecemeal" method of amendment* refers to the legislature's presentation of proposed amendments to the voters. To be on the general election ballot, the measure must have the approval of three-fifths (at present, thirty) of the senators elected to the legislature. Since 1968, if four-fifths of the elected members (forty senators) approve, proposals to amend can be submitted to the voters at a special election. The legislature has chosen to interpret the words *special election* to include primary elections. The rationale is that a special election is any except a general election. To date, no special constitutional amendment elections have been called.

Beginning three weeks before the next legislative or special election, the measure must be printed once a week in at least one newspaper in each county where a paper is published. Amendments must be printed on a ballot separate from the one containing the names of candidates, and the amendments must be so printed that voters can mark each one separately. The measure becomes part of the constitution if the majority voting in favor is equal in number to 35 percent of the votes cast in the election. Through the use of this procedure, 120 amendments have been added to the constitution in the years since 1920.

The convention approach to constitutional revision requires three-fifths of the legislature to launch the process. If a majority of the electorate, equal in number to not less than three-fifths of the votes cast at the next legislative election, approves, then a convention, consisting of no more than one hundred delegates, shall assemble. The legislature is given the power to prescribe the exact number of delegates to be chosen and the districts they shall represent. Delegates are elected and required to convene within three months of their election. No constitutional amendments or changes proposed by the convention shall take effect until approved by a majority of the electorate. Since the 1919–20 convention, no proposal to hold a new constitutional convention has been approved by the legislature.

The popular initiative amending process is invoked by a petition of 10 percent of the electorate. Signatures on the initiative petition must be obtained from at least five percent of the electorate from each of two-fifths of Nebraska's ninety-three counties. The initiated amendment, along with the necessary signatures, must then be filed with the secretary of state, who is required to place it on the next general election ballot, provided that not less than four months shall pass between the time of submission and the election. The constitution also specifies that an initiated proposal that fails at the polls cannot be resubmitted for consideration more than once every three years in either an affirmative or negative form. The referendum portions of the initiative procedures follow the same rules as prescribed for legislative "piecemeal" amendments. Since 1914, eight out of a total of sixteen popularly initiated proposals have been accepted.

The Nebraska Constitutional Revision Commission was a statutory innovation created by the legislature in 1969. The commission consisted of twelve members: six appointed by the legislature, three by the governor, and three by the supreme court. According to its charter, the commission was to "make a complete study of the Constitution of Nebraska to determine what changes, if any, should be made therein."[11]

The commissioners were selected and worked energetically for

11. *Report of the Nebraska Constitutional Revision Commission,* September 24, 1970, p. 142.

over a year. In 1970, they submitted a report to the Executive Board of the Legislative Council with over one hundred proposals for constitutional change. Approximately fifty proposals were accepted by the legislature and referred to the voters at the general election of 1970 and the primary and general elections of 1972. Of all the proposals offered at these three elections, the voters chose to approve thirty-eight. For those who wish future constitutional revision without resorting to "piecemeal" amendments, the reestablishment of another constitutional commission may prove easier than generating the political pressure necessary to bring about a constitutional convention.

Significant Constitutional Changes since 1920

In the period 1920–81, the most significant change in Nebraska's basic law was the installation of the nonpartisan unicameral legislature in 1934. Both from an institutional and political point of view, that probably represents the most radical innovation in the history of American state government. Although the unicameral plan has often been studied by other states, none has dared to make such a bold change in the traditional structure of its government. Also significant were the judicial reform amendments passed in the 1960s (see chapter 5). Another area of fundamental reform, whose political implications are still being worked out, was brought about by the measures in the 1960s that eliminated the general property tax and substituted for it the sales and progressive income taxes. Table 1 presents a summary of all amendments passed since 1920.

The foregoing history of 128 years of constitution making illustrates one central point about such documents: however basic they may be and however detailed their language may be, they are always being changed. No constitution can last unless it has the ability to grow. After the original uncomfortable experience with the 1875 document, Nebraskans now have a number of methods for changing the constitution. The record shows clearly that they are not hesitant to experiment with their government. But the amendatory process is only one way in which a constitution grows; it is, moreover, too cumbersome a process to give much effective guidance to those officials and citizens who have to know the meaning of the document here and now.

Table 1.1: Nebraska Constitutional Amendments: Passed by
Legislative Piecemeal and Popularly Initiated Methods, 1920–82

Number in each Category	Topical Categories Relating to or Affecting:	Years in which Enacted
7	Business and economic matters	'30, '38, '60, '64, '72(2), '82
4	Constitutional procedures	'52(2), '68, '72
14	Courts	'52, '58, '60, '62, '66, '68, '70(3), '72(4), '80
4	Criminal justice	'56, '72(2), '78
5	Educational finance	'66(2), '68, '70, '72
8	Education	'40, '52, '54, '66, '68(2), '72, '74
20	Executive departments and agencies	'36, '58(3), '60, '62(3), '64(2), '66(2), '68, '70(2), '72(4), '80
5	Executive and legislative salaries	'56, '60, '68(2), '72

continued

Table 1.1: *continued*

Number in each Category	Topical Categories Relating to or Affecting:	Years in which Enacted
5	Gambling and liquor control	'34(2), '58, '62, '68
16	Legislative branch	'34, '62(2), '66(3), '68, '70(2), '72(4), '74(2), '76
5	Local government and finance	'60, '68, '72, '78, '82
3	Suffrage	'70, '72(2)
24	Taxation, assessment, and revenue matters	'52, '54(3), '56, '58(2), '60(2), '64(3), '66(4), '68(2), '70, '72(2), '78, '80, '82
7	Other	'46, '60, '72(3), '76, '78

Total: 127

SOURCE: *Nebraska Blue Book,* 1981–82, 100–104.

It remains, then, to investigate the second major way in which constitutions are changed—namely, judicial interpretation.

Constitutional Interpretation: The "Final Word"

In all American jurisdictions, the ultimate limits of constitutional development are fixed by the courts. As Chief Justice John Marshall stated, "It is emphatically the province and duty of the judicial department to say what the law is."[12] Also, before he became chief justice of the United States, Charles Evans Hughes made a similar statement: "We are under a Constitution, but the Constitution is what the judges say it is."[13] Both Marshall and Hughes were, of course, referring to the judicial interpretation of the U.S. Constitution, but the same ground rules apply to all state constitutions as well.

How has this come about? As noted above, the legislature and the people are empowered to change the text of the constitution, that is, to make constitutional law. How then do the courts get into the act? It is quite simple: the court system was established to decide cases and controversies. Of these, the larger portion concern disputes that do not raise constitutional questions. But where such cases arise requiring the interpretation of the meaning of any words in the constitutional text, it is up to the judges to decide the precise definition of constitutional language. Thus, as time passes, a collection of constitutional law cases grows. It is these cases which must be examined, along with the text of the constitution itself, in order to find the complete meaning of that document. Although the text is written by legislative and popular action, the final legal meaning of an American constitution depends on the judiciary. Through their interpretive role, they make the law.

How can we have responsive government if the laws are ultimately interpreted by a group of people appointed for life, as they are in the federal system, or somehow insulated from popular control, as is often the case in state government? It seems anomalous, but at the same time, one must agree that it would not do for each branch of govern-

12. *Marbury* v. *Madison*, 1 Cranch 137 (1803).
13. Quoted in Harold Chase and Craig Ducat, *Constitutional Interpretation*, 2d ed. (St. Paul, Minn.: West Publishing, 1979), p. 1.

ment, or individual citizens, to decide on their own what the powers and limitations of the constitution are. If chaos is not to result, some organ of government must be the final word on the constitution.

Fortunately, the dangers of judicial despotism are overblown. The courts do make law, but their powers of enforcement of that law are very limited. Moreover, the judges are forbidden from soliciting business; the courts are only permitted to decide questions that are brought to them in actual cases and controversies. Most of the disputes, whether they raise constitutional issues or not, are settled at the trial court level. Only a few cases that cannot be resolved by a trial court are appealed to the Nebraska Supreme Court. Even assuming that the court does rule on a constitutional issue, the impact may be minimal. The immediate consequences of a court decision extend only to the parties to the suit—except in class actions, where it may be that all persons in the "class" are affected. In contrast, when the legislature passes a law, it affects every person in the state to whom it applies at the instant it becomes effective.

Furthermore, when the Nebraska Supreme Court is faced with questioning the constitutionality of a legislative act, it must construe the statute on the basis of a set of self-imposed restrictions. Among these limitations, (1) the court will not pass on contrived, friendly, nonadversary suits; (2) the court will not question the constitutionality of a statute if the issue can be resolved in a less drastic way; (3) the court will not pass on a statute if the complainant has not been injured by its operation; and (4) the court will not pass on a legislative act at the request of a person who has already taken advantage of its benefits. In short, as the court stated in a 1963 case, "courts will not declare [an] act of [the] Legislature unconstitutional except as a last resort."[14]

Some topics are obviously more controversial than others. Table 2.2 displays the topical distribution and number of constitutional law cases decided since Nebraska became a state. The short commentary below, based on selected cases, illustrates how the Nebraska Supreme Court makes new constitutional law.

14. *Stanton* v. *Mattson*, 175 Neb. 767 (1963).

Table 2.2: Court Decisions Interpreting Articles
of the Nebraska Constitution, 1867–1981

Article	Topic Covered	Number of Decisions*
I	Bill of Rights	973
II	Distribution of Powers	79
III	Legislative	475
IV	Executive	186
V	Judicial	302
VI	Suffrage	15
VII	Education	151
VIII	Revenue	282
IX	Counties	13
X	Public Service Corporations	34
XI	Municipal Corporations	68
XII	Miscellaneous Corporations	83
XIII	State, County and Municipal Indebtedness	45
XIV	Militia	1
XV	Miscellaneous Provisions	96
XVI	Amendments	6
XVII	Schedule	36
		Total: 2,707

SOURCE: Shepard's Nebraska Citations, 51–60; *Shepard's Nebraska Citations, July 1981 Supplement*, 192–95.

*These are primarily Nebraska Supreme Court decisions; approximately 1–2 percent are U.S. Supreme Court and lower federal court decisions.

Selected Illustrations of Constitutional Cases

Section 9 of Article I, part of the Nebraska Constitution's Bill of Rights, declares: "Excessive bail shall not be required, nor excessive fines imposed, nor cruel and unusual punishment inflicted." Recently, Charles Irwin Simants was convicted of murder and sentenced to death by a Nebraska district court. In an appeal to the state supreme court, Simants's lawyer argued that the death penalty constituted "cruel and unusual punishment" and was, therefore, in violation of Section 9. The court did not agree. "The death penalty," it held, "may defer offenders, is not invariably disproportionate to the severity of the crime of murder, and is not per se cruel and unusual punishment."[15] Although the text of Section 9 will not come out in a new printed version, the effect of the *Simants* decision was to "amend" Section 9 to read: "nor cruel nor unusual punishment inflicted—and the death penalty is not per se cruel and unusual punishment." The impact of the court's work will not be changed until the legislature or the people pass an amendment to accomplish that purpose or until a future high court decision changes the rule in *Simants*.

As originally written, Article IV vested in the governor the "supreme executive power" but it did not elaborate on a critical executive power, namely, that of removing (or firing) appointed officials in the executive branch. Yet, through judicial interpretation, the words *supreme executive power* were expanded in 1951 to confer specific removal power on the governor: "All officers and employees of the executive department who are not appointed for a definite term are removable at the will of the Governor."[16] The question was later clarified by a constitutional amendment broadening the authority of the governor.

Occasionally, the constitution writers failed to cover all possible situations; it then becomes the task of the court to provide a workable ruling. An example of this is Article XVII, Section 4, which established the dates for election of all state, district, county, precinct, and township officers, except for school district and municipal officials. A

15. *State* v. *Simants,* 197 Neb. 549 (1977).
16. *State ex. rel. Beck* v. *Young,* 154 Neb. 588 (1951).

problem arose over the status of police magistrates in second-class cities. As judges, they could be considered state officials, but their connection with city government gave them municipal status. Should they be chosen at a municipal or a state election? The supreme court had to clarify the matter by concluding: "Being within exception of this section, the Legislature may provide that police magistrates in cities of the second class shall be chosen at either municipal or general elections."[17]

From the examples, one can see that the courts not only have the "last word" on strictly legal constitutional questions, but they also serve as a kind of constitutional convention in continuous session. But there is also a more negative side to the work of policing the constitution. Higher courts correct constitutional errors by reversing the decision of lower courts; courts strike down unconstitutional executive acts; and courts will declare as void the unconstitutional acts of legislative bodies. The power to say what is or is not constitutional often puts the courts in apparent conflict with the popularly elected agents of government and is worthy of further comment.

Unconstitutional Legislation in Nebraska

The most effective judicial weapon in the arsenal of checks and balances is the power to strike down a legislative act. This power has been used to void 162 statutes from 1871, when it was first used, until the end of 1980, a number representing 5.9 percent of the total of 2,707 Nebraska constitutional law cases. Sometimes the court found that one legislative act violated more than one section of the constitution. Closer examination reveals that the 162 legislative acts were declared contrary to 55 different constitutional sections in 221 cases.

In terms of distribution, over half of the total violations were repugnant to only five sections, as indicated below:

1. Twenty-nine violations of Article III, Section 14, which provides, "No bill shall contain more than one subject, and the same shall be clearly expressed in the title. And no law shall be amended unless

17. *State* v. *Reilly*, 94 Neb. 232 (1913).

the new act contains the section(s) . . . as amended and the section(s) . . . so amended shall be repealed;''

2. Twenty-seven violations of Article III, Section 18, which provides that no special laws be passed;

3. Twenty-six violations of Article I, Section 3, which states that no person shall be deprived of life, liberty, or property without due process of law;

4. Fifteen violations of Article I, Section 16, which prohibits bills of attainder, ex post facto laws, and laws impairing the obligations of contracts;

5. Fourteen violations of Article II, Section 1, which organizes state government on the basis of a separation of legislative, executive, and judicial powers.

The remaining 110 cases concerned violations of 50 other parts of the constitution, ranging from 1 to 11 violations per section. For a period of 109 years—from 1871 to 1980—this amounts to about two constitutional violations per year by the legislature and 1.45 legislative acts per year overturned by the supreme court.

The following excerpts from the three most recent Nebraska Supreme Court decisions voiding unconstitutional legislative acts may give an idea of how the court "speaks" in such cases.

1. *State* v. *Adkins* ruled, ''A statute providing it shall be unlawful just to be in a place where a controlled substance is being used illegally is unconstitutionally vague and overbroad.''[18] The court found the act to be in violation of three parts of the Bill of Rights—the equal protection, due process, and free speech sections.

2. A legislative act amending Article VIII was struck down with the court holding, ''The proposed amendment . . . adopted by the Legislature . . . violates the equal protection clause of the 14th amendment by creating nonuniform taxation and violates the due process clause of the 14th amendment by failing to provide taxpayers with notice and an opportunity to be heard. It is therefore void.''[19]

3. In *State ex. rel. Douglas* v. *Thone*, the supreme court declared,

18. *State* v. *Adkins*, 196 Neb. 76 (1976).
19. *State ex rel. Douglas* v. *State Board of Equalization and Assessment*, 205 Neb. 130 (1979).

"Section 66–825, *R.S. Supp.*, 1979, which authorizes a plan for the development of alcohol plants and facilities in Nebraska in effect authorizes the state to guarantee payment of bonds . . . to be issued and thus is unconstitutional and void as a violation of this section of the constitutional limitation on debt."[20] The constitutional debt limit of $100,000 does not provide any exception for the development of alcohol plants and facilities.

This final case is also a good illustration of American constitutional practice. Understand that the court is not saying that Nebraskans can never finance alcohol plants; rather, it said that under the ground rules that the people have established for themselves, such a project is not authorized. If the advocates of gasohol are intent on getting state financial support, then they will have to ask the people to amend the constitution. The court is simply not able to sanction an amendment to the constitution which has not gone through the rigorous amendatory process.

Conclusion

By the end of this book, it is hoped, the reader will appreciate why the chapter on the constitution had to be placed at the beginning. The written document is the place to begin the study of any American government, but it is only a start. The real constitution is to be found in the practices of officials and citizens. The specific details of the various branches, local governments, and even political parties and interest groups are also critical parts of the patterns and processes by which we govern ourselves. In this sense, the entire volume is a commentary about Nebraska's constitutional system.

20. *State ex rel. Douglas* v. *Thone,* 204 Neb. 836 (1979).

SUSAN WELCH

THREE

The Governor and Other Elected Executives

To the average Nebraskan, the governor is the focal point of state government and politics. He (all Nebraska governors have been men) has name recognition and visibility that other state officials do not have. Unlike members of the legislature, he does not have to share his office with forty-eighty others. When this typical citizen thinks about state government at all, the governor probably gets most of the credit or blame for what goes on. But is that deserved? Exactly what powers does a governor have and what does he do with them? In this chapter, I will describe the role of the governor in Nebraska state government, examine some of the characteristics of the people who have served in that office, and look at some recent history of the governors and their accomplishments. Since the governor is only the most prominent and powerful of several elected state executives, I will also examine briefly the functions of these officials.

The Job of Governor

Constitutional Position

The authorization for the duties, method of selection, and role of the governor is found in Article IV of the Nebraska Constitution, which vests the "supreme executive power" in the governor and directs him to "take care that the laws shall be faithfully executed and the affairs of the state efficiently and economically administered." To this general grant of administrative power, the constitution gives the governor the following specific duties: (1) prepare and submit a state budget to the legislature; (2) convene special sessions of the legislature to undertake certain specified business (the legislature must confine itself to only those subjects identified in the governor's call); (3) nominate and appoint, with the consent of the legislature, certain executive officials; (4) remove appointive executive officials from office and appoint replacements; and (5) veto entire bills passed by the legislature or specific items in appropriation bills (known as an item veto). The governor has five days (not including Sundays) to review each bill passed. He may sign the bill; ignore it, in which case it becomes law after five days; or veto it in total or, with appropriations, in part. If the veto is used, the legislature may override it by a three-fifths vote, in which case the bill becomes law without the governor's approval.

Other powers specifically granted the governor are those of the commander-in-chief of the Nebraska National Guard, including the right to call it into service in emergency situations. The governor, along with the secretary of state and attorney general, also serves as a member of a board that has the power to grant reprieves, pardons, and commutations of sentences except in cases of treason or impeachment.

On the whole, then, the grant of constitutional power to the governor is fairly large. In comparison with governors of other states, Nebraska's governors have been found to have more constitutional powers than most in such areas as budget making, the appointment and dismissal of officials, veto power, and tenure potential. Some states, for example, do not permit the item veto, while others do not allow wide latitude in making appointments or preparing the budget. By having fairly extensive powers in each of these areas, Nebraska's governor rates slightly above the mean of all states in terms of formal gubernatorial power.[1] Constitutionally, Nebraska has a fairly "strong" governor.

1. For a method of comparing gubernatorial power, see Joseph Schlesinger, "The Politics of the Executive," in Herbert Jacob and Kenneth Vines, eds., *Politics in the American States* (Boston: Little, Brown, 1971).

The Governor and Other Elected Executives

While the constitution grants to the governor the supreme executive power in the state, it also gives executive power to several other elected officials who are quite independent of the governor. The secretary of state, state auditor, state treasurer, attorney general, and the members of the State Board of Education, the Public Service Commission, and the University of Nebraska Board of Regents are all state executives whose offices are mandated by the constitution and whose powers, responsibilities, and method of selection are entirely outside the governor's control. The lieutenant governor, even if now elected in tandem with the governor, is not legally required to follow gubernatorial commands. Still other appointed bodies are described in the constitution and may serve to inhibit free action by the governor. The constitutional dimensions of the Nebraska executive branch are sketched in Table 3.1. This proliferation of independent executives is quite common in the states, although there is no counterpart at the national level. Each independent executive heads a separate bureaucracy (which we will discuss later) and has a constituency independent of, and sometimes in conflict with, the governor.

Exercise of Power

The power of a governor rests not only on constitutional authority, but also on the willingness and ability of the incumbent to make use of that authority. In practice, Nebraska governors, with some exceptions, have tended to be weak in terms of using political power to shape public debates, influence the legislature, and lead their party. This has long been the case. In 1952, John P. Senning, a political scientist with much experience in Nebraska politics, noted that the job of the governor is "to administer the laws the Legislature enacts; not to dictate the laws. His recommendations, rightfully, should be limited to such measures as will make for better administration. Under the system he is to keep his fingers out of general policy matters."[2] A later

2. Quoted in Bernard Kolasa, "The Nebraska Political System: A Study in Apartisan Politics" (Ph.D. diss., University of Nebraska–Lincoln, Political Science Department, 1968), p. 387.

Table 3.1: The Nebraska Executive Branch
(Constitutional requirements)

Office	Constitutional Provision	How Chosen	Term
Governor	Art. IV	Elected at large	4 Years
Lieutenant Governor	Art. IV, Sect. 1	Elected at large	4 years
Attorney General	Art. IV, Sect. 1	Elected at large	4 years
Auditor of Public Accounts	Art. IV, Sect. 1	Elected at large	4 years
Secretary of State	Art. IV, Sect. 1	Elected at large	4 years
State Treasurer	Art. IV, Sect. 1	Elected at large	4 years
Board of Equalization	Art. IV, Sect. 28	Ex officio, governor, secretary of state, auditor, treasurer and tax commissioner	indefinite
Board of Pardons	Art. IV, Sect. 13	Ex officio, governor, secretary of state, attorney general	indefinite
Commission on Industrial Relations	Art. IV, Sect. 9	Five members, appointed by governor	6 years

continued

student of Nebraska politics observed in 1968, ''The executive in Nebraska has been looked upon basically as an administrator . . . the expansion of the executive's role into other areas . . . has been very slow.''[3]

Despite some instances of strong executive leadership, such as Norbert Tiemann's program to restructure the tax base, the verdict in 1983 must remain that Nebraska governors have generally chosen to play a weak role. Recent governors, such as Charles Thone, have taken a more active role in mobilizing legislative support through appeals to party loyalty, and both J.J. Exon and Thone worked to build

3. Ibid., p. 386.

Table 3.1: *continued*

Office	Constitutional Provision	How Chosen	Term
Board of Educational Lands and Funds	Art. VII, Sect. 6	Five members, appointed by governor	5 years
Public Service Commission	Art. IV, Sect. 20	Five members, elected by districts	6 years
Tax Commissioner	Art. IV, Sect. 28	Appointed by governor	indefinite
State Board of Education	Art. VII, Sect. 2	Eight members, elected by district	4 years
Board of Regents of the University of Nebraska	Art. VII, Sect. 10	Eight members, elected by district	6 years
Board of Trustees of the Nebraska State Colleges	Art. VII, Sect. 13	Six members appointed by the governor; ex officio, the commissioner of education	6 years
Commissioner of Education	Art. VII, Sect. 4	Appointed by Board of Education	indefinite

the strength of their parties. But most bursts of legislative political activity have been directed toward holding the line in budget matters or toward legislation directly affecting party fortunes (such as apportionment), rather than toward undertaking new policy initiatives. Generally, the governors have been content to let the legislature define much of its own agenda, stepping in to veto whenever budgets are felt to be too high. More often than not, vetoes are sustained by the legislature, giving the governor the "last word." Kolasa's examination of gubernatorial vetoes from 1937 to 1966 found only 18 of 100 overturned by the legislature.[4] Since then, the proportion of overrides

4. Ibid., p. 430.

has increased, largely because of the 84 of 161 Exon vetoes overridden by the legislature.

In view of the relatively large grant of constitutional powers to the governor, how do we explain gubernatorial performance? Some of the explanation may lie in the nature of executive-legislative relations when the legislature is formally nonpartisan. In other states and the national legislatures, there is a system of organization by political party, with various types of party floor and committee leaders. A chief executive can often expect a sympathetic hearing for a program from his or her party leaders in the legislature. Indeed, the executive's program and agenda may have been worked out in consultation with party leaders from the early stages and may even have served as a platform on which they jointly ran. So, in other states, the executive has a built-in, visible bridge to the legislature with these common party linkages. As explained in chapter 4, this system simply does not exist in Nebraska, thus making the governor's leadership in legislative matters far more problematic.

A second factor in explaining the ''weak governor'' stance taken by most Nebraska governors is simply the nature of the state's political culture or climate. While there is a populist strain in the political tradition, certainly in recent decades the conservative elements are much more predominant. Nebraska voters seem to prefer statewide officeholders, both Republicans and Democrats, who are conservative but not extremists, and who often, though not always, have quite bland public personas. Charisma is not critical to success in Nebraska politics. Cut from that mold, the typical behavior of governors has been to play very much a caretaker role, emphasizing the administrative rather than the political functions of the office. Voters have been content with governors who come to office with few programmatic goals beyond those of fiscal conservatism, and seem content, if not wildly enthusiastic, with a gubernatorial performance that does not rock the boat.[5] Whether the defeat of Charles Thone in 1982 will be an

5. For example, a statewide opinion poll showed 61 percent of the public satisfied with the performance of the governor and state agencies, although only three percent were ''very satisfied.'' Only 13 percent expressed varying degrees of dissatisfaction. See Alan Booth and Susan Welch, *Nebraskans' Evaluations of Their State Government*, NASIS–79, no. 4. Lincoln: University of Nebraska, Bureau of Sociological Research, 1979.

exception to this generalization or the beginning of a new era remains to be seen.

The existence of competing centers of power within the executive branch, as represented by other elected executive officials and by several large agencies outside the governor's direct control, seems to be a minor factor in the governor's passive stance. Since the governor does not tend to articulate forcefully and fight for specific programs, conflicts among various parts of the executive branch, when they have occurred, have tended to be more administrative squabbles than real political contests for power.

The Governors

Qualifications and Term of Office

The constitution provides only a few requirements for becoming governor. A governor must be at least thirty years old, a resident of Nebraska, and a citizen of the United States for at least five years before election. No other state office may be held while serving as governor. The term of office is four years, with eligibility for one further consecutive term. If further service as governor is desired, four years must elapse following retirement from the second four-year term. Until 1966, governors served two-year terms; in that same year, voters approved a limit of two consecutive four-year terms. Before these changes, fifteen governors had served two years or less, eleven governors had been in office for four years, and only four had served as long as six years. A pattern of two two-year terms was typical in the earliest years of the state, the one two-year term the norm from 1891 to 1913 (with some exceptions), and the two or three two-year term was prevalent from 1913 until the change in 1966. No clear pattern can be discerned from the careers of the four governors since the change to four-year terms.

Personal Characteristics

All have been white males with Protestant religious backgrounds. Their average age on election as governor was forty-eight years. They

Following is a list of Nebraska governors in the postwar period.

1941–47	Dwight Griswold (R.)
1947–53	Val Peterson (R.)
1953–55	Robert B. Crosby (R.)
1955–59	Victor E. Anderson (R.)
1959–60	Ralph G. Brooks (D.; died in office)
1960–61	Dwight W. Burney (R.; was lieutenant governor, served from Sept. 9, 1960, to Jan. 5, 1961)
1961–67	Frank Morrison (D.)
1967–71	Norbert T. Tiemann (R.)
1971–79	J. James Exon (D.)
1979–83	Charles Thone (R.)
1983–	Robert Kerrey (D.)

have come from a variety of professional and white collar occupations, including banking (Griswold and Tiemann), education (Peterson, Morrison, and Brooks), publishing (Peterson), law (Crosby, Morrison, and Thone), business (Anderson, Tiemann, Exon, and Kerrey), and farming (Burney).

Like most American political leaders, Nebraska's governors have tended to have more formal education than the general population. Although five men without a high school education served in the 1800s, since World War II, all eleven of the governors have had some college education. Peterson, Crosby, Brooks, Morrison, Thone, and Kerrey had advanced degrees of some type, and only three did not have at least a bachelor's degree. All postwar governors except Crosby and Burney received some of their education at the University of Nebraska (or, in one case, the former University of Omaha).

Most of Nebraska's postwar governors have been natives of the state, with only Morrison (from Colorado) and Exon (from South Dakota) being born outside the state. This represents a change from earlier years, when most governors, because of the short history of the state, were born elsewhere and moved to Nebraska in childhood or early adulthood. No postwar governor has been from Omaha, although four (Anderson, Exon, Thone, and Kerrey) made their homes in Lincoln. The others have had a small town or rural background.[6]

Such personal characteristics supply evidence for the impression of the basically conservative orientation of these men. The strong ties to small-town Nebraska and the parochial educational background combined with the business-oriented careers of most of them would seem to provide an environment supportive of a conservative outlook. While stereotypes can, on occasion, be misleading, this picture is largely borne out by the behavior of the men while in office.

Political Background

The political party affiliations of the governors show no dramatic changes over time. There have been thirty-five governors through 1983; three lieutenant governors, all Republicans, succeeded to the office by the death, resignation, or impeachment of their predecessors. Of the thirty-two elected governors, twenty have been Republicans and twelve have been Democrats.

It was not until 1891 that the first Democrat was elected governor, but during the years from 1901 to 1945, they held the office for twenty out of forty-four years. Although nine Republicans and only five Democrats were elected in that period, the longer tenure of the Democrats resulted in a near equality of total years in office. Much the same pattern has been evident in the years since 1947. Five Republicans have been elected while one succeeded to office on the death of the Democrat Brooks; four Democrats have been elected since the war. By the end of Robert Kerrey's term in 1987, Democrats will have held the governorship for twenty years in the postwar period, compared to twenty-two for the Republicans.

6. The information in this section is drawn from Kolasa, "The Nebraska Political System," pp. 407–16; additional material on Exon and Thone is found in Robert Sobel and John Raimo, eds., *Biographical Directory of the Governors of the United States: 1789–1978*, vol. 3. (Westport, Conn.: Meckler Books, 1978), pp. 916–17, and the *Nebraska Blue Book*.

Table 3.2: Political Experience of Nebraska's Elected Governors

	Prewar*	Postwar
Member of state legislature	15 (68%)	3 (30%)
Office in political party	7 (31%)	6 (60%)
No government service or party office	1 (5%)	2 (20%)
Total number	22	10

*Griswold is counted as a postwar governor. He had
legislative experience but no recorded party office.

Aside from political loyalties, what kind of "job training" do the
governors have? What political experience do they bring to the job?
Kolasa found that eighteen of the twenty-nine elected governors at the
time of his study in 1968 had state legislative service, nearly as many
had served in local government, eleven had held positions in a political party, and a few had served in judicial positions, the federal
government, school boards, or other positions in state government.[7]
Thus, most governors came to the job with previous political experience of some sort. The legislature was a training ground for many, at
least from statehood to Tiemann. However, since the adoption of
nonpartisanship, it has become less important as a recruiting ground
for governors.[8] We can see from Table 3.2 that, whereas 68 percent of
the prewar elected governors served in the legislature, only 30 percent
of the ones elected since 1946 have done so, including Griswold, who
served only in the partisan bicameral. Thus, only two of the elected
governors have ever been members of the unicameral, although Burney had been a senator. Other political experiences of postwar governors include service as mayor by Tiemann and Anderson, experience in a variety of federal positions, including U.S. representative by
Thone, and a state appointive position filled by Peterson. Brooks,
Morrison, Exon, and Kerrey, all Democrats, held no government

7. Kolasa, "The Nebraska Political System," p. 415.
8. Susan Welch and James Bowman, "The Nonpartisan Legislature: Does It Affect
Careers?" *National Civic Review* 61 (October 1972): 451–56.

position before their election as governor, although Morrison and Exon had been very active in party affairs. Only one elected postwar governor has ever served as lieutenant governor. Interestingly, for five of these postwar governors, election to that office was their first successful try for elected public office; for Peterson, Exon, and Kerrey, it was their first attempt, successful or not.

Sixty percent of the postwar governors have had important positions in their political parties, indicating that they are generally experienced in politics, either through government service or party activity. It appears that the legislature is becoming less important as a stepping stone to the governor's office and that party activity is now more important. However, as the legislature becomes more overtly partisan, this trend may be reversed.

Retirement from Office

The way in which the governor leaves office sheds light on the nature of the position and the people who have held it. There are six ways of voluntary or involuntary retirement from office that the governors have taken since 1867.

1. *Impeachment.* Only one Nebraska governor, David Butler in 1871, was impeached, convicted, and removed from office. This rather nasty episode led to a novel change in the state's impeachment process (see chapter 5) and, apparently, chilled any enthusiasm for the method, for no governor since the first has faced this sort of challenge.

2. *Resignation.* Charles Dietrich resigned in 1901, four months after his inauguration, to accept appointment as a U.S. senator.

3. *Defeat in Reelection Bid.* Seven governors have been retired involuntarily through defeat at the polls. An eighth was denied renomination by his party in the era before party primaries. One of the seven defeated governors, Ashton Shallenberger, was defeated in the primary election in 1910. Three of the remaining unsuccessful bids (Anderson, Tiemann, and Thone) took place in the postwar period; in fact, a Republican incumbent has not been reelected since Anderson in 1956.

4. *Death.* Only one governor—Ralph Brooks in 1960—died while in office.

5. *Constitutionally Mandated Retirement.* Governor J.J. Exon was the first to be affected by the restriction on the number of consecutive terms. After eight years in office, he became ineligible to succeed himself.

6. *Voluntary Retirement.* The majority of governors have retired after completing one, two, or three terms of office. In some cases, the retirement may have been brought on by the anticipation of electoral defeat; in other instances, the person wished to run for another office; and in most cases the governor appeared simply to have wanted to quit. Of the twenty-one men who retired voluntarily, three were later elected to other offices and five ran unsuccessfully for office. Three of these five failed in an attempt to regain the governor's seat.

Is There Life after Being Governor?

What does one do after moving out of the Governor's Mansion? Kolasa concluded that in Nebraska, as elsewhere, the governor's office is the apex of a political career. However, if we examine the careers of the postwar governors, that conclusion may not hold. Two former governors (Griswold and Exon) were later elected to the U.S. Senate, and two more were elected to other offices (Peterson and Griswold to the University of Nebraska Board of Regents and Morrison as Douglas County Public Defender). Three (Griswold, Peterson, and Tiemann) held important federal appointive offices, and Morrison and Anderson were rewarded with temporary appointments by Washington. Governors Crosby, Anderson, and Thone pursued active careers in law or business following service as governor. Thus, most of the postwar governors did not retire to their porch swings, but rather went on to other active careers, in and out of politics.

The Governor and Politics in the Postwar Era

One of the main issues that has shaped the nature of Nebraska's postwar politics is taxation policy. Despite the centrality of the issue, however, most governors drifted along with a policy aimed more at avoiding immediate crises than constructing a long-range solution to the revenue problem. Insofar as there has been a typical response to the issue, it has been to try, fruitlessly in most cases, to hold down the cost of government to a level that could be supported by an increasingly outmoded tax base.

By the 1960s, most states had turned to more reliable sources of tax money, such as personal income or general sales taxes. Nebraska continued to depend on the general property tax, despite that tax's failure to keep pace with increased demands for public services. Political leaders in the state, however, were reluctant to be identified with the introduction of new taxes. Thus, for example, Governor Crosby, after taking office in 1953, continued to preach the doctrine of limiting government. His response to the issue of taxation was "Operation Honesty," a campaign of moral suasion urging all persons to report fully their taxable property.

Crosby's successor, Victor Anderson, also did not see fit to propose dramatic changes in the state's tax laws. Arguing that the governor was an administrator and not a policy maker or legislative leader, he pressured for fiscal austerity during his 1957–58 administration. In the election of 1958, Democrats made the inequalities in the enforcement of the property tax a major issue, and relied heavily on it en route to electing Brooks as governor. Brooks, while more activist than his recent predecessors, did not favor a new tax structure but only a more vigorous and impartial enforcement of the existing laws.

Brooks's elected successor, Frank Morrison, was pledged to no new taxes but instead to a study of the whole state tax situation. Although Morrison was elected to three terms, he too played a generally passive role in the issue. During the last year of his administration, the legislature did approve a state income tax law, which Morrison allowed to go into effect without his signature.

During the 1966 election, voters, led by farm groups, took matters into their own hands by voting to terminate both the state property tax and the newly passed income tax, leaving the state with practically no revenue. The incoming Tiemann administration was forced to take action to straighten out the state's shaky financial affairs. Tiemann, the first governor to serve a four-year term, exercised considerable effort behind the passage of a more balanced state tax system that included both an income and a general sales tax. These measures were passed by the legislature. Tiemann also worked for the passage of a new system of state aid to local schools, a measure designed in part to provide some relief in local property taxes.

The reaction to these initiatives on the part of the taxpayers was mixed. On the one hand, an initiative calling for the repeal of the state income tax was soundly defeated in 1968. On the other hand, Tiemann, renominated by a slim majority, was defeated for reelection in 1970 by Exon, who stressed in his campaign Tiemann's responsibility for the new taxes and higher levels of spending. Thus, after staving off a challenge from the conservative wing of his own party, Tiemann was defeated by a Democrat who preempted the conservative position and portrayed Tiemann as a big spender.

Although neither Exon nor other political leaders made a serious effort to roll back the new taxes, Exon went on in his career as governor to endorse fiscal conservatism at every opportunity. Exon's successor, Charles Thone, emphasized even more the need for frugality in state government. Exon, however, was able to parlay his tight-fisted image into reelection and a U.S. senatorship. Thone may have been undone by his resistance to tax increases when the state's finances were overwhelmed by a combination of federal tax changes and a faltering economy. In the successful campaign of the Democrat Kerrey in 1982, the charge was made that Thone's failure to exercise positive leadership had made a bad situation even worse.

The handling of the tax issue over a twenty-year period is indicative of the role played by Nebraska governors. Until driven to it by crisis, none of the state leaders acted to bring about fundamental changes, even though most of them recognized the inadequacies and inequities in the system. And, after the unhappy example of the most activist governor in the period—Tiemann—there is probably little incentive for future governors to deviate from a "hold the line" philosophy.

A second topic that illustrates the tendency of Nebraska governors to maintain a low political profile regarding substantive issues concerns water resources. As an agricultural state, Nebraska is becoming increasingly dependent on the wise management of its water. Groundwater in particular is essential to the economy of the state because it is used widely for irrigation and supplies much of the water for nonagricultural use. Fear about the eventual depletion of groundwater has pervaded discussions of the issue since the 1940s. For at least two decades, water law has been a political morass from which the legislature has been unable to extricate itself in any systematic fashion. Despite the urgency, none of the governors has seen fit to exercise leadership on this issue by laying out and working for a coherent program. Rather, they have tended to abdicate responsibility in the area to the legislature (which has not been able to do much either). The governors (and legislators) have continually called for further study of the problem, so that the state has compiled a record of much research and little substantive action.

It is not argued that a governor is likely to be without any policy interests. Obviously this is not true. The governors have been interested in a variety of issues ranging from mental health to educational television to agriculture. The passivity of the governors in the two important issues of tax policy and water resources simply illustrates the general patterns of gubernatorial behavior, not the entire range. Perhaps in Nebraska, more than in other states, the burden rests with a governor because of the fragmented nature of the legislature. The combination of a passive governor and a fragmented legislature has meant little state action in many areas. To some Nebraskans, this type of gubernatorial behavior is desirable and in keeping with a preference for a low profile for state government. However, in a period of American history when state passivity has been complemented by increasing federal activity, persons of a conservative bent have not necessarily been pleased with the ultimate outcome of limited state action. Then too, passivity not only means passivity in terms of fighting for more state programs, but also passivity in achieving aims that might be more consonant with conservative ideologies.

Other Elected Officials

Nebraska's constitution specifies the election of other officials whose duties should be discussed. Some issues surrounding the elections of these officials will also be considered.

Lieutenant Governor

The office of lieutenant governor was created by the constitution of 1875. Originally, the lieutenant governor, like the governor, was to serve a two-year term and was elected separately. In 1962, the voters approved a constitutional amendment extending the term of office to four years; another amendment in 1970 provided for a jointly elected governor and lieutenant governor. Under this system, each voter casts one vote for a governor–lieutenant governor slate, thus ensuring that the two offices will be filled by members of the same party.

Actually, it would seem to make little difference, under most circumstances, to which party the lieutenant governor belongs since the office carries few duties and little responsibility. The major constitutional function of the office is to preside over the legislature. The right of the lieutenant governor to vote in the legislature was confused by apparent contradictions in two parts of Article III of the constitution. Section 10 says the lieutenant governor "shall vote only when the Legislature is equally divided," and Section 13 states that no bill becomes law "unless by the assent of a majority of all members elected." In the 1981 session, Lieutenant Governor Luedtke broke a tie on a controversial issue with his vote, and the opponents, including Governor Thone, argued that the bill had not been approved by the constitutionally required majority. The issue went to the Nebraska Supreme Court, where, in a four to three decision, the lieutenant governor was denied the right to vote on the final passage of a law, although he does retain the vote, in case of a tie, on all other issues before the legislature.

Aside from the presiding function, the lieutenant governor is mostly a "spare tire," as former Governor (and Lieutenant Governor) Robert Crosby noted.[9] He (and Nebraska lieutenant governors have also always been men) is on call should death, disability, or the inclination to resign strike the governor. As Crosby said in an article written while holding the office, the low mortality rate of governors has meant "worse luck for aspiring lieutenant governors." Only two have

9. Robert Crosby, "Why I Want to Get Rid of My Job," *State Government* 20 (July 1947): 193–94.

achieved the governor's seat through the death or resignation of the incumbent, and only two have ever been elected governor in their own right. Part of the reason for the failure of lieutenant governors to be elected governor was sometimes attributed to the constitutional stipulation against running for other offices while already holding an elected position. But since this ban was lifted in 1962, no lieutenant governor has been elected governor, although three (Burney, Sorensen, and Whelan) have tried.

The lieutenant governor is also on call for the occasions when the governor leaves the state. He can, at the governor's discretion, serve as a gubernatorial substitute at meetings of various boards and commissions. Thus, the office of lieutenant governor, while undoubtedly conferring some prestige to its occupant, has rarely been a route to higher office, and the occupant has never been weighted down by heavy responsibilities of state. Whether these are arguments for its abolition is a matter of preference. Nine states do without such an office. The main question in abolishing the office is the line of succession should the governor die or resign. Currently, the speaker of the legislature is next in line following the lieutenant governor; in some states the secretary of state is next in line. Clearly, this question could be worked out should the voters decide that the lieutenant governor is superfluous. At this time, it does not appear that there is any such sentiment.

The Secretary of State, Auditor, Treasurer, and Attorney General

The secretary of state, like the other officials discussed here, is elected by the voters to a four-year term. The secretary provides a variety of services, although the only constitutionally prescribed one is to keep the Great Seal of the State of Nebraska. The office is largely a record-keeping one, with the job of recording and maintaining laws passed, election returns, articles of incorporation, trademarks and labels; receiving the certificates of nomination of candidates for office; certifying petitions for popular initiatives; and general supervision of the election machinery in the state. The secretary of state serves on a number of boards and commissions. The secretaries of state tend to have long tenure and since 1915, only seven different people have held the office. Between 1927 and 1971, the Frank Marshes, father and son, held the office for thirty-four out of forty-four years.

The auditor of public accounts manages an agency whose function is to examine and certify financial records of the state and many of its subdivisions. The auditor is required to report, when requested, to the legislature and to the Department of Administrative Services concerning the findings of the accountants. Low turnover rates have also been a feature of this office. Ray C. Johnson served from 1939 to 1971 and Ray A. C. Johnson (no relation) has served since then.

The state treasurer handles the money of the state with the aid of an office employing a dozen people. While the position sounds impressive, in reality it is mostly a technical job; it involves ensuring that money received is deposited, interest is earned, and receipts of the inflow and outflow of cash are kept. The treasurer has no discretion in deciding how state money is spent, but only that the actual dollars received and disbursed by the state are efficiently and honestly handled. There is some discretionary activity in the sometimes controversial matter of choosing where and how state money shall be invested. To ensure some turnover, the constitution permits no more than two consecutive terms. This office is the only one of the six discussed in this chapter ever held by women. Bertha Hill was appointed to finish the unexpired term of her husband in 1958. Kay Orr was also appointed to a vacancy in the office in 1981 and was elected to a full term as treasurer in 1982.

The attorney general is the state's chief legal expert. He represents the state in legal issues to which it is a party. He also consults with and advises county attorneys in certain matters. When requested, he offers advisory opinions to the governor, other executive departments, and the legislature concerning the legal meaning of any proposed or actual law or activity. While these opinions are not binding, as a supreme court decision would be, they do have a good deal of influence on the other officials who want to avoid court challenges of their actions. Only three men have held the office since 1950.[10]

10. This does not include Harold Caldwell, who was elected to a term of approximately thirty-one hours.

The other elected officials do derive some policy-making power through their association with the governor on constitutional boards. The Board of Pardons, made up of the governor, secretary of state, and the attorney general, is one of these. Another more important body is the Board of Equalization and Assessment, discussed in chapter 8.

On the Future of the Independent Executives

Why do we continue to choose the secretary of state, treasurer, auditor, and attorney general by popular vote? Should not the governor appoint them just as he appoints the heads of the welfare and public roads departments, agencies more important and expensive than all the executives combined? The existence of the independent elected officials has often been decried by state government reformers as an impediment to responsible government. By dividing power among several officials, not necessarily of the same party or political outlook, concerted government action is made even more difficult than it otherwise might be. Whatever programs and plans the governor wants to promote may be thwarted by the officials with a base of political power beyond the governor's control. This reasoning has led to attempts in many states, including Nebraska, to limit the number of elected executives or to shorten the so-called long ballot. These attempts have not been as successful in Nebraska as they were in some other states, although two elected state positions in Nebraska—the commissioner of public lands and buildings and the superintendent of public instruction—were eliminated. The first was removed in 1936 and the latter replaced in 1952 by the multimember State Board of Education. The major effort in the state to shorten the ballot was an amendment proposed by the legislature in 1938. The proposal, providing for the appointment of the secretary of state, attorney general, and treasurer by the governor with the consent of the legislature was defeated by the voters by a huge margin—233,319 to 89,357. The issue has come up sporadically since then, but it does not seem to be high on anyone's list of priorities.

Proponents of the existing arrangement might argue as follows:

1. We have always had these independently elected officials and, in

the absence of an impending breakdown in government, tradition argues for keeping them.

2. Similarly, having this arrangement has never done any great harm. There is no evidence that it has impeded the functioning of state government to any perceptible degree. Indeed, most of the officeholders have been dedicated and distinguished citizens.

3. The existence of these offices offers a check on unfettered gubernatorial power. Some would argue that it is especially important to have an independent treasurer and auditor to guard against fraud and corruption.

4. The independent officials also provide a certain amount of continuity in state government. Governors come and go, but secretaries of state and auditors tend to remain. More cynically, some would argue that the retention of these positions ensures job security for politicians who enjoy the public visibility and prestige but would rather not risk their careers in less secure and more controversial offices.

The arguments for having some or all of these executives appointed by the governor include the following.

1. There are already substantial checks and balances, most notably the legislature and judiciary, affecting gubernatorial power. In fact, the existence of many other independent agencies outside the direct control of the governor suggests that we need more, not less, gubernatorial control and accountability.

2. The fact that the lesser officers have been held almost exclusively by Republicans may mean that governors of that party hold some advantage over the Democrats, especially if the offices are meant to serve as a check on one another. One-party domination of the offices can also put the minority at a disadvantage on multimember boards. For example, Governor Exon never had a Democratic majority on the Board of Equalization and Assessment during the eight years of his administration. Governor Kerrey, whose campaign alleged failures in Republican fiscal policy, also lacked a majority. In the highly partisan matter of setting tax rates, this may be a significant factor.

3. Even if a check on the governor is wanted, it is hard to see how these officials, with tiny staffs and budgets, as well as rather routine functions, provide much of a curb on gubernatorial power. The

officials might slow down a power-hungry governor, but it is difficult to see how they could defeat completely such a potential despot.

4. Eliminating two to four elected executives will focus voter attention on the top of the ticket, and reduce the problem of voters making choices about little-known candidates. Are there many voters who care how candidates for the auditor's job stand on the issue of accrual accounting or what a potential secretary of state intends to do as chairman of the Nebraska Brand Committee? No matter how well minor officeholders perform, they are not highly visible or salient to the average voter.

5. Eliminating these offices as elected ones might save money. The savings will not come because of elimination of the office, since someone will still have to perform the functions of auditing, record-keeping and fund disbursing. But surely some tax money could be saved by avoiding the cost of electing these officials; and there probably would be some savings possible in the consolidation of the functions of these offices with other units of state government.

6. In the case of the attorney general, it makes particularly good sense for that officer to be part of the governor's "team." After all, the attorney general does have a legal obligation to represent the state, whose policies should largely be set by the governor.

Overall, there is probably not much chance that in the next few years the offices will be made appointive. The Governor's Task Force for Government Improvement, in its 1980 report, did not even publicly consider this move as an option. They did call for more regular consultation between the governor and the other elected executives, perhaps indicating an awareness of a lack of coordination. But in the final analysis, it probably does not make much difference one way or the other whether these officials are elected or appointed. The departments they head are, in fact, "small potatoes," and with the exception of the attorney general have little in the way of policy-making power.

Conclusion

The assessment is that Nebraskans prefer executive leadership that is passive in pursuing policy goals. Unexciting leaders, however, may offer some compensating advantages. For one, the state has generally been free of any deep, rancorous political feuds, and politics is conducted with a generally high degree of civility. For another, Nebraskans have enjoyed a long tradition of honest government, little touched by the scandals, frauds, and corruption to be found in some other states. Whatever other faults they possess, the governors have been models of probity.

What about the future? If the past is any guide, we can expect a gradual move toward strengthening the formal power of the governor, with more of the executive branch brought under gubernatorial control. If the legislature continues to become more openly partisan, then we might also expect that the nature of gubernatorial-legislative relations will change. It may be that the governor will be forced to take on a more active stance in order to serve as the leader of his party in the legislature. Whatever direction the future takes, we can reasonably expect that the changes will be slow and incremental and that no drastic shifts will occur overnight in Nebraska's political landscape.

JACK RODGERS, ROBERT SITTIG, AND SUSAN WELCH

FOUR

The Legislature

Nebraska makes life a little bit harder for authors of state government textbooks; especially when making generalizations about the legislature, they must include phrases like "except for Nebraska" or "only Nebraska." It is the only state with a one-house (unicameral) rather than a two-house (bicameral) legislature, and it is the only state to elect its legislators on a nonpartisan ballot, rather than on one with party labels. Because of the single house, it also has the smallest total number of state legislators. In this chapter, we will examine the background of this legislative structure, what kinds of people serve in the legislature and how they are elected, and how the legislative system works. An overarching question in this chapter is whether all these unique features make much difference in general legislative performance.

The Birth of Unicameralism

Under our federal system, each state is free to determine the structure and nature of its own government, subject only to the vague and unimportant provision for a "republican form of government" in Article IV of the U.S. Constitution. Even with this latitude, there are more similarities than dissimilarities among the fifty state governments, this high degree of uniformity being fastened on them by history and tradition. In addition, major alterations in, or departures from, these accepted governmental institutions are rare. Nebraska, however, did make such a major change in the 1930s when it adopted a nonpartisan, unicameral legislature. The question is often raised as to how and why this occurred. It was not sudden.

Actually, there have been momentary spurts of interest in unicameralism in a number of states since just before World War I. Governors in some states have recommended it; in others, various "good government" groups and constitutional conventions have given it serious consideration; it has even been voted on by the people in a few states. The most recent stirring of interest grew out of the "one man, one vote" requirements in the apportionment of both houses of state legislatures; the supreme court decisions effectively undermined the "federal analogy" supporting the argument for a second house in state government. All of this interest flared only briefly and soon disappeared—except in Nebraska.

One of the recommendations made to the 1915 Nebraska legislature by a joint committee created in 1913 to suggest ways of improving the operation of the state government was the establishment of a unicameral legislature, and a joint resolution was introduced during the 1917 session proposing a constitutional amendment to create a one-house legislature of sixty members. At the 1919–20 constitutional convention, a proposal to establish a legislative assembly of one house reached a final vote but died on a tie vote. Following the failure of a campaign to place the issue on the ballot by initiative petition in 1923, unicameral proposals were defeated in the 1925 and 1933 legislative sessions.

A major reason why the issue of unicameralism stayed alive in Nebraska throughout the 1920s was the influence of Senator George W. Norris. In his article in the *New York Times* of January 28, 1923, "A Model State Legislature," he inaugurated his long and eventually successful campaign against bicameralism. In numerous articles and speeches, he set forth the major faults of the traditional system and his vision of the merits of unicameralism.

A primary target of Norris's criticism was the conference committee, that group set up to reconcile differences in a bill that had passed both houses. Among its defects, he asserted, was that it met in secret with no record kept of its proceedings, that its reports were not subject to amendment when returned to the respective houses, and that the need to compromise in order to get something passed often resulted in provisions being included without the support of a majority of the legislators. He was strongly opposed to and suspicious of those parts of the political system which functioned hidden from public view.

Senator Norris was also unimpressed with the traditional defense of bicameralism that one house served as a check on the other, thus preventing the passage of hastily considered legislation. It was his opinion that what actually happened too often was the shifting of responsibility from one house to the other, with bills being passed by one with the knowledge that they would be killed across the rotunda. In any event, he believed that there would be ample checks on the one-house legislature through judicial review, the gubernatorial veto, and the availability to the people of the referendum. He also felt unicameralism was valuable because it would result in a smaller number of legislators. In his view, most state legislatures had too many members, thus frustrating the personal efforts of individual legislators. They were forced to cede many of their individual rights as lawmakers to the committees, they found it difficult to offer amendments to bills, and their opportunity to debate freely was severely curtailed. This argument was part of Norris's basic feeling that sheer numbers operated to hide from public scrutiny the operation of state legislatures.

Norris also was convinced that corruption was more likely in a two-house legislature since it would be easier for unscrupulous legislators to cover their tracks. In this connection, he stressed the increase in what he considered to be the "baneful influence" of lobbyists, a natural result, he felt, in legislatures that were too large, too cumbersome, too secret, and too irresponsible. Finally, he contended that salaries could be more easily increased in a one-house legislature because of the smaller size, and this in turn would result in a better type of person being elected. The dedicated legislators would also be capable of functioning independently since they would be less likely to have to rely on the lobbyists.

Norris saw unicameralism as only one aspect of a model state legislature. Equally important, in his view, was the principle of nonpartisanship. He contended that the partisan election of state legislators was usually colored by national issues, most of which did not affect directly the activity of the state. If not hampered by partisan connections, therefore, the legislators could give their full attention to the state's interest and welfare. Because the state's responsibilities were in no sense partisan, he felt, his plan would enable the legislature to function more like a business corporation.

The successful initiative campaign resulting in the establishment of the nonpartisan unicameral legislature was launched in 1934. One citizen committee was formed to draft the proposal, another to seek signatures on the petition (although only 57,600 signatures were required, they collected 95,000), and a third campaign committee to seek support for the proposed constitutional amendment. This latter committee was headed by Senator Norris. He personally campaigned vigorously throughout the state, as did other supporters of the proposition.

There was intense opposition to the proposal, largely organized into the nonpartisan Representative Government Defense Association, which referred to the idea as "dangerous" and "un-American." The press was nearly unanimous in its opposition and editorials pictured the whole concept as an absurd, harebrained scheme. At the 1934 general election, the amendment was approved by a vote of 286,086 to 193,152. It carried in all but nine of the state's counties and seventy-three of the 2,029 precincts. The 1935 legislature made the necessary arrangements for the transition and the first session of the unicameral legislature convened on January 5, 1937.

From the above, we know how, but not why, Nebraskans scrapped a traditional political institution. There is no definitive answer to the more important question, but instead a great deal of speculation. It is safe to say that many contemporary factors undoubtedly contributed to the final result. First, two other popular proposals were on the same ballot—the repeal of prohibition and the authorization for pari-mutuel betting at horse races. However, the legislative issue did not merely ride in on their coattails because, while it received fewer votes than the repeal of prohibition, it outpolled pari-mutuel betting and carried in more counties than either issue. Second, there was a general feeling that the 1933 session of the legislature had performed poorly. The proposal may have benefited from a reaction against the performance of the incumbents — many of whom were inexperienced at the time — and not the institution itself.

The 1930s, furthermore, were years of acute agricultural distress and general economic dislocation, and the possibility of saving some money from a smaller one-house legislature probably had some influence. Finally, the educational efforts of Senator Norris, by keeping the issue before the voters for several years, must have contributed to the outcome. In summary, a combination of circumstances converged at one time to enable the proponents of unicameralism to carry the day. Certainly it was more complex and subjective than the result of a detailed and dispassionate weighing of the relative merits and demerits of bicameralism versus unicameralism with an objective and enlightened electorate tipping the scale toward the latter.

Even if it can be argued that the citizens were uncertain what they had wrought with their new legislature, they have not been eager to undo the actions of 1934. A good test of the public acceptance of the system, then, would be the incidence and fate of attempts to abolish it and return to the traditional partisan bicameral system. Remarkably, there have been few serious attempts, either through legislation or the initiative procedure, to propose an amendment for a return to the two-house structure.

The more vulnerable part of the reform has been the feature of nonpartisanship. In 1953, a petition campaign was inaugurated to go back to a partisan legislature and to consider the desirability of returning to bicameralism. The effort was the brainchild of the chairmen of the two major political parties, and a bipartisan committee was formed to sponsor the movement. Using many of the same arguments against the performance of the 1953 session that had been made about the 1933 bicameral legislature, the group soon found that there was little public enthusiasm. The proposal was almost unanimously opposed by members and former members of the Unicameral (by popular usage in Nebraska, this adjective has been converted into a noun). In the face of this resistance, it was decided by the sponsors to drop references to bicameralism, but the plan fared no better. It was difficult to find canvassers for the petition, few signatures were acquired, and the movement soon collapsed.

In addition to the abortive 1953 petition campaign, bills were introduced in 1951 and 1957 proposing a constitutional amendment to return to partisan elections. They were both killed in committee and aroused little discussion. Since 1957, nine bills have been introduced proposing a return to partisanship, the latest in 1981, but they all died, and usually at an early stage in the legislative process. The Nebraska legislature is likely to retain its distinctive characteristics for the foreseeable future.

Undoubtedly, part of the reason for the quick acceptance of the new legislative system was the fact that it continued to mirror the generally conservative views of a majority of the state's people. The traditional opposition to a broadened tax base was not disturbed. Attempts to adopt sales and income taxes were easily beaten back and the state became the only one continuing to rely on the general property tax for a significant portion of *state* revenue. One result was that at the end of this period Nebraska had the lowest per capita state tax burden of all the states save one.

There had always been a decidedly rural flavor to Nebraska politics and to legislative policy making, and this continued throughout these formative years. For example, efforts by educational groups to bring about compulsory school district reorganization failed and the state ended up with more school districts than any other state. Attempts to adopt some plan of state aid to schools, which could also be used to reorganize school districts, likewise foundered, in part because such a program would have demanded the unwanted broadened tax base already referred to. Events, of course, were ultimately to change all this, and sales and income taxes were adopted, a program of state aid to public school districts became a reality, and the number of school districts began to shrink substantially.

Through the 1960s, there were few changes in either the organization or the procedures of the Unicameral. However, the members began to feel that some changes might provide for a more adequate consideration of legislative proposals, particularly in connection with the committee stage of the legislative process. As the result of an interim study, two innovations were adopted in 1957. A new committee alignment was developed, resulting in one additional and smaller existing committees; standing committee hearings were set to begin at

1:30 P.M. rather than 2:00 P.M. The purpose was to speed up the hearing process so that all-day floor sessions could begin sooner, an essential change since all bills introduced had to be given a public hearing. More extensive modernization, however, would not occur until the 1970s.

Later Developments

Just because the Nebraska legislature's two fundamental features have remained intact after nearly fifty years of hard wear and tear is not to say that the system works according to the ideals of the original advocates or that it has remained static. The system has been refined by usage and by a number of formal changes, both in the constitution and in the rules of procedure.

The Constitutional Provisions

Article III of the Nebraska Constitution outlines the structure and functions of the legislative branch in rather great detail. For present purposes, it will suffice to sketch only some of the more important constitutional requirements. Most notably, the legislature is to have only one chamber of not fewer than thirty nor more than fifty members, with each member elected from a separate district. The number of members (called senators) was set at forty-three by state law from 1937 to 1963, but the legislature added six seats in response to a long and wrenching dispute over an acceptable reapportionment standard (three separate legislative plans were rejected by the federal courts for deviating too widely from an equal distribution of population). The additional seats served as a cushion and allowed the requirements to be met without any absolute reduction in the outstate representation, since all the new districts went to the Omaha and Lincoln urban areas. Another complicating factor in reapportionment is the constitutional requirement that district lines, as far as practicable, coincide with county lines. See Map 4.1 for the latest district boundaries.

A person may serve in the legislature if he or she is a U.S. citizen, a registered voter, and twenty-one years old. A senator must have resided for at least one year in the district from which elected and

Map 4.1: Legislative Districts Established
by LB 406 (1981 Legislative Session)

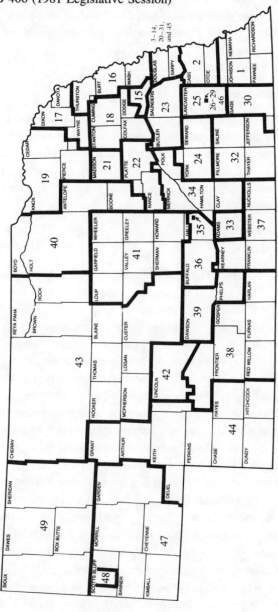

continue to live there after election. Since the approval of a constitutional amendment in 1962, the term of office is four years, with one-half of the members elected every two years. There is no limit on the number of terms one can serve. The salary of a senator is four hundred dollars a month (or forty-eight hundred dollars a year, as compared to the five thousand dollars a year earned by a member of the Lincoln city council). This figure is fixed in the constitution, so the voters must approve any increase; and since the last raise in 1968, they have not been eager to do so, rejecting nine different proposals for an increase in compensation. The senators have been quite inventive in their proposals for fixing their salaries, but the voters persist in disproving Norris's argument for an adequately compensated legislature.

Another major constitutional change, approved in 1970, replaced biennial with annual sessions. Many felt that Nebraska, like other states (forty-three now have annual sessions), could no longer set state policy in a few months and then adjourn for periods up to eighteen months. At the same election, the voters approved the setting of limits on the length of the sessions—ninety legislative days in odd-numbered years and sixty legislative days in even-numbered years. Artificial limits such as these are often found in state constitutions in order to encourage the prompt consideration of public business each year. Many critics of the practice assert that it causes the concluding days and hours of each legislative session to become increasingly hectic, if not chaotic, as time runs out. In Nebraska, the senators, sometimes reluctantly, have with one slight exception adhered to these limits, even though sessions can be extended provided forty senators are in favor. The legislature can also be called into special session by itself or by the governor. The regular sessions are directed by the constitution to start precisely at 10 A.M. on the first Wednesday after the first Monday in January.

Both the constitution and the rules of the legislature act to ensure that no bill will become law without the opportunity for deliberation by the senators and the public. Each bill, with the exception of certain technical revisor's bills, after introduction by a senator, is referred to the appropriate committee for public hearing and detailed consideration. After favorable action by the committee, it is placed on general file, from which it will eventually be extensively debated and voted on by the entire house. If the bill is advanced from general file, it is reviewed by the legal staff for technical errors and placed on select file. A second vote by the full legislature is then taken, again, after extensive debate. The bill next undergoes a further technical review (called engrossment) before final reading and passage. If approved by the required majority, the bill is signed by the presiding officer, certified by the clerk, and sent to the governor for approval or a veto. If passed by a simple majority and signed, the new law takes effect in three months from the final adjournment of the session. The legislature, however, can attach an emergency clause by a two-thirds vote, making the law effective the day following the governor's signature.

The steps leading to the passage of a bill are outlined here.

1. *Introduction of the bill*. Generally, bills can be introduced only during the first ten legislative days. The bill is read aloud by title only and referred to a standing committee.

2. *Committee hearings*. The committee sets a date for a public hearing on the bill. At the hearing, proponents and opponents may testify.

3. *Committee report*. Following public hearing, the committee reviews and votes in executive session. The committee may postpone indefinitely any further action or report the bill to general file. The committee may also combine similar bills or propose amendments.

4. *General file*. The bill and committee amendments are read and debated. Other amendments may be added from the floor. After consideration, the legislature votes on the disposition of the bill.

5. *E & R initial*. If advanced, the bill is checked by the Committee on Enrollment and Review for spelling, punctuation, and phraseology.

6. *Select file*. At this second reading, the bill can be advanced, postponed indefinitely, or recommitted to general file or to the committee. The bill may also be amended at this stage. A second vote is taken to advance the bill.

7. *E & R final*. A positive select file vote sends the bill back to the Committee on Enrollment and Review for "engrossment" or final printing.

8. *Final reading*. At the third reading, the bill must be read in full.

The bill may be recommitted to E & R, to the standing committee, or to select file for further amendments. If a vote is taken and the bill receives a majority, the presiding officer declares that the bill has passed.

9. *Gubernatorial action.* The bill is sent to the governor. If the bill is signed, it becomes law. If it is neither signed nor vetoed within five days, the bill becomes law. If the governor vetoes the bill, it is returned to the legislature, where a three-fifths vote is required to put the law into effect without the governor's signature.

The required majority of votes necessary for passage at different stages varies, depending on the issues under consideration. It should be noted that in most cases, the majority refers to all members elected and not to those present and voting on a particular date.

Action	*Votes Needed* (with 49 legislators)
Advance from committee	Majority
Advanced from general file	25
Pass on final reading	25
Pass with emergency clause	33
Increase appropriations above governor's request	30
Override governor's veto	30
Propose a constitutional amendment: general election	30
Propose constitutional amendment: special or primary election	40

The Organization of the Legislative Branch

Although Norris and the other reformers hoped that a smaller, nonpartisan, relatively simple legislature would give each representative a greater sphere of independent action, they were fighting a trend in all

legislative bodies toward greater centralization and growing disparities in the distribution of power. All deliberative bodies need some
rules, some structure, if anything is to be accomplished. Even in
Nebraska, the sheer increase in the amount of legislation, to say
nothing of the stringent time limits for a session, has forced a greater
consideration of ways to expedite the business of making law.

Thus, beyond the constitutional and statutory changes mentioned so
far, the rules of the Unicameral have undergone considerable change.
These rules are matters internal to the chamber and can be altered, in
most instances, by a three-fifths vote (thirty votes) at any time;
recently, rule changes occur most often at the beginning of a session,
when the procedures under which hundreds of bills do or do not
become laws are reviewed. Many of the rules concern fine points of
parliamentary procedures, but in two important areas—the officers of
the legislature and the number or jurisdiction of standing committees—some significant trends are discernible.

In terms of legislative officials, perhaps the most important change
has been the steady strengthening of the position of the speaker. As
was shown in chapter 3, the lieutenant governor's role as presiding
officer is largely meaningless, but, unlike the speaker of the U.S.
House of Representatives and those of most state lower houses, the
Nebraska speaker played, until recently, only a ceremonial or honorific role. In the past ten years, rule changes have empowered the
speaker to set the daily agenda for bills to be debated on the floor and
to coordinate the committee system. Either of these new functions
would have been a significant change, but together they indicate the
central role of the office. In 1981, the trend toward institutionalization
of the speakership became clear when the tradition of not reelecting
top officers was ended and the incumbent speaker, Senator Richard
Marvel, was unanimously reelected. In its new appreciation of the
speaker's function, the legislature has moved away from its original
system of decentralized, or nonexistent, formal leadership.

The evolution of the committee structure shows a similar move
toward greater centralization. For example, the committee chairmen
were, until recently, scarcely distinguishable from other members of
the committee in terms of previous experience on the committee. The

old method for selection of chairmen was appointment by the Committee on Committees, a rather large body (three senators from each of four regions in the state, plus a chairman elected at large), which assigned individual senators to committees. The Committee on Committees apparently perceived its job as the selection of whomever *it* believed to be the best choice. One study revealed that, from 1963 to 1971, 56 percent of the appointed chairmen had no previous service at all on the committees they had been assigned to lead.[1] In 1973, the rules were changed to provide for the election of chairmen by the entire Unicameral. Although some had doubts about a body of forty-nine members electing some fifteen leaders, the result has been that the elections are largely pro forma. Incumbent chairmen are often not even challenged and only rarely are they unseated. When vacancies occur, a good qualification for the chair is tenure on the committee or, best of all, to have been the vice-chairman, a position each committee bestows on one of its members. Thus, continuous service on a committee is now being rewarded and senators are adjusting their internal career plans accordingly.

The developments involving the centralization of power in the speaker and the committees reflect current legislative reality. Dealing with growing numbers of increasingly controversial and complex issues requires structure and restraint, if not discipline. This the Nebraska nonpartisan legislature, with its long-standing tradition of individualism, seemed unable to provide, and the desire for change has emerged. So while concessions have been made to a changing legislative environment, some senators are still sensitive about what they see as their prerogatives. The ambivalence is illustrated in proposals for speeding up the process for handling the workload. In one problem area—the impact of committee decisions—a satisfactory solution has emerged. In another—the number of bills any senator can introduce—there are still strong feelings about retaining the old ways.

In the first area, the committees have been helped by a rule change

1. Buster Brown, "Committees in State Legislatures," unpublished research paper, Political Science Department, University of Nebraska–Lincoln, 1974.

that makes overturning a committee decision by the full Unicameral more difficult. Upon introduction, a bill is referred to the committee having jurisdiction over the particular subject matter. After a public hearing, the committee then decides whether or not to recommend passage of the measure. Bills may be reported out of committee favorably or unfavorably to the full legislature. It is unusual for measures to be "bottled up" in committee and never heard from again, as is typical in many other states. This may result in an open and responsive system, but it also means that a negative committee report (typically given to about 40 percent of the bills considered by committees) could be reversed by the other members, who are perhaps not so familiar with the subject matter or the public input, by a simple majority vote on the floor. In 1975, the required majority for overturning the committee decision was raised to at least thirty votes, thus strengthening the committee's role. This change, especially since the committees are fairly small in size (seven to nine members), is another reason for senators to concentrate their time and energy on their committee assignments rather than on more general legislative activities.

The bill introduction problem remains, however. Despite continued efforts to resolve the matter, basic disagreement remains over the question of the number of bills and the efficient use of legislative resources. At present, there is no limit on how many bills a senator may introduce, although one short-lived experiment set the limit at ten per session. Proponents of the limits argue that the current high workload precludes thorough consideration of all bills, whereas the opponents believe that legislators should remain free to propose whatever is perceived to be in the best interest of their constituents. In order to avoid a complete breakdown, recent speakers have been forced to devise some system for allocating debate time toward the end of the session. Given the calendar limit on session duration, the openness of the bill introduction process, and the large number of bills reported favorably by committees, some priorities had to be set. The answer, if somewhat arbitrary, is quite practical: individual senators are allowed to designate one bill; committees, two bills; and the speaker, other bills as deemed necessary. This permits the speaker to schedule some floor time for at least these designated measures.

Staff and Facilities

The relatively small group of men and women assembled in a single room to vote on bills is only the most visible part of the legislative branch. To survive in the contest with an increasingly powerful executive, with a massive bureaucracy, and with a more active judiciary, legislators throughout the country have had to increase their own resources. Nebraska legislators today are expected to form an intelligent opinion on groundwater control, energy from milo, the educational needs of the mentally retarded, abortion, minority rights, and the candidates for the state reptile. Even a secluded scholar would be exhausted by the very range of questions now demanding a legislative answer, and senators are far from seclusion, since citizens are more vocal than ever in demanding to be heard on issues or to complain about the action of government. And each citizen expects personal service from his or her senator. The demands of the job are too much for any single individual.

Only in the last twenty years have the senators begun to provide themselves with a decent level of staff support. According to the *Lincoln Sunday Journal and Star,* in a July 20, 1980, article, the total legislative staff, including senators, had increased from 220 to 333 people, or 51 percent, from 1973 to 1980. Naturally, some critics pointed out that this growth was far greater than that of the executive branch, but such a comparison is unfair since the legislature was starting from a point in the vicinity of zero. Not too long ago, senators had no office facilities other than their desks in the chamber and all except committee chairmen had to share a secretary. Even today, by national standards, the Nebraska legislature is hardly profligate.

Most citizens would agree that their legislators need competent research and clerical personnel if they are to be effective participants in the governmental process. Today, each senator has an individual office in the state capitol and clerical and research aides are available to each one. Committees are also much better served by a permanent staff.

The general auxiliary services of the Unicameral are directed by the Legislative Council, which, since 1949, consists of all members of the legislature. The eight-person Executive Board, the chairmanship of which is a coveted post, supervises the services and personnel of the legislature. A major function of the council is the provision of information for the senators. To this end, it commissions interim reports on significant issues likely to come before the legislature. The permanent staff of the legislature includes the director of research, the clerk of the legislature, and the revisor of statutes.

Two of the newer offices established within the legislative staff are the public counsel, or ombudsman, and the legislative fiscal analyst. The work of the ombudsman is discussed in chapter 6, but it should be noted here that this office has relieved some of the burden of handling citizen complaints from the senators. The establishment of the legislative fiscal analyst is a sign that the Unicameral is anxious to retrieve some of its power of the purse lost to the governor. All bills must now include an estimate by the fiscal analyst of the relative financial impact of the measure. In considering the governor's budget proposal, the analyst staff scrutinizes the data supplied by the agencies and the executive budget experts. Overall, this office is an important element in the move to bring greater competence to the fiscal process, always the most pivotal item on the legislative agenda.

The Legislators

Regardless of the structure of the legislature, the ultimate determinant of legislation will always be the sort of men and women who seek and win office. Each senator is a unique person, but some generalizations can be made here.

Background

We learn quite a bit just from the fact that membership in the Unicameral is a part-time job with part-time pay. This means that a potential legislator must have another source of income and the sort of occupation that provides some flexibility in hours. Senators must be free to spend several months each year in Lincoln as well as be able to break away from regular pursuits to attend to other legislative business throughout the year. Therefore, one might expect the Nebraska legislature, like those of other states, to contain self-employed people (e.g., persons in insurance or real estate), farmers and ranchers who can afford to pay for help when away, retired people, younger people not yet established in a career outside of politics, and housewives.

Studies in other states have found the legislatures to contain a disproportionate number of lawyers. One reason for this may be that lawyers see state politics as a way to gain name recognition and establish contacts useful to their practice. Another reason is that many who go into law have an interest in politics, and the state legislature is a good place to begin a political career. One study of the Unicameral showed that the proportion of lawyers declined from about 25 percent in the last session of the bicameral system to only ten percent in the 1969–70 session, a ratio that has remained steady in the years since 1970.[2] Farmers have consistently constituted a large part of the membership, as have men and women involved in business. Blue-collar workers are seldom well represented in numbers.

Legislative membership also dramatically underrepresents women, with normally only one or two women serving; in the 1981 and 1983 legislatures, the number of females increased to six, for a ratio of men to women approximately the same as found in other state legislatures. Racial minorities have scant representation, but this is reflective of their small share of the statewide population.

Does this skewing of representation make any difference? It is difficult to say with certainty since it is plausible that a bank president could represent the interests of a blue collar worker on some or all issues. However, it is difficult to sustain an argument that a legislature comprising only bank presidents would in fact represent blue-collar interests, or those of teachers, civil servants, or housewives. It is easy to imagine that a legislature of housewives or blacks or manual laborers would produce legislation different from that enacted by the existing body. How different and whether it would be an improvement or not are other questions. But clearly, the occupational composition of the membership, like that of other legislative bodies, is biased toward professional, business, or farm interests. In the American context, this suggests a predominance of middle-class values and

2. Susan Welch and James Bowman, "The Nonpartisan Legislature: Does It Affect Political Careers?" *National Civic Review* 61 (October 1972): 451–56.

economic concerns, which, in turn, translates into generally conservative public policy.

Legislative Service in a Political Career

We may also learn something about Nebraska legislators by examining how legislative service fits into an overall career in politics. Is the typical senator a "professional" politician or an ordinary citizen performing a civic duty? Obviously, these are not ordinary people since election to any office is not a random event, and most of the members of the Unicameral report much involvement in community, fraternal, or party organizations. For the great majority, however, election to the legislature is the first, and only, successful run for office. In the 1981 session, for example, only twelve members served previously as an elected member of governing boards of cities, counties, schools, or special districts, while three had been mayors.

In many states, the legislature is a steppingstone to higher office, serving as a training and recruitment place for those wishing to become governor or other statewide officers or a member of Congress. One study of top officials in Nebraska found that between 1937 and 1970, only 25 percent of the governors, 38 percent of lieutenant governors, none of the secretaries of state, 30 percent of U.S. senators, and 11 percent of U.S. representatives had ever served in the state legislature.[3] Since 1970, the pattern has not changed much, with former senators winning two U.S. House seats and two lieutenant governorships. Service in the legislature, in other words, does not seem to be a great advantage in the quest for higher offices.

It may be that the legislature, in comparison to other states, does not produce many members of the state's political elite because of the nonpartisan feature. Higher political offices are all partisan; while nearly all legislators are also members of a party, running and winning in a nonpartisan election requires somewhat different sources of support and techniques than running for partisan positions. As parties become more involved in the legislature, this may change and the state legislature may again be a recruiting ground for other political office.

3. Ibid.

For most senators, the legislature is the apex of a political career. Turnover rates seem to indicate that it is a not altogether satisfactory prize, although this may be changing. In a typical election year, about ten of the twenty-five incumbents will not return for another session and since incumbents are rarely defeated (1980 was an exception, with five incumbents losing), turnover stems largely from personal decisions to not serve any longer. This pattern of voluntary retirement means that a typical session of the legislature finds about 40 percent of the members still in their first four-year term; the average member of the 1983 session had served 5.7 years. Although a case can be made for encouraging "new blood," most observers argue that this high turnover deprives the legislature of the experience of a large corps of legislative veterans. In short, a small minority make the legislature a long-term political career (in 1983, only seven members had served for more than twelve years). Part of this is no doubt caused by the meager salary earned by senators, but it may also be that, in their first taste of it, the senators do not derive much satisfaction from the life of an elected official.

Legislative Elections

How do people become candidates for the legislature? In states and communities with strong political parties, the party leadership may encourage potentially attractive candidates to file for office. Sometimes the party finds candidates, even if there is no chance of winning, just to contest every election. In Nebraska, nonpartisanship has discouraged the parties from playing a major role in selecting candidates for the legislature. A study done in 1967 in thirty-nine legislative districts found no district in which party leaders of both parties were actively involved in recruiting legislative candidates, although some party leaders admitted encouraging people from time to time to run.[4] Since 1967, there is general agreement that party involvement in legislative politics has become more intense, even if largely informal.

4. Bernard Kolasa, "Party Recruitment in Nonpartisan Nebraska," in John C. Comer and James B. Johnson, eds., *Nonpartisanship in the Legislative Process* (Washington, D.C.: University Press of America, 1978).

The activity can range from simple encouragement of potential candidates to financial support and campaign help, such as providing mailing lists and volunteers. One of the more ambitious party efforts, and perhaps a clue to the future, was the state Republican party's 1980 contribution of nearly thirty thousand dollars to candidates in districts where incumbent "Democratic" senators were running. In the absence of strong party involvement, we must assume that most candidates for the legislature are self-starters. Perhaps they receive some encouragement from friends, coworkers, or local civic and business interests, but most candidates are "on their own." This factor no doubt accounts for the independent attitude of legislators once in Lincoln.

Candidates for the legislature face two elections. The primary election reduces the field to two candidates. Sometimes, of course, when only one or two candidates have filed for the office, the primary election is just a formality (unless there is a successful write-in campaign). The two candidates receiving the most votes in the primary meet again in the general election.

Competition for Legislative Seats

The democratic ideal presents us with a picture of competitive elections, with several candidates running for each office. In such a situation, the voters are given a choice among candidates, if not always among radically different political alternatives. Norris and the other supporters of the nonpartisan ideal felt their plan would eliminate the party barrier and encourage greater participation in the electoral process by candidates and voters. If nonpartisanship has had any impact, however, it has been in the opposite direction.

In the wide-open nonpartisan system, with its minimal requirements for candidacy and small filing fee, one would anticipate more candidates and thus greater competition. In fact, in Nebraska the competition for legislative seats has declined, by some measures rather dramatically, since the partisan system was replaced by nonpartisanship. In the last decade of partisanship, almost three-fourths of primaries were contested, while the figure had fallen to a bare majority during the 1960s.[5] In the 1980 primaries, an average of only 2.5 candidates per district filed for the two nominations to be won, which means that anyone filing had an excellent chance of making it to the general election. In sixteen of the twenty-six districts with elections in 1980, there was no contest at all since only one (six districts) or two (ten districts) candidates were running.

Competition in the general election has also decreased. From 1927 to 1937, only a third of the winning candidates received more than 60 percent of the votes (which is considered a landslide), while from 1962 to 1972, almost half won by this margin. In the 1980 general election, the average margin of all winners was just over 70 percent of the vote. Incumbents do especially well, as evidenced by their 15 percent higher winning margin when compared with nonincumbent winners. While it is true that the advantage of incumbency obtains in all elections, it is probably more important in the nonpartisan setting.

The impact of nonpartisanship in the decline of competition is not easy to assess precisely, and it is true that many partisan legislative elections in other states are not overly competitive either. But the promise of nonpartisanship was that many more otherwise well-qualified candidates would seek public office if the political parties were forced into the background. Despite those hopes, closely competitive elections with large numbers of candidates have never been a feature of the nonpartisan Unicameral.

Nonpartisanship and the decline of competition may have effects on voters as well. In partisan systems, party labels are cues to voters who may lack any other type of information about the candidates. While parties in the United States are not highly disciplined or cohesive, there are differences in general orientation of the parties toward economic and social issues. Thus, party labels provide a broad indication about where a candidate might stand. Without such labels, voters may have no information at all and simply abstain from voting. This seems to be a very common pattern in Nebraska. Over one quarter of the voters who vote for the ''top of the ticket'' (president, governor, or

5. Susan Welch, ''Election to the Legislature: Competition and Turnout,'' in Comer and Johnson, *Nonpartisanship in the Legislative Process.*

U.S. senator) do not cast ballots for legislative candidates. This figure is very high compared to those of other states, where only about 6 percent of voters abstain from voting in legislative races; it is also in contrast to the partisan era in Nebraska, when ten percent ignored legislative contests.

In sum, it appears that the nature of the nonpartisan system has adversely affected competition for the legislative as well as voter interest and participation. Like it or not, political parties are a valuable means for providing voters with information about candidates and in forming a linkage between the public and their elected officials. It may be that the loss of competitiveness and voter participation is compensated by some other features of the legislature. However, in weighing the merits of a nonpartisan system, we cannot ignore the aspects discussed above.

Influence on Legislative Voting Behavior

The Structure of Legislative Voting and the Influence of Party

Legislators have many policy choices to make in the legislative process. They may choose to sponsor or cosponsor a bill, vote for or against it in committee or on the floor, decide to override a veto, or exercise their influence to gain others' support for their position at each stage. The informal "influence" behavior is difficult to study, so most analyses of legislative behavior focus on voting. In voting the legislator must take a public stand; the outcome of these public stances determine whether a bill will succeed or fail and thus whether a particular policy will be adopted. It is of great interest, therefore, to know what factors influence legislative voting decisions even if voting is not the only matter we would like to know about.

In most state legislatures and in Congress, the political party is one of the most important influences on voting behavior. Intraparty consensus on issues is almost never total, but differences between Democrats and Republicans are apparent on a wide variety of policy issues. In any partisan legislature, over the course of a session Democrats and Republicans do on the whole vote differently. There is a certain predictability about these differences, which all but the most uninterested citizen can observe. Thus, party labels, as we have noted earlier, do give voters cues not only to the general orientation of the candidates but also to their eventual voting behavior. What happens, then, in a nonpartisan legislature? What, if any, cues can the interested voter get in trying to predict how a prospective legislator might vote?

Overall, the answer seems to be that there simply are not very many good predictive factors for the average voter on how such a legislator might vote. In a detailed examination of voting in several sessions over a period from 1927 to 1969, one study found that voting patterns are very unstructured; that is, on different votes there are very different coalitions of legislators supporting and opposing the bills.[6] The structure in the Nebraska Unicameral had declined over time, from a relatively predictable, structured voting pattern in the pre-1937 partisan session. Voting in the Nebraska legislature was shown to be more random, in terms of aggregate patterns, than Congress or than other state legislatures that have been studied. This situation has been noted by other observers too, such as Reichley, who states that the nonpartisan legislature has "a tendency to fragment into small blocs, some of which contain only a single member."[7] A frequent observation is that the Unicameral is "an army of all generals."

Even those votes that are cohesive (that is, situations in which similar coalitions vote in favor of several bills) are not predictable by the few factors that might be obvious to voters, such as urban or rural residence. Since surveys show that most voters do not even know the name of their legislator, it stretches the imagination to assume that the typical constituent would be informed about the legislator's personal background, political ideology, or party membership. The evidence suggests, further, that even personal or party factors do not predict voting records in the Nebraska legislature more than a small percent of the time.

Some observers believe this pattern of voting is healthy, since it suggests a certain amount of independence—each legislator making

6. Susan Welch, "The Impact of Party on Voting Behavior in a Nonpartisan Legislature," *American Political Science Review* 67 (1973): 854–67.

7. James Reichley, *States in Crisis: Politics in Ten American States* (Chapel Hill, N.C.: University of North Carolina Press, 1964), p. 254.

up his or her own mind on each issue and then voting, regardless of party positions or anything else. The other view is that the legislative voting pattern just described does not allow constituents to fix responsibility for legislative actions. The voter cannot identify who is in charge and cannot vote out those responsible for bad policies (or reward those responsible for good ones). Generally, in a partisan legislature, one of the two parties has a majority and can, with some justice, be given credit or blame for legislative actions. The voter can then use this shared party responsibility in casting a vote for legislators. Of course, in no U.S. legislature does complete party-oriented voting exist—parties are only a rough guide to behavior in the legislature. But at least they are some guide for the average voters who know very little about their representatives.

The Influence of Lobbyists

Since legislators must get voting cues from somewhere, and it is clear that party and gross constituency characteristics are not that influential, what is left? One possible explanation is that legislators are guided by special interest groups and their lobbyists in Lincoln. In general, studies of state legislatures have noted that where parties are weak, interest groups and lobbyists are strong (and vice versa). Since the influence of party in the Nebraska legislature is quite weak, we might expect the influence of interest groups to be strong.

There are, of course, problems in assessing the influence of interest groups and lobbyists. One way is to ask legislators about their views of lobbyists. A 1968 study found that Nebraska legislators were much more positive toward lobbyists than were legislators in five other states studied. Only 2 percent of Nebraska's legislators had negative feelings about lobbyists, compared with 20 to 40 percent in the other states; and over 60 percent of Nebraska's legislators had positive feelings compared with 23 to 43 percent in other legislatures.[8] Another study of Nebraska lobbyists done at about that time showed that the lobbyists themselves felt they had a positive impact on

8. James Johnson, "Representational Orientations and Nonpartisanship," in Comer and Johnson, *Nonpartisanship in the Legislative Process.*

legislative behavior, with 59 percent believing they had some effect in changing votes at least some of the time.[9] Lobbying groups rated most successful in the legislature included education, state government, banking, ranching, livestock, farming, business, and public power. Labor, liquor, communications, real estate, and citizen lobby groups were ranked at the bottom of the list of influentials.

Since lobbyists are required to register with the clerk of the legislature, we can determine the great variety of interests seeking to influence voting. The list for 1981–82 shows over one hundred business interests with lobbyists. These interests range from the association of funeral directors to gas and oil companies. In addition, thirty-six insurance interests have representation, and there are sixteen banking lobbyists. Forty-one labor interests are represented, most of them serving public employees such as police, firefighters, and state employees. Education is also well represented, ranging from individual school districts to the University, and including as well a coalition of college students. Associations representing counties, cities, power districts, and health systems agencies serve the interest of governmental units. Farm and ranching organizations and professional groups make up another sizable portion of the legion of lobbyists. Finally, there are dozens of other groups such as "public interest groups" (for example, Common Cause, League of Women Voters), conservationists, both sides of the abortion issue, veterans' groups, religious groups, the Junior League, citizens against the death penalty, the Knights of Ak-Sar-Ben, and many others. Any examination of the list of registered lobbyists gives one an appreciation of the level of lobbying activity as well as a feel for the incredible diversity of issues considered by the legislature.

All these lobbyists must feel there is some point in their contacting senators and it seems a reasonable conclusion that some of them have an impact on some votes by some legislators. The setting certainly seems conducive to such influence. However, it is probably impossible to determine exactly how much influence lobbyists do have, since legislative ties with lobbyists are even less public than party ties. In

9. Kolasa, "Lobbying in the Legislature: The Influence of Nonpartisanship," in Comer and Johnson, *Nonpartisanship in the Legislative Process.*

contrast to some states, there have been few allegations of gross improprieties, such as bribes or payoffs to legislators, so there has been no stimulus for a thorough public airing of the question.

The Legislature and the Governor

As noted in chapter 3, Nebraska eliminated the partisan ties that often serve to unite the executive and legislative branches in other states. Since legislative organization does not center on the party, this link, while present, is less obvious and less regular. The lack of formal party organization has at least two implications for gubernatorial-legislative relations. First, it means that there is no group of party leaders in the legislature publicly bound in terms of party loyalty to carry the message of the governor to the "troops" in the legislature. Second, there is no group of "loyalists" in the legislature publicly committed to the governor's program on the basis of party ties. The governor's task in mobilizing legislative support for a coherent program is made more difficult.

Of course, a popular governor can certainly influence voting by some legislators on some matters. Governors Exon and Thone used party ties as well as more general appeals for support. The point is that nonpartisanship denies to the governor an institutional means of working through established party leadership in the legislature. Like any other supplicant before the Unicameral, governors must also strive to overcome the "forty-nine generals" syndrome.

Other Influences on Voting

Idiosyncratic influences must also play a role in voting behavior in Nebraska, as they do elsewhere. Given the volume of bills, one cannot expect a legislator to be interested in or informed about all of them, so advice from a friend, relative, influential constituent, or other source may well influence votes in quite random ways. Some observers of the legislature assert that certain senators in any session are looked to by their colleagues for voting cues in certain policy areas. All these factors make it very difficult to identify exactly why senators vote as they do.

We have portrayed a situation in which voting in the Unicameral is relatively unpredictable in light of the kinds of information that the citizen is likely to possess. If party ties are weak and lobbyists are strong, what does this tell us about the responsibility of legislators to the electorate? If one of the reasons for the nonpartisan system was to give the people more power, it is difficult to see how a system with little consistency in behavior on the part of the elected and little knowledge on the part of voters can lead to greater citizen control. In fact, the opposite result can be expected.

Evaluating the Legislature

Just how well does the Nebraska legislature work? How does it compare to other legislatures? One evaluation of the capability of all state legislatures was done in 1971 by the Citizens Conference on State Legislatures (CCSL). In their index, Nebraska was ranked ninth.[10] The score was a composite of rankings according to five criteria. In their view, an effective legislature should be:

1. *Functional*. The legislature should make good use of its time, have adequate staff and facilities, a small size, a relatively small number of committees with clear jurisdictions, and efficient procedures. Nebraska rated thirty-fifth among the states on this criterion, undoubtedly because it had at that time a small staff and very limited physical facilities.

2. *Accountable*. A legislature should have a clear system for redistricting, comprehensible rules and procedures, means of public access to information, and internal accountability. Here Nebraska ranked first, largely because of its single house, small size, emphasis on public access to committee hearings, and availability of voting and debate records.

3. *Informed*. The legislature should have adequate professional staff resources for research and fiscal review. On this item, Nebraska ranked sixteenth.

4. *Independent*. The legislature should be independent of the executive and interest groups and free from conflicts of interest. Nebraska

10. Citizens Conference on State Legislatures, *The Sometime Governments* (New York: Bantam Books, 1971).

ranked thirtieth on this criterion, probably because of the lack of a comprehensive lobby registration and financial reporting law, the generally close relationship with lobbyists, legislative powers then thought to rest with the lieutenant governor, and the nonpartisan structure.

5. *Representative*. This criterion is based on citizen awareness of legislators, reasonable qualifications for office, adequate salaries, and a streamlined operating procedure that allows each member to represent constituents in the best way possible. Here, Nebraska was ranked eighteenth.

CCSL also made some specific recommendations for improving Nebraska's legislative process. These included (1) discontinuation of rotating leadership; (2) a return to a partisan system; (3) the removal of legislative powers from the lieutenant governor; (4) increased compensation (salary and reimbursement for expenses); (5) public roll calls on committee votes; (6) more regulation of conflict of interest; (7) improved staff support; (8) individual offices for senators; (9) removal of restrictions on meeting times so the legislature can convene whenever it feels necessary; and (10) improved facilities for media.

In the decade or so since CCSL's original study, progress has been made to correct many of the deficiencies, especially those concerning staffing, offices, and legislative leadership. However, the criteria of the CCSL were largely concerned with institutional structure and formal procedures. A full evaluation should also include more behavioral measures. Professor John Comer, in analyzing the Unicameral in these terms, used four evaluation criteria.[11]

1. *Responsibility*. By this, Comer meant the way in which the legislature has dealt efficiently and effectively with public problems. He compared the responses of Nebraskans to questions about the performance of the legislature with responses from a national study and found little difference. That is, the unique features of the Unicameral do not lead citizens to give it higher or lower marks than conventional legislatures.

11. John Comer, "The Nebraska Nonpartisan Legislature: An Evaluation," *State and Local Government Review* 12 (September 1980): 98–102.

2. *Responsiveness.* To what degree does the Nebraska legislature respond to the appeals of interested parties? As has been said already, the legislators tend to be positively oriented toward interest-group activities. However, as Comer points out, such openness may "not extend to unorganized interests or individual citizens." Thus responsiveness may be skewed toward those with substantial organizational resources, a characteristic not unique to Nebraska's legislature.

3. *Accountability.* Do citizens know whether their votes for candidates will influence decisions by the legislature? Since voters cannot see how their votes will affect any legislative majority, the Nebraska system ranks low on this form of accountability. One cannot choose to support a particular group in the legislature since there are no such stable coalitions.

4. *Leadership Structure.* Does the legislature have a well-defined and stable leadership structure? As we have seen, the roles of the speaker and the chairmen are evolving but, as Comer argues, this strengthened leadership is still largely an administrative matter, or more effective clerkship, necessary to shepherd legislation through the process. Policy leadership, such as might be found in party caucuses, is not much in evidence.

Some Conclusions

In general, it would appear that where the Nebraska legislature rates highly it is largely because of its unicameral feature and its small size. A unicameral legislature is simpler and theoretically more comprehensible to the typical voter. A voter living in another state is represented by one representative of the upper house and at least one representative of the lower (and more if multimember districts are used). The voter has to try to comprehend the leadership, operation, and committee structure of two houses to follow legislative affairs closely. Further, because of the two houses and the larger size of other state legislatures, there are simply more legislators to be aware of. So Nebraska voters do not have to work as hard as voters in other states to remain informed about legislative activities. However, the assumption that the simple unicameral system does lead to such situations as identification by constituents of their representatives is cast into some doubt by the findings that only 32 percent of Nebraskans know the name of their senator, a figure not much different from percentages in studies of other bicameral legislatures.

The Unicameral's low ranking in some categories seems to be due in large part to the nonpartisan nature of the body; nonpartisanship makes the legislature vulnerable to outside pressures and is a contributing factor in the weak leadership system within the Unicameral. Another general reason for low scores is the fiscal conservatism of Nebraskans which had led to very low salaries and limited facilities for the legislators.

Even if the legislature made all the changes suggested by the reformers, there is no gurantee that it would make better laws. Political scientists have had a great deal of difficulty in proving conclusively that any sort of governmental reform makes a significant difference in the sort of policy that is eventually made. However, there undoubtedly is some virtue in having a legislative structure and procedures that maximize those characteristics that most citizens believe important; reform may also make the legislature more efficient. It appears that the unicameral structure aids representation and citizen comprehensibility. The nonpartisan feature appears to impede those ends. These contrasting outcomes of Nebraska's unique legislature should be seriously considered in any attempts at reforming that body.

ROBERT SITTIG

FIVE

The Judiciary

Of the traditional three branches of government, the judiciary is often the most obscure for ordinary citizens. The judges and the legal profession may have caused some of this obscurity by convincing others that the business of dispensing justice is somehow divorced from political affairs. But anyone interested in politics must take into account the courts because, while not as publicized as the governor or the legislature, they are an integral part of the political process. Consider the general impact of two recent Nebraska Supreme Court decisions: the distribution of $70 million in state funds to local government as a replacement for certain property taxes was prohibited because of flaws in the distribution formula; and a long-established policy preventing the transfer of water from one river basin to another was overturned, thus intensifying the struggle of the "haves" and "have-nots" among the state's many irrigators.

Lesser state courts can also have a significant impact far beyond that of a single case. A district court judge in North Platte attempted to limit pretrial publicity about a sensational murder case by issuing what the press called a "gag order." The attempt at prior restraint of the press was overturned by the U.S. Supreme Court in *Nebraska Press Association* v. *Stuart* (1976), a case called "the most important constitutional victory for freedom of the press since the Pentagon

Papers case.''[1] Such examples of judicial decision making underscore
the need for an examination of the organization and operation of
Nebraska's courts. Admittedly, these examples recount relatively rare
events, but they also point out that the courts serve a number of
important roles in our system of government, roles that go beyond the
adjudication of disputes between individual citizens or between the
state and accused wrongdoers.

State Court Reform

In 1906, the renowned legal scholar, Roscoe Pound, then dean of the
Law College at the University of Nebraska, issued a manifesto calling
for a thorough reform of state judicial systems. The multiplicity of
courts, with very little central direction, caused wasteful administration. The archaic nature of the judiciary was the major cause of
popular dissatisfaction with the administration of justice. Other critics
at the time were unhappy with the lack of proper training of many
judges and the introduction of partisan politics into the selection
process of almost all state judges.

Pound's remarks are generally considered as the beginning of the
reform movement in the American judiciary. Unlike concurrent reforms in the executive and legislative branches, however, court reform has not always been the result of a great deal of popular demand.
Instead, it has tended to be the result of the slow, steady work by the
legal profession and the judges themselves. Among the goals of the
reformers have been the following:

1. The rationalization of the court structure. A state judiciary should
be a single system with a central source of direction. Overlapping
jurisdiction should be eliminated so that responsibility can be easily
identified.

2. The professionalization of the judiciary. A selection method that
produced many nonlawyer, part-time judges should be replaced by a
process stressing "merit," with merit understood as legally trained,
full-time judges without overt partisan ties.

1. Benno Schmidt, "The Nebraska Decision," *Columbia Journalism Review* 15
(November–December 1976): 51.

3. The simplification of court procedures. A single set of readily understood rules should replace the older mix of case law and codes.

4. Professionalization of court administration. A single office should have coordinating power in order to ensure the orderly assignment of judges and the smooth disposition of pending cases.

5. State financing of the courts. Justice should not depend on the financial ability of local entities, and above all it should not depend on fees generated by the legal process itself, as it did in the justice of the peace system.

If these are the major goals of the revolution that Pound began, there is still much work to be done in many states. And in Nebraska, from the reformer's point of view, the situation is far from perfect. It is not literally true that Pound was a prophet without honor in his native state, for he was recently enshrined in the Nebraska Hall of Fame. But he was certainly a prophet without immediate impact, since it was not until well into the postwar period that Nebraska began a sustained effort at court reform.

From statehood until 1970, the court system remained virtually unchanged. The supreme court and the district courts were the only tribunals supported directly from the state treasury. County courts enforced state law but were maintained as a function of county government. At the lowest level were the justice, municipal, and police courts. The justice courts were the most questionable feature of the entire system. These courts were presided over by elected justices of the peace. The exact number of such courts is uncertain but, according to the *Nebraska Blue Book,* there was authority for as many as two thousand. The justices received no salary from state or local government, but supported themselves by commissions and fees for their work. In short, the system was highly decentralized and largely nonprofessional.

The beginning of serious reorganization work came in 1970, when voters approved a constitutional amendment allowing the legislature to revamp the regional and local courts. Under the leadership of the Nebraska Bar Association, legislation was approved in 1972 to implement the amendment. As a result, the structure and operation of the local and district courts were more fully integrated into a unified system. The justice courts, as well as the justices of the peace, disappeared from the judicial landscape. These changes, together with the earlier modifications in the selection process, meant Nebraska was well on the way to achieving that professionalized, centralized pyramid that is the ideal of court reformers.

Space does not permit an exhaustive review of all the important but somewhat technical reforms of the Nebraska system. Instead, attention will be directed toward the two most important areas of reform: court personnel and court structure.

Selection and Tenure of Judges

Direct citizen involvement in the selection of state and local judges is an American tradition, even though the federal court system has always remained insulated from direct popular control. The appropriateness of various appointive or elective arrangements for selecting state judges is a subject of continuing debate, but Nebraska in the past two decades has moved steadily in the direction approved by court reformers. Beginning with a 1962 constitutional amendment, supreme court and district court judges have been selected under the so-called Missouri Plan. This approach, as described below, was subsequently deemed so beneficial that it was extended to include all other judges. Major emphasis in this section will be given to the process by which the present mix of appointment and election of judges developed.

Nebraskans, like other Americans, have been guided by changing philosophies about a central question of representative government, namely, the uncertain line between democratic accountability and the neutral professionalism of government personnel, including judges. The advocates of what came to be called Jacksonian democracy took accountability to an extreme; public officials, from president and governor down to village constable, were to be elected. Public office had to be open to all; that, in their view, was a reasonable proposition since no real expertise was needed to handle the business of government. Eventually, the excesses promoted by the democratization of the public sector brought about another school of reformers. These opponents of the Jacksonian ideal, gaining strength after the Civil War, stressed the need for neutral experts in government. Professional knowledge, especially in an area so complex as the law, was to be protected from the vagaries of partisan politics.

During the colonial period, judges at all levels were most often selected by the legislature, with occasionally some involvement by the governor. Appointment of judges by the chief executive became more fashionable once the U.S. Constitution went into effect in 1789, since it provided for presidential appointment with senatorial confirmation of all federal magistrates. Once a selection system or, for that matter, any other political device is established, it acquires increased status and durability with age, and so a few states still employ a purely appointive method for selecting their judges.

For most states, however, the emergence of Jacksonian democracy had a direct impact on the judicial selection process. The emphasis on political participation by all citizens led to the long ballot, in which all manner of government offices were filled by election. Although this democratization effort was directed more toward executive and administrative officials, by the late 1800s two-thirds of the states had constitutional provisions for the popular election of judges. In addition, the term of office tended to be short (two years, in most cases) so that the "will of the people" could be injected frequently and directly into judicial affairs. By this time, the political parties were well established and growing in influence, so most often judges were included on the partisan ballot along with other legislative and executive officials. Finally, the power of judges to determine the constitutionality of legislative and executive acts was so firmly established that the advocates of further democracy were all the more convinced that the courts must be directly accountable to the public.

Nebraska's original constitution was colored by the Jacksonian ideal, but by the turn of the century a new brand of reformism had arisen to lead a challenge to the existing system and to the supposed bane of partisanship in government. That group of reformers known as the Progressives began to succeed in implementing nonpartisanship in city, county, school, and judicial elections. They were especially powerful in the plains states, where, for a number of reasons, the political parties had never been able to sink deep roots. In Nebraska, the Non-Partisan League was instrumental in getting the provision for elections without party designation of the candidates applied to all judicial elections, except for justices of the peace. The nonpartisan movement reached its zenith in Nebraska with the establishment of the nonpartisan legislature, but today the movement has run its course. We are left with an important legacy, however, in that the state's judges are still selected in a nonpartisan manner.

For court reformers, removing the judges from partisan politics was not enough. These reformers, led by the American Judicature Society, a body of legal professionals, scored a coup in the area of public relations by claiming for their proposal the honorific term *merit plan*. While a fervent democrat might well argue that the merit of government personnel is precisely the matter to be decided at the polls, the reformers were able to sell the idea that judges should possess professional training in order to carry out what is a highly specialized job. And if professional training determines merit, it then follows that the body most capable of evaluating who has merit is not the uninformed voter but instead the professionals themselves; that is to say, lawyers are the most qualified to assess the capability of a judge.

One of the earliest reform plans was implemented by Missouri in 1940, following a scandal with the political machine in Kansas City. Contrary to what its advocates say, this Missouri Plan does not take politics out of the judicial process and, as one authority noted, "the appointment of judges by the governor from lists supplied by nominating commissions is every bit as political as a popular election or as appointment by the governor in response to a deal with a political boss."[2] However, reformers have seen the plan as an improvement and fifteen states, including Nebraska in 1962, moved in this direction.

The Missouri Plan for selecting judges establishes a shared responsibility among citizens, lawyers, the governor, and sitting judges in the filling of court vacancies. A nominating commission is appointed for all types of judgeships by district. This means that there are presently a total of fifty-five such commissions. The membership of a commission consists of four citizens from the district, four lawyers from the district, and a supreme court judge who serves as the

2. Victor Rosenblum, "Courts and Judges: Power and Politics," in James Fesler, ed., *The 50 States and Their Local Governments* (New York: Alfred A. Knopf, 1967, p. 422.

nonvoting chair. The citizens and the judge are appointed by the governor and the members of Nebraska Bar Association selects the attorneys. A commission is activated when a vacancy occurs. The credentials of those applicants who respond to the announcement are received by the commission and a public hearing is subsequently held to allow for any additional testimony or comments by or about the candidates.

After closed deliberations, the commission may nominate as many candidates as it deems to be qualified, except that it must forward at least two names on a public list to the governor. The governor then selects the judge. In the event that the governor fails to select anyone within a specified time period, the supreme court is required to fill the position from among those nominated. This has occurred only once in Nebraska's experience with the plan, when Governor J.J. Exon apparently found neither of the candidates on a list to be acceptable.

The newly appointed judge, after taking office, serves a probationary period in order to establish a record for the voters to evaluate. The initial term is somewhat indefinite because of the irregularity with which vacancies ocur. However, it must be at least three but not more than five years in duration. The election that follows the probationary term (and all later elections) is uncontested since the voters are restricted to a simple yes or no choice about the retention of the incumbent. If successful with the voters, the judge serves a full six-year term, at the end of which the electoral phase is repeated. If a sitting judge is rejected by the voters, the post is considered vacant and the nomination commission is again called to duty.

In terms of the actual operation of the merit plan, in Nebraska and elsewhere, one could have predicted that certain unanticipated effects would occur because ideals, political or otherwise, are seldom realized completely. We have now had sufficient experience with its operation to provide us with some basis for assessing its advantages or shortcomings. At the most tangible level—electoral impact—the major result has been that the voters rarely exercise the prerogative of terminating an incumbent judge, either after the probationary period or at the end of a full term. In Nebraska, of the hundreds of judges who have sought "reelection" since 1966, only two have been defeated, both after a public airing of information about personal matters and not on the basis of their judicial records. The low level of judicial turnover is comparable to that of other states using a merit plan.

In recent elections, voters have given an 80 to 90 percent approval rate for those "running," regardless of the circumstances (level of court, age and experience of incumbent, region of the state) surrounding the election. Another 10 to 30 percent of all voters do not even bother to express any preference at all in these contests. We have no evidence to explain this indifference. Overall, the minimal response of the public seems to deviate significantly from the ideal of the Missouri Plan proponents, who argued that the general citizenry had an important role to play in the determination of state and local judges.

Some critics take this low voting turnout as validation of their assertions that the lawyers and the governor dominate the selection process. The lawyers would probably respond that, because of their professional involvement, they are entitled to a special role. Governors would argue also that, from among *qualified* nominees, they should have the latitude to pick those with some affinity to the governor, the political party, or both. There have been enough instances in Nebraska to indicate that pure merit is not always the determinant for selection, although we must admit that there has been no empirical study of the factors that influence the decisions of the commissions or the governor. This is not mentioned as a condemnation of the entire process, but it does point out that the real choices are made by the more active participants, while the public plays a much more passive, reactive, and probably less effective part in the system.

Given the increased length of tenure in the Missouri Plan states, the circumstances under which an incompetent jurist can be terminated are becoming more important. Under normal conditions, judges in Nebraska may retire with full benefits at age sixty-five, and they must retire at seventy-two. A bad judge who refuses to retire poses a problem. The impeachment process is available but never used. Impeachment is a rather ponderous and basically ineffective means of dealing with the common variety of incompetence that is far less than criminal.

To provide a method of policing the judiciary on a regular basis, the constitution was amended in 1966 to establish the Commission on Judicial Qualifications. The commission, made up of judges, attorneys, and citizens, considers, upon complaint, whether a judge should be removed or involuntarily retired. More recently, the power to discipline judges short of removal from office has been authorized. The commission recommends the appropriate action to the supreme court, which then makes the final determination. This is an approach far more sensitive to a variety of circumstances than the impeachment "blunderbuss." The Commission on Judicial Qualifications investigated 161 complaints between 1967 and 1982. The largest number of cases were found to be without merit, while seven were serious enough that the judge involved either resigned or applied for early retirement. In the 1981–82 period, three cases resulted in punishment in the form of a "private reprimand" from the chief justice. No judge has been removed from office by the commission.

Given all the debate about the selection of judges, one might ask if the method really makes any difference. While it is impossible to answer that question with complete accuracy, studies done so far suggest that the answer may be no. It has been found that there are few differences in the educational qualifications, experience, or social background of judges chosen by appointment compared to those elected or selected through the Missouri Plan. Furthermore, a study comparing decisions of state supreme courts concluded that any differences in decisions were not related to the means of selecting the judges. The propensity of judges to decide in favor of defendants rather than plaintiffs, the state rather than private citizens, landlords rather than tenants, and so forth bore no relationship to the method of judicial selection.[3] Thus, perhaps it makes less difference how judges are chosen than reformers would have us believe.

A final aspect of the selection process of supreme court judges, not associated with the Missouri Plan, has caused some controversy over the years. The issue concerns the equitable apportionment of the districts for the judges. The chief justice is chosen without regard to geographical factors and one judge is selected from each of the six regional districts. From 1930 until 1971, the district boundaries were

3. Bradley Canon, "The Impact of Formal Selection Processes on Characteristics of Judges—Reconsidered," *Law and Society Review* 13 (1972): 570–93; Burton Atkins and Henry R. Glick, "Formal Judicial Recruitment and State Supreme Court Decisions," *American Politics Quarterly* 2 (1974): 427–49.

never redrawn by the legislature, despite great population changes within the state. In 1970, the constitution was amended to require apportionment of the districts after each decennial census, a move made necessary by the fact that judicial election districts are not governed by the one-person, one-vote standards imposed by the federal courts on legislative bodies. The change remedied the then-existing disparities, but in the 1970s, the traditional urban-rural rivalries cropped up as some Omaha legislators sought another amendment to eliminate what was seen as gerrymandering. The Omahans argued that their metropolitan area was split among four of the six districts so that only one judge actually lived in Omaha. They also noted that 30 percent of the state's population, 40 percent of the state bar association membership, and 50 percent of the supreme court cases came from Douglas County. Voters in 1980 defeated an amendment to change the situation. In 1981, the Unicameral took up the matter again in the course of its regular reapportionment of all electoral districts and defused temporarily the issue by approving new district boundaries.

The Court Structure

As currently constituted, the Nebraska court system consists of three tiers of courts with general jurisdiction and a few more specialized courts. (See Figure 5.1).

The Supreme Court

The Nebraska Supreme Court, consisting of a chief justice and six judges (not justices), is the apex of the statewide system. The court hears and decides appeals from the district courts, juvenile courts, Workmen's Compensation Court, and such regulatory agencies as the Public Service Commission. The constitution provides the right of appeal to the supreme court in all felony and civil cases, and the appeal of misdemeanors is permitted by statute.

As noted in chapter 2, the greatest power of the Nebraska Supreme Court is that of judicial review, which enables the court to issue definitive statements about the meaning of the constitution and resultant statutes, executive orders, regulations, and other action by public

Figure 5.1: Court Structure and Process of Appeal

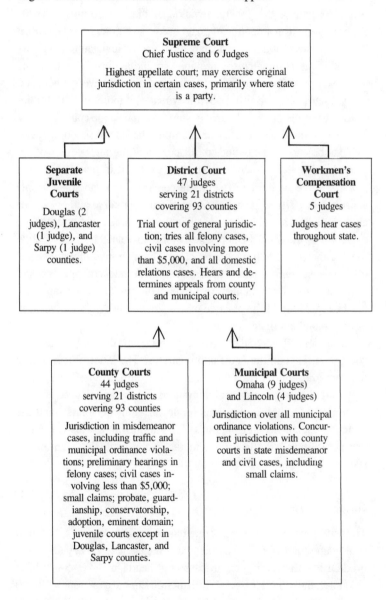

SOURCE: State Court Administrator, *The Courts of Nebraska, 1980.*

officials. However, there is a curious limitation to this power of the court. As part of the general revision of the constitution in 1920, voters approved an amendment that requires an extraordinary majority (five of the seven judges) to declare an act of the legislature unconstitutional. This eliminated the previous simple majority requirement, which still prevails in the federal courts and virtually every other state court system. The provision obviously makes it more difficult for the court to overrule the legislature. In some instances, the court majority of four has found major acts (for example, the sale of school lands in 1960) to be outside the bounds of the constitution, but, because of the extraordinary requirement, the statutes were left in place.

A more recent source of supreme court power is an amendment, approved in 1970, that says, "General administrative authority over all courts in this state shall be vested in the Supreme Court and shall be exercised by the Chief Justice. The Chief Justice shall be the executive head of the courts and may appoint an administrative director thereof." The supreme court can issue uniform rules of practice and procedures for all other courts in the state; the court is also responsible for the regulation of the practice of law, including disciplinary action against members of the bar.

The major officers of the supreme court include the clerk, a supreme court reporter, and the court administrator. The latter officer assists the supreme court in the exercise of its administrative functions, including the preparation and administration of the budgets, the development of training programs for lower court personnel, and the review of record-keeping methods. The administrator is also in charge of staff support for all other elements of the judicial system of the state.

District Courts

The district courts serve as intermediate appeals courts for cases from county and municipal and courts and some agencies. They also have original jurisdiction in certain cases not heard in lower courts. For example, they have original jurisdiction in most serious (felony) criminal cases. There are twenty-one district courts staffed by forty-seven district judges. Juvenile courts in Douglas, Lancaster, and

Sarpy counties share with the district courts some of the jurisdiction over domestic relations. The judges are appointed and elected from the district and paid by the state, while the clerk of the district court is elected and financed at the county level.

The probation function is served by the Office of the Probation Administrator and the Field Probation Service as an integral part of the district court operation. General supervision is provided by the Nebraska Probation Services Committee. The state probation administrator oversees the probation officers in the field and serves as a liaison between officers and the courts. The Field Probation Service works out of seventeen probation districts. The officers cooperate with district and county judges by providing presentence information on offenders so that the most appropriate sentence can be determined. They also keep track of those persons placed on probation by the courts.

County and Municipal Courts

The lowest courts in the state are the county courts; the municipal courts in Omaha and Lincoln serve a similar purpose although they are financed by the cities. The county courts have jurisdiction over probate, adoption, guardianship, eminent domain proceedings, and juvenile matters (outside of Douglas, Lancaster, and Sarpy counties). These courts share with the district courts jurisdiction over civil cases involving five thousand dollars or less. They have jurisdiction over criminal cases involving misdemeanors and violations of city ordinances. County courts are financed and overseen by the state. In 1981, there were forty-four county judges.

The newest judicial innovation is the small claims court, which is operated as an adjunct of the county and municipal courts. These were set up in order to allow people to avoid some of the cumbersome and expensive procedures found in regular courts. The small claims court affords a citizen an opportunity to settle minor grievances with another party under somewhat relaxed conditions. No lawyers are allowed and the litigants have to present their own cases before a presiding judge who renders an immediate decision. Only cases involving one thousand dollars or less can be considered.

Specialized Courts

Because certain bodies of law require a great deal of specialized knowledge, courts have been created to handle a single subject matter. Juvenile courts, as mentioned above, handle cases pertaining to neglected, dependent, or delinquent children in the more populous parts of the state. At the state level, the Workmen's Compensation Court adjudicates the claims of workers for compensation from their employers arising from occupational injuries. Although not part of the judicial branch, the Commission (formerly "Court") of Industrial Relations concentrates on disputes in labor-management relations between employee groups and units of government. Other state agencies combine adjudication with administration; the Power Review Board and the Public Service Commission are examples of such regulatory agencies.

Court Workloads

The daily course of judicial business deals most often with the disposition of criminal and civil cases rather than with political or public policy matters. In the area of criminal law, local prosecutors and enforcement officials are in the pivotal initiatory role and, through the exercise of their considerable discretion, make it possible to settle a large number of cases outside of court. This avoids the activation of a time-consuming jury trial with its sometimes unpredictable outcome. The burden on the courts is thus relieved by the simple fact that many potential cases never make it to the courtroom; the dismissal of charges, plea bargaining, and other practices help to avoid a breakdown in the system. In civil actions between two private parties, the volume of cases continues to increase as society becomes more complex and individuals become conscious of their legal rights. The nationwide trend of resorting to litigation to counter perceived wrongs is evident in Nebraska as well. As in criminal cases, efforts are made to encourage and facilitate the resolution of these disputes short of an actual trial. Still, the court dockets continue to grow and, as elsewhere, judicial resources are always strained. For example, the supreme court, faced with almost one thousand cases each year, began in

1983 the use of settlement conferences for all appeals coming before it; the conferences, in some cases using retired judges, attempt to get lawyers to settle appeals out of court.

Impeachment

Finally, special note must be made of the unique impeachment mechanism in Nebraska. The federal and most state constitutions prescribe that the action commence in the lower house with the passage of a bill of impeachment. Next, the prosecutors (called *managers*) are appointed by the house and the trial proceedings shift to the senate, which sits as a court of impeachment. If, after presentation of the evidence, the upper house finds the impeached official guilty, usually by a two-thirds vote, the culprit stands convicted and is removed from office.

Until 1875, Nebraska followed the national pattern. The delegates to the constitutional convention of that year were extremely dissatisfied with the method because of the politically motivated impeachment in 1871 of Governor David Butler. In order to prevent a recurrence of the public furor and bitterness that developed in the Butler case, they proposed and the people approved a new procedure whereby a public official would be impeached by a joint session of the legislature; any trial would then take place before the state supreme court, with the two-thirds rule for conviction still in effect. If a member of the supreme court were impeached, the trial would be held before the district court judges sitting as a body. Essentially, the same impeachment plan is still in effect with, of course, adjustments made for a unicameral legislature.

This procedure is no minor curiosity. In Nebraska, impeachment trials are on a par with criminal prosecutions in a regular court of law. The assignment of the crucial trial phase to the supreme court has given substantial protection to the accused, since the court is more restrictive in matters of rules, rights, and jurisdiction. Since most impeachment attempts are inevitably political in nature, and quite often blatantly partisan, the meticulous standards of the court may well account for the fact that there have been no impeachments initiated within the state since the 1890s. Political trials cannot be so easily brought to a "satisfactory" finish before a court of law as they can before a legislative body.

Conclusion

The Nebraska judicial branch has experienced considerably more change in the past two decades than it did in the first one hundred years of its existence. Structurally, the courts in the state have been realigned into a nearly centralized system, with the supreme court and the chief justice exercising wide authority for the overall administration of justice in the state. In the area of judicial personnel, the major change came with the introduction of the merit plan for the selection and retention of judges; additionally, the matter of ensuring acceptable conduct and performance by judges has been formalized and refined by the creation of the Judicial Qualifications Commission. Many other more technical features have undergone much modernization in the past few years. A comparative study of state courts in 1975 ranked Nebraska in the top half of the fifty states in terms of court modernization.[4]

How should one evaluate this rather impressive activity? It would be hard to believe that the reforms have not been to the benefit of the state and its people. It is certainly doubtful whether many look with fondness back to the "good old days" of a decade ago, when largely untrained, partisan justices of the peace made their livings from dispensing justice at the local level. Despite the positive accomplishments, however, one might have hoped for a little more popular involvement in the changes. In many respects, court reform has been the work of judges and lawyers and so it could be suggested that some changes were based on the premise that "what is good for the Nebraska Bar Association is good for everybody."

Carl Baar, a political scientist, is one who argues that state court reform "should shift from a consideration of the needs of judges and court administrative personnel to a consideration of the needs of litigants and other members of the public serviced by the courts." As

4. James A. Gazell, *The Future of State Court Management* (Port Washington, N.Y.: Kennikat Press, 1978), p. 11–12.

evidence of the closed nature of reform, he cites the attempt at further modernization in Nebraska in 1977. The Nebraska Bar Association played the central role by employing consultants from the National Center for State Courts to evaluate how closely the state approximated American Bar Association standards. Those surveyed for their views were judges, lawyers, and experts from outside Nebraska.[5]

One must readily concede the obvious response from the lawyers. A public meeting for consideration of court reforms, even if publicized during halftime of the Oklahoma game, would probably not draw enough citizens to fill one of the state capitol's notoriously tiny elevators. If we had depended on some mass expression of popular demand for court reform, we would undoubtedly still have nineteenth-century conditions. The lawyers have assumed leadership by default. It is to be hoped, then, that Nebraska citizens will someday show more interest in the shaping of their judiciary. As is true in so many other areas, the law is too important to be left to the experts.

5. Carl Baar, ''The Scope and Limits of State Court Reform,'' paper delivered at the Symposium on Administrative Reform and Public Policy, University of Nebraska–Lincoln, April 14, 1978.

SIX

The Bureaucracy

Perhaps one could have used the more neutral term *public administration* in the title of this chapter, but any discussion of administration will get eventually to the thing called bureaucracy. It is a value-laden word, a word that often sums up all the animosity that Americans and Nebraskans have toward their government. At the same time, it is the word that best captures the condition of the modern world, for no matter how long or loudly we curse bureaucracy, it endures. This chapter examines the growth of Nebraska state bureaucracy, the reasons for its durability in a hostile environment, and the means now used to keep it under control.

The Growth of Bureaucracy

Life was simpler in the immediate postwar period. No one brooded about the perils of insecticides or feedlot runoff, and the environmental movement was far in the future. The great majority of women worked in the home, or aspired to, even though many had worked elsewhere during the war. Urbanization was developing, but a majority of Nebraskans lived in rural areas. Natural fuels were plentiful, and the groundwater level in the Ogallala Aquifer was an obscure academic topic. As a result, the administrative functions of the state in

1945 still reflected for the most part a traditional understanding of government's role in providing services for the citizens.

Thus, most agencies in 1945 provided straightforward services or performed the basic functions enabling government to maintain itself. The Department of Agriculture and Inspection and the Department of Roads and Irrigation are examples of the former. Agriculture and Inspection oversaw various agricultural activities to provide protection against obvious dangers (for example, the European corn borer and Bang's abortion disease) and to monitor and regulate the behavior of people in certain occupations (for example, itinerant merchants and operators of frozen food lockers). The work of Roads and Irrigation was clear: to provide for and maintain a system of roads in the state and to monitor the use of water for irrigation, power supply, and drainage. In the maintenance category, the Office of Tax Commissioner was to ensure uniformity and propriety in the performances of county assessors.

A more recent inventory of state departments and agencies reflects the greater complexity of Nebraska society. The latest *Nebraska Blue Book* describes agencies and functions that were practically nonexistent in 1945. For example, the Department of Environmental Control (established in 1971) helps to develop and administer rules, regulations, and standards regarding water, air, and land quality. The Commission on the Status of Women reflects the changing role of women in society. The Equal Opportunity Commission is a source of support for people who have suffered discrimination in employment because of race, sex, or age. And speaking of age, the Department on Aging tries to improve the lot of elderly Nebraskans.

Even old, familiar organizations have undergone great changes. The Department of Institutions (established in 1961) exists to manage all state activities for the mentally retarded and visually impaired and to combat alcoholism and drug abuse. While this department began its life in the nineteenth century as the Commission for the Control of the Feeble-Minded and the Board of Control, its operation today reflects a more active orientation toward preventing certain problems and rehabilitating those who suffer from them. Today's Department of Motor Vehicles (established in 1957) administers all laws regulating the use of motor vehicles. This function was formerly performed by a division in the Department of Roads and Irrigation. The growth in the number and diversity of motor vehicles as well as the regulations concerning them grew to a point justifying the creation of a separate bureau.

These agencies evolved into their present form because there are more Nebraskans who are more active, thereby creating a need for state government to protect the common interest and those who cannot help themselves. The agencies also suggest the utilization of more sophisticated technologies—on the farm, highways, hospitals, and elsewhere—requiring some form of regulation. Finally, these examples suggest that Nebraskans, like other Americans, are demanding more benefits from their government: comprehensive mental health care, reduced alcoholism, cleaner air and water, and a number of other elements of the modern version of the "good life."

The conventional wisdom is that Nebraskans cherish the ideal that the least government is the best government. Data describing the growth of the state bureaucracy raise the possibility that Nebraskans do not practice what they preach. For example, the number of state employees per 10,000 of population for the entire country was 46 in 1946; for the same year, the rate for Nebraska was 61.[1] In 1979, the national rate was 140 while Nebraska's was 177. Thus, although the national figures rose at a slightly higher rate than Nebraska's, the state continues to exceed the national norms in terms of number of state employees. The state had 7,000 full-time employees in 1946 and by 1982, the number was about 27,800.

Another way of looking at the growth in Nebraska's bureaucracy is to examine the salaries paid to public employees. Between 1946 and 1979, the monthly payrolls of all state employees in the United States grew by a factor of twenty-five. This is clearly a sizable rate of growth, yet Nebraska's was greater. The monthly payroll for the state in 1946 was about $1,000,000; by 1979, the figure had grown to $29,377,000, just under thirty times larger. Thus, Nebraskans have been simul-

1. These and other figures here and in the following paragraph come from *State and Local Government Quarterly Employment Survey,* also published annually as *Public Employment* (Washington, D.C.: Bureau of the Census).

taneously protesting bigger government and spending proportionately more money than the national rate on their state administration.

It is necessary to add some qualifying remarks about the number of full-time employees and payrolls, for a number of other midwestern and western states have experienced similar growth. Some government functions require a minimum number of employees regardless of the state's population. For example, the number of people needed to promote agricultural products outside the state depends more on crop productivity than it does on population. In addition, the physical size of Nebraska plays a role in these matters. The Department of Roads employs a sizable proportion of the total work force, which is likely a function of area rather than people. Finally, the rate of growth for Nebraska stands out because the state was starting from a lower base and the figures reported here may not mean that the state has caught up with the rest of the country in terms of the quality or quantity of its public services.

Obviously, no state official has the title of bureaucrat, and no one is formally in charge of doing "bureaucratic things." The much maligned bureaucrats are, after all, ordinary men and women performing a variety of jobs—jobs that at least some segment of society feels are very important. The state patrol officer aiding a stranded motorist, the librarian ordering braille books for blind students, the hatchery employees stocking streams and lakes, even the head football coach at the University of Nebraska are, in the crudest sense, bureaucrats.

It would be hard to make the argument that the growth of the bureaucracy is the result of the mindless proliferation of new programs. The biggest agencies can trace their lineage back to the early days of statehood. This is certainly true of the University of Nebraska, with its 11,996 employees in 1980. Other state agencies with more than 1,000 employees are Public Institutions, Roads, Correctional Services, and the Nebraska State colleges. None of these units could be accused of foisting novel and useless services on the long-suffering public—unless the critic is in favor of an illiterate population, gravel roads, and criminals and the mentally disturbed walking the streets.

A rough count reveals twenty-seven agencies created since 1945; this number includes only those agencies performing a wholly new function of state government and excludes some large and important bureaus, such as Public Institutions and Corrections, that were officially created in the 1970s but that had existed in some earlier form. Of the twenty-seven new agencies, thirteen had fewer than ten employees in 1980. None of the new units employed more than one hundred people; the two largest are Environmental Control (eighty-eight employees) and Economic Development (eighty-six employees). Again, the point is that the growth of state government has occurred largely because of the improvement and expansion of nineteenth century programs.

In any event nobody tricked Nebraskans into hiring all these people. Every one of them occupies a line in a budget approved by the legislature and signed by the governor. The politicians voted for the growth of bureaucracy because they saw an opportunity to give their constituents a valued service. This is true regardless of where the germ of the program came from—on the banks of the Potomac or the mighty Platte. Elected officials, after all, want to be survivors and there is no better way of surviving than finding and supporting groups of citizens with particular needs. True, one group may find another group's favorite bureau to be a shameless boondoggle, and vice versa, but for better or for worse, that is the way government tends to grow in a democratic society.

Another factor contributing to the growth of state government was the tremendous increase in the number of programs promoted by the federal government. Many state agencies, including several of the largest, are influenced by federal mandates. Budget figures show the impact of federal policy making on state bureaucracy. In 1946, the national government contributed 18.7 percent of Nebraska's total revenues.[2] In 1979, this share was 23.9 percent. This may not look like such a large increase. However, during the 1960s, when the federal presence was particularly strong, the proportion peaked at 35.3 percent in 1967. In other words, the state decided (sometimes with encouragement bordering on coercion) to adopt federal pro-

2. The figures in this paragraph come from *Compendium of State Government Finances and State Government Finances in 1979* (Washington, D.C.: Bureau of the Census).

grams. Even as federal funds recede, the state may not be in a position to terminate all the programs that had been created.

There was more than a financial relationship involved in the expansion of federal and state programs during the period between 1946 and 1979. The 1950s and 1960s were periods of sustained prosperity in the United States. Rates of inflation were modest by later standards and most incomes seemed to be rising. As a result, the politics of appropriations was not a "zero-sum game." If some group benefited from government spending, another group did not necessarily have to suffer. Taxpayers might not always like new programs, but they could afford them. This was true in Nebraska as well as the rest of the country.

The 1960s were also a period of growing awareness of serious social problems in areas such as education, poverty, housing, race relations, and the environment. Nebraskans came to share this awareness, prompted undoubtedly by increasing urbanization. The percentage of Nebraskans living in urban areas was 39.1 percent in 1940. By 1960, a majority of the population, 54.3 percent, was living in urban areas and the trend continues. Urban life, by definition, means more people living near each other and potentially getting in each other's way; urban life usually requires higher levels of government activity to make and enforce regulations coordinating human interaction. A rancher in the western part of the state who sees more coyotes than people on a given day will probably be less inclined to see the need for many jobs in government than the person in Omaha who faces daily the problems associated with traffic, pollution, crime, and urban deterioration.

Thus, while Nebraskans were experiencing the expansionist impact of federal programs, some might also have been increasingly inclined to accept the idea that their state government should be doing more. Combined with general levels of prosperity, this may have facilitated the adoption of many state programs and the establishment and enlargement of many agencies and the employment of more public officials.

Of course, there is no natural law that says bureaucracy must continue to expand. A few years ago, a political scientist studied the federal government in a book called *Are Government Bureaus Immortal?*[3] After finding that only a small number of federal agencies ever went out of business, he answered his title in the affirmative. The same situation probably exists in Nebraska, although the cast of characters may seem to change. For example, the *Blue Book* for 1946 lists the Crippled Children Committee, the Chemurgy Project, and the Penitentiary Medical Board, which are absent from the 1981 edition. However, readers interested in smaller government should hold their applause since these agencies did not die but were rathered merged into newer and larger departments. Very few agencies, or government functions, are ever eliminated completely. The Nebraska Song Committee closed up shop after completing its work. The Bicentennial Commission, by definition, faced a short lifespan. A small bureau set up to support volunteer work lasted about a year in the Thone administration. There are not many more examples of agencies that did not survive.

The Challenge of Bureaucracy

If we reject the notion of spontaneous generation for bureaucracy, then we must concede that the bureaus that survive are fulfilling, in the eyes of some politically significant part of society, useful functions. An elderly couple may feel too much money is spent by the Department of Education while couples with school-age children might question the Department on Aging. The Sandhills rancher wonders about the Mexican-American Commission while the minorities in Omaha have no use for the Brand Committee. We will always question the other person's priorities, but if we were assured that all the agencies were performing efficiently we would be less concerned about bureaucracy.

The central challenge of government bureaucracy is controlling the system so that it does perform socially useful functions. Bureaucracy is typically viewed as a tool that society uses to solve its collective problems. Elected officials are entrusted with the responsibility of

3. Herbert Kaufman, *Are Government Organizations Immortal?* (Washington, D.C.: Brookings, 1976).

deciding which problems are most pressing and therefore deserving of a larger share of tax resources. Making sure that the departments do what they are directed to do and in a manner that is acceptable to broad segments of society is the basic challenge.

There are a number of reasons why controlling bureaucracy is a continuous struggle. According to scholars, in its ultimate form, a bureaucracy represents a self-contained collection of specialists who resist outside intrusion into their little spheres of activity. Bureaucracy tends to be fragmented along professional lines and this inherent fragmentation is often exacerbated, as it is in Nebraska, by constitutional or statutory provisions insulating certain bureaus from general oversight. Since these professionals also tend to be appointed on a permanent basis, they sometimes feel that they can wait out transitory politicians who have any large-scale plans for changing things.

Controlling a public organization is not the same as running a business firm. Private enterprises are supposed to maximize profit and therefore are encouraged by the rules of the game to maximize their productivity and minimize their inefficiencies as much as they can in pursuit of the goal of making money. Having a general commitment to rationality and efficiency, most of us want our public organizations to function along the same lines as private firms. As casual observers, we want our public agencies to have specific, obtainable goals and the capacity to accomplish those goals efficiently. Without going into the discussion about the real efficiency of private organizations, it is clear that bureaucracies are often guilty of considerable wastefulness and lack of accomplishment. Public agencies are often criticized for having hazy, unattainable, or inappropriate goals; for taking too long to do anything; for being tools of powerful interests; for being more committed to paperwork (red tape) than goal achievement; and for using standard operating procedures designed more for the convenience of administrators than the satisfaction of public needs.

The fact is, however, that the writers of the U.S. Constitution never intended for government and its many parts to function in a smooth, well-coordinated way. Having just fought a war with the British and being familiar with the dangers of an overcentralized and coordinated government, they designed a system with checks and balances that literally forces participants with different interests to work in the same arena to produce and execute policy. They knew that there would probably be as much disagreement as agreement when this occurred. The founders were more interested in creating a government that could be checked by inaction than they were in creating one that could do some things well.

Many difficulties of controlling the bureaucracy are in large part intentional. There is no single authoritative source that can enforce absolute conformity with clear goals. Public organizations, therefore, often have multiple objectives. For example, the largest and most expensive bureaucracy in the state is the University of Nebraska. Despite the money spent on it, most participants would have difficulty in coming to total agreement on its mission. Students or parents may see it as providing education for a career while the faculty views it as a center for research and farmers look at it as a source of practical advice. The picture is fuzzy enough that no one is ever sure if the whole institution is moving in the same direction.

Of course, some publicly stated goals are not even meant to be seriously attempted. As its participation in the National Highway Safety Program, the state has an Office of Highway Safety within the Department of Motor Vehicles. This office, however, is a very feeble tool for the securing of what most people would agree in principle is a fine goal—the reduction of highway accidents. It is largely a data-collecting agency, even though the means for drastically reducing traffic accidents are known: enforce ruthlessly the fifty-five-mile-an-hour speed limit, send convicted drunk drivers to long prison terms, and raise the driving age to twenty years. But any agency trying to implement any or all of those approaches would so threaten the lifestyle of Nebraskans that the political backlash would be fatal.

Public goals, then, are far from concrete directives. They tend to be general statements that are given meaning only in the day-to-day operation of the agency. This means that the people with the greatest impact in a single policy area are the bureaucrats within a substantive field along with outsiders having a strong interest in the subject. For example, who will decide which public relations firm will receive money for the promotion of the state's wheat products? The ordinary citizens, probably much to their relief, are unlikely to be asked about this matter. Instead, the decision will be made by members of the Department of Agriculture, influential wheat growers, and perhaps some members of the Institute of Agriculture and Natural Resources at the university.

Political scientists have described these impediments to popular control of the bureaucracy as "iron triangles" (other terms include "policy clubs," "whirlpools of influence," "governmental subsystems," "cozy triads"). These are essentially three-cornered sets of relationships among key legislative committees, agencies, and interest groups. A good example on the national level is the triangle commonly known as the military-industrial complex. The members of the congressional committees overseeing national defense and the private military contractors share a common interest with the Pentagon. Everyone can win who plays the game. The military gets more appropriations for weapons development and acquisition. The industries (and the unions associated with them) get contracts and provide their communities with greater prosperity. And the members of Congress get reelected. It does not happen so neatly every time, but it is possible to see a pattern resembling this dynamic in the long haul.

The same thing happens at the state level. The power of a triangle is a function of a host of factors, including the influence of individual legislators and their committees within the Unicameral, the number of organized interests and the skill of their lobbyists, and the general mood of the public toward the subject matter.

An iron triangle in the area of education, for example, includes (1) members of the Unicameral Education Committee and the Appropriations Committee, when dealing with education spending; (2) the Department of Education; and (3) the Nebraska Association for Childhood Education, Nebraska Association of County Superintendents, Educational Service Units Boards Association, Nebraska State Education Association, Nebraska Association of Elementary School Principals, Nebraska School Boards Association, and many more interest groups. For public roads, the triangle may be formed of (1) members of the Agriculture, Business and Labor, Public Works, and Appropriations committees, when dealing with public works spending; (2) the Department of Roads; and (3) Chambers of Commerce; Associated General Contractors of America; County Engineers, Highway Superintendents, and Surveyors Association; Petroleum Council; Sand, Gravel, and Ready-Mixed Concrete Association; and many other interest groups. A characteristic triangle concerned with health issues may include (1) members of the Public Health and Welfare Committee and the Appropriations Committee, when dealing with health spending; (2) the Department of Health; and (3) the American Academy of Family Physicians, American Academy of Pediatrics and State Pediatric Society, American College of Dentists, American College of Surgeons, American Lung Association, Chiropractic Physicians Association, Dental Hygienists Association, and others.

In the iron triangles, the central element is the bureaucracy itself. Agency officials with their considerable expertise and some tenure in their jobs maintain close ties with interest-group constituents and legislators. Within each triangle, there is little substantial disagreement about the preferred direction in which the policy area should move and thus the bureaucrats are generally free to take the lead through their choice of means of implementation of policy. The question remains, then, How does a more general interest get represented in each triangle? How do the citizens at large effect any real control over the bureaucracy as a whole?

Coping with the Challenge

The use of the word *coping* is purposive. As long as our system of government, with its separation of powers and checks and balances, retains its essential form, there will be continuing efforts to control the work of the state bureaucracy. Gimmicks such as sunset laws or zero-base budgets will come and go, giving their practitioners more or less influence over individual agencies; but the basic structure and process of bureaucracy will continue and so will the challenge of controlling it. Once again, this is not the result of a devious plot by special interests and bureaucrats. It is the way the system was designed to operate.

The job of trying to control the bureaucracy has traditionally fallen to a set of public actors who can best be described as centralizers. As centralizers, their perceived role has been that of making sense out of all the disparate functions of government and giving some overall purpose to these functions. In their role they are not confined to particular issue areas. Rather, their role requires that they become involved with a variety of areas with a view toward coordinating several issues.

All U.S. legislators love to orate about their oversight function, but they are not often able to perform it very well. As we have seen, the inherent fragmentation of the legislative process makes the members and their committees a part of the problem, not the solution to the lack of coordination in government. In Nebraska, as elsewhere, the main centralizing unit within the legislature is the Appropriations Committee. Although this committee has in the office of Fiscal and Program Analysis a source of assistance in reviewing the governor's budget, it has had little success in formulating comprehensive responses to the initiatives originating in the executive branch.

Nebraska legislators are as frustrated as their counterparts in other states in getting a handle on administration. Thus, the state was one of several to jump on the sunset law bandwagon during the 1970s. Sunset legislation, so it is argued, is a systematic way to review the operation of government and to weed out unnecessary bureaus. Each agency, instead of enjoying an indefinite authorization, is handed a death sentence from which it must earn a reprieve. In Nebraska, in a law passed in 1977, a number of minor regulatory boards and commissions—for example, the Board of Hearing Aid Dealers and Fitters and the Board of Examiners in Embalming—as well as a handful of more important agencies—such as Revenue and Economic Development—were scheduled for close investigation over a five-year period. In the year an agency was scheduled to be terminated, the Performance Review and Audit Committee, assisted by legislative fiscal analysts, conducted a performance audit to determine if the agency should be renewed. As might have been predicted, the procedure had minimal impact on the agencies. Afer all, if the legislature were really serious about ending unnecessary bureaucracy, it could do so at any time. Designing a formal timetable is not going to make the messy business of angering an agency and its allied interest groups any more palatable. Indeed, the law may have been counterproductive since it committed a disproportionate amount of staff resources to looking at minor and noncontroversial agencies.

Governors and Reorganization

Many people make the mistake of assuming that the governor of Nebraska is in full control of a coherent executive branch. In this respect, however, the office is similar to most in the nation. Because of constitutional or statutory provisions, the governor is excluded from full participation in a number of important functions of government. It is a familiar lament, but the most recent group studying the reorganization of the executive branch came to the same conclusion: the governor does not have the authority needed to fulfill popular expectations about leadership.[4]

The state constitution, as we have seen, charges the governor "to take care that the laws be faithfully executed and the affairs of the state efficiently and economically administered." That same document, however, reflects in its other parts a long-standing distrust of too much executive power, and so the means for ensuring that economical and efficient administration are often denied to the governor. Since the turn of the century, governors have attempted to rearrange the structure of the executive branch in such a way as to bring more of it under their control.

The move for consolidation of a number of independent departments and boards began in 1913, but it was not until the major changes were made in the constitution in 1919–20 that much was accomplished.[5] Under the 1875 constitution, the reorganization of the administration was effectively stalled by a prohibition against the creation of new executive offices. Many Nebraskans found this limit detrimental to the progress of a growing and changing state. The attempt to get around the restrictions resulted in the creation of a multitude of

4. Governor's Task Force for Government Improvement, *Summary of Findings and Recommendations* (Lincoln, Nebr.: Governor's Task Force for Government Improvement, 1980), p. 14.

5. See Arthur Buck, *The Reorganization of State Governments in the United States* (New York: Columbia University Press, 1938), pp. 151–56.

boards and commissions headed by the governor and other constitutional officers. The actual operation of these entities was left to deputies who exercised some discretion.

After a time, this rather awkward answer to the problem fostered more fragmentation than was tolerable and so, in 1919, a civil administrative code was approved that abolished twenty-four boards and replaced them with six departments, each headed by a gubernatorial appointee. This reform met with considerable opposition and was a matter of hot partisan dispute at least through the 1930s. The agencies created in 1919 and 1920, as well as several others added in the intervening years, came to be called code agencies. Today, there is no precise definition of a code agency; the major criterion for classifying a bureau as one is the governor's ability to hire and fire the department head. This is the latest division of code and noncode agencies.

Code Agencies and Offices

Commission on Law Enforcement and Criminal Justice
Department of Administrative Services
Department of Aeronautics
Department on Aging
Department of Agriculture
Department of Banking and Finance
Department of Correctional Services
Department of Economic Development
Department of Environmental Control
Department of Health
Department of Insurance
Department of Labor
Department of Motor Vehicles
Department of Personnel
Department of Public Institutions
Department of Public Welfare
Department of Revenue

Department of Roads
Department of Veteran's Affairs
Department of Water Resources
Military Department
Policy Research Office
State Athletic Commissioner's Office
State Energy Office
State Fire Marshal's Office
State Patrol

Noncode Agencies and Offices

Abstracters Board of Examiners
Auditor of Public Accounts
Board of Barber Examiners
Board of Educational Lands and Funds
Board of Examiners for Professional Engineers and Architects
Board of Pardons
Commission for the Hearing Impaired

continued

Noncode Agencies and Offices
continued

Commission on Industrial
Relations
Commission on the Status of
Women
Coordinating Commission for
Postsecondary Education
Department of Education
Department of Justice (attorney
general's office)
Educational Television
Commission
Equal Opportunity Commission
Game and Parks Commission
Gasohol Committee
Library Commission
Lieutenant Governor's Office
Liquor Control Commission
Merit System Council
Mexican-American Commission
Motor Vehicle Industry Licensing
Board
Natural Resources Commission
Nebraska Arts Council

Nebraska Brand Committee
Nebraska Investment Council
Nebraska state colleges
Office of the Governor
Oil and Gas Conservation
Commission
Political Accountability and
Disclosure Commission
Power Review Board
Public Employees Retirement
Board
Public Service Commission
Real Estate Commission
Secretary of State's Office
State Board of Agriculture
State Board of Landscape
Architects
State Board of Public
Accountancy
State Claims Board
State Electrical Board
State Historical Society
State Racing Commission
State Treasurer's Office
University of Nebraska

Other state agencies are still headed by elected officials or appointed boards and commissions. Although these multiheaded agencies create problems for those interested in controlling or coordinating bureaucracy more closely, their continuation by the legislature shows the vitality of the tradition of having boards or commissions to deal with specific policy areas. In 1981, there were forty-one such organizations, with lines of authority and accountability going in every direction. Some examples of these commissions cover the important areas of liquor control, educational television, and game and parks. The multiheaded nature of their leadership makes it difficult to know who is accountable to whom.

Reorganization has taken place sporadically, but some governors have made more energetic efforts at increasing their control. Governor

Tiemann set up a "little Hoover Commission," which reported its findings in 1968. Governor Thone, at the beginning of his administration, launched the most ambitious attempt at large-scale reorganization by appointing the Governor's Task Force for Government Improvement. The recommendations of the group were issued in 1980. Following a two-year implementation effort, during which a few important changes were made, the task force issued its final report and disbanded. In general, the task force illustrated the difficulty of overcoming the centrifugal force of the bureaus and interest groups.

Staff Aids to the Governor

Whatever formal authority a governor possesses, it may be dissipated if the struggle for control of administration is one person versus the combined weight of the bureaucracy. Therefore, a major move in state government in the past thirty years has been the strengthening of staff assistance of the governor. *Staff* refers to groups of administrators, reporting directly to the governor, who help in designing and executing a policy for the state. Staff functions, such as budgeting and personnel, are naturally centralizing since they reach across all agencies.

A major innovation in Nebraska government was the creation, in 1965, of the Department of Administrative Services. The department combines a number of basic government-wide services. The functions of the department include accounting, budgeting, data processing, general transportation, purchasing, printing, telecommunications, and building maintenance. In terms of the operational control of government, the most important function is provided by the Budget Division.

The governor is charged by the constitution to present to the legislature "by message, a complete itemized budget of the financial requirements of all departments, institutions and agencies of the state and a budget bill." The annual budget message is a summary of the general philosophy of government and a listing of the governor's priorities. As well as informing the public and legislators, the budget message is also a clear signal to the bureaus about their standing in the eyes of the governor. A generous recommendation is a sign that their conduct has been found satisfactory by the governor. A suggested cutback in funds is a clear sign of trouble on the horizon.

The development of the budget is the closest process there is to generating a coordinated overview of state policy. However, the policy-making potential of the budget is often inhibited by the specific details reported by the agencies. The Nebraska budget process in 1982 was still primarily based on the traditional line-item method (so much money for very detailed lines—personnel, supplies, travel, and so forthwith) with only a very general description of broad program proposals. As a result, after reading the budget bill, one may still be very confused about where the state is moving. Output-based budgets stressing long-range goals are resisted by officials who want to know "who is spending how much and for what"; shortsightedness is also encouraged by an annual appropriations and revenue cycle.

The situation might cause greater confusion in the federal government or the larger states. It may be less of a problem in Nebraska, where, despite the growth described above, the state government is still of less than gigantic proportions. It is possible for governors and their chief assistants to know key department people personally and to know what can be expected in terms of performance. The biggest factor in a governor's ability to see beneath the details of the budget document may be the turnover in the budget staff. The less turnover there is, the more the budget office can establish an unwritten understanding of the strengths and weaknesses of various bureaus and what they are doing with their money.

The Policy Research Office (PRO) is another staff tool to be used by a governor in directing the bureaucracy. Named the State Office of Planning and Programming when established in 1969, PRO has the job of coordinating and promoting comprehensive planning, reviewing, and evaluation among all levels and parts of state government. In theory at least, all substantive policy programs are reviewed in this office to ensure against duplication in effort. PRO is interesting, despite its success or failures in practice, because it does indicate that governors and others in state government do place some value on being able to see the bigger picture.

Policy Research is also an example of the federal impact on state government since it plays an important role in the system of inter-governmental relations. In the 1960s, federal leaders as well as governors became concerned about the proliferation of federal grants to state and local government. The major problem was that individual agencies applying for an array of federal grants were duplicating programs and generally getting into each other's way. The so-called A-95 review process was created to provide some direction.[6] Under this process, most applications for federal grants must be reviewed by a central clearinghouse. PRO was designated as the A-95 review unit for state agencies, and, supposedly, no federal grants to agencies are approved until they have been cleared by that office.

Americans have been ambivalent about a major means of controlling the bureaucracy, namely, the hiring and firing of personnel. The bad experiences with the "spoils systems" in the 1800s led many jurisdictions to establish civil service or merit systems to protect government employees from political pressure. In many places where civil service extends even to department heads, this development has also meant considerable bureaucratic freedom from democratic accountability. In several states, high officials are chosen according to objective standards of merit (passing an exam or having the right professional training). They can be removed, but only for demonstrated incompetence on the job, not for policy disagreements with the governor. This means that the governors cannot appoint people known to be sympathetic to a certain policy, nor can they threaten to fire officials who disagree with them.

Nebraska was relatively slow in adopting modern personnel practices and even now two systems exist side by side. The older one is the Joint Merit System. It was initiated in 1940 for use by those state agencies that were required to operate under a merit system in order to receive federal funds. At present, eleven state agencies participate in this system. The other system, covering most state employees (excluding higher education), is administered by the State Department of Personnel.

6. See Michael Steinman, "The A-95 Review Process: Suggestions for a New Perspective," *State and Local Government Review* 14 (January 1982): 32–36.

The role of the governor in the personnel process is unclear. In comparison to most states, Nebraska seems to have more possible "patronage" positions, although no official figures are available to confirm this. Governors do appear to have some leeway in placing friendly faces in certain agencies. This is perhaps more an unwritten rule arising from the political culture of the state; the use of patronage is not likely to cause the same excitement in a state where citizens are not accustomed to honest government, where the civil service ethos is firmly entrenched, or where government employees are highly organized.

Regardless of formal personnel procedures, gubernatorial control of public employees have become more tenuous because of their participation in elections. For some years, observers have been predicting that the growth of the government workforce would eventually create a body of voters who are quite sensitive to reductions in budgets and who are highly motivated to go to the polls. Many post mortems of the 1982 elections indicate that this may have come true in Nebraska. By the end of his term, Governor Thone, by his actions and words, had alienated a large percentage of state employees. An extraordinary turnout of voters in Lincoln (once referred to by Thone as an atypical "company town") gave Robert Kerrey a large enough majority to ensure a narrow statewide victory. A wise candidate in the future will surely be cautious about antagonizing public employees—unless confident that the votes will come from somewhere else.

Citizens and the Bureaucracy

The discussion of controlling the bureaucracy has thus far focused on the efforts of centralizing actors in Nebraska government, particularly certain legislative committees and the governor's staff. There are also a number of avenues by which individual citizens can apply pressure to government agencies. Beyond the simple act of walking into fairly accessible state offices, citizens are encouraged by state law and tradition to attend a wide variety of public meetings about the business of state government. Almost all state agencies have integrated into their structure some form of citizen advisory body.

Ordinary citizens who are unhappy with their treatment by an administrator have two important ways to seek satisfaction. The first involves members of the Unicameral working with specific agencies to help individual citizens resolve their problems. An agency will typically be as responsive as it can to a senator for reasons that should be obvious; and senators are usually willing to be liaisons with agencies for their constituents for equally obvious reasons. Senatorial staffers are continuously involved in this kind of work, making their senators appear invaluable to the folks back home.

The second opportunity for individual effort to hold an agency accountable concerns the Office of Public Counsel, better known as the ombudsman.[7] First developed in northern Europe, the ombudsman is an official who investigates complaints against particular agencies and officials. The idea was widely discussed during the 1960s as a way of helping citizens cope with an increasingly complex and occasionally unresponsive bureaucracy. Nebraska was an early adopter of the idea and remains one of only four states to have the office.

The office was established in the early 1970s to investigate citizen complaints about any administrative act and to initiate independent investigations. Agencies are required to help in these investigations and to provide information necessary for their completion. The ombudsman can use a subpoena to compel uncooperative agencies to give needed information. Most agencies find it to their own benefit to cooperate and there have been few controversies as a result.

While there has not been a crying need for this kind of office, it seems to have found a place for itself in Nebraska. Citizens do seem to find their way to the ombudsman if they have a problem and the office handles several hundred cases every year. Many of these cases are resolved simply by giving information about the proper agency to contact; other cases are usually treated quickly through mediation

7. See Allan Wyner, *The Nebraska Ombudsman: Innovation in State Government* (Berkeley: University of California Institute of Governmental Studies, 1974); Robert Miewald and John C. Comer, ''The Nebraska Ombudsman: An American Pioneer,'' in Gerald Caiden, ed., *The Ombudsman: An International Handbook* (Westport, Conn.: Greenwood Press, 1983).

between officials and citizens. Many cases have to be turned away because they concern local governments, and the ombudsman's jurisdiction is limited to state agencies.

Conclusion

Nebraska's state bureaucracy has grown considerably over the last thirty to forty years. The number of people working in it has increased, as have the scope and complexity of the jobs they perform. This growth has brought with it a challenge that is characteristic of bureaucracies: trying to control what they do and how they do it. This accountability problem is probably not resolvable in any final sense. Although the tools to cope with the challenge exist, we must expect varying degrees of success in their use over time because of fluctuations in the skills of those using them and the difficulties—if not impossibilities—presented by the basic structure of our system of government: the separation of powers and checks and balances.

Only the most fanatical believers in the ideal of small government would suffer never-ending anxiety on this account, however. The size of Nebraska's population and its relative homogeneity in almost every possible sense combine to keep government and bureaucracy reasonably close to its people. There will always be the occasional controversy and problem; but the main tendency has been and probably will continue to be one of bureaucratic behaviors mirroring mainstream preferences fairly closely. This may be one of the benefits of those iron triangles. All in all, then, if people get the kind of government they deserve, Nebraskans have little to complain about and much to applaud.

JOHN C. COMER

SEVEN

The Citizens:
Their Political Attitudes
and Behavior

The preceding chapters have set the institutional scenery on the Nebraska political stage. We need now to bring out the living actors, playing their roles of citizens. Put another way, the constitution, statutes, executive orders, and administrative regulations create a perfect world from a multitude of "oughts." Citizens ought to be concerned and public-spirited; politicians ought to be honest and dedicated to the general interest; officials ought to be efficient and industrious. However, all the political prescriptions cannot make a system work the way it should. The introduction of real people into the complex equation leads to a number of deviations from perfection. The ways in which the general population thinks about or acts toward government is what political scientists refer to as political culture. Here the culture of Nebraska will be identified in order to learn more about the actual operation of the institutions of the state.

The concept of political culture became popular in academic circles in the 1950s. Scholars wanted a theory that would tell them why the same institutions performed so differently when transplanted to another country. The British, for example, scattered replicas of their parliament, perfect in every detail down to the powdered wigs, across the globe; yet the legislatures in India and Ghana did not behave in the same way as the model in London. Research efforts then focused on the attitudes and values of the participants within a particular system. Especially important were the attitudes toward political institutions, such as courts and the bureaucracy; the mechanisms by which citizens influence those institutions, such as elections and political parties; and the citizen's self-image as a political actor.

The attitudes of citizens toward these factors can be significant for the operation of a political system. If, for example, citizens are unfamiliar with the major institutions of government, it is improbable that they will be able to influence them. Likewise, if citizens do not know about the various mechanisms by which they can influence political institutions, it is probable that they will not have much impact. If citizens expect little from the political process, that is all they are likely to get. A widespread feeling on the part of the citizens that they can influence the system will affect not only levels of participation in politics but the nature of the political system itself as well as its policies.

Although most often applied to entire nations, the concept of political culture is also relevant for the study of state government. While there exists an American political culture, distinct from that of Albania or Zambia, each of the fifty states, it can be argued, also has its peculiar version of that culture. One does not have to be too sophisticated a political pundit to know that politics in California is not the same as that in Alabama. Thus, while the institutions may be superficially the same in all states and while all states have Democrats and Republicans, the ways in which the organs of government and the parties are regarded by most of the citizens may lead to different policy outcomes.

The exact components of a state's political culture are very elusive. In many cases, our impressions are highly subjective. In a state such as Nebraska, writers may view the same phenomena and come to startlingly different conclusions. A local historian, for example, celebrated Nebraskans as a "self-reliant, physically vigorous, elemental, and long-lived" people who "have learned to adapt to the land, to change it, and, in increasing ways, to control it."[1] Another Nebraskan

1. Dorothy Weyer Creigh, *Nebraska: A Bicentennial History* (New York: W. W. Norton, 1977), p. 3.

felt that this hardy stock was depleted by the Great Depression: "The young, the imaginative and the creative population moved away and a normally cautious farm population withdrew into every deeper conservatism."[2]

Although the state is too young to have been described by distinguished political observers such as De Tocqueville or Bryce, later commentators on the American scene have tried to define the state's politics. In the 1950s, John Gunther wrote that Nebraska, along with North Dakota, Wisconsin, and Minnesota, was one of the chief repositories of progressivism in the United States.[3] Professor Reichley thought Nebraskans in the 1960s were not very keen on significant reform; instead, they could "be relied upon to dig their heels in hard against any innovation that might threaten their pocketbooks or their personal freedom."[4] Neal Peirce, in 1972, described the Nebraskan's political creed as "I've always done for myself, so should other folks; government should stay away from giveaways."[5] Both Reichley and Peirce agreed there were certain qualities lacking in the Nebraska political character: imagination, generosity, daring, compassion, and tolerance.

Provocative as these journalistic accounts may be, they are far from scientific. Scholars do not have a wide repertoire of devices by which to measure objectively the elements of a state or national political culture, beyond basic registration and election statistics. Students of Nebraska politics have a great advantage over students in many other states because of the data from the Nebraska Annual Social Indicators Survey (NASIS). Each year since 1977, the Bureau of Sociological Research at the University of Nebraska has conducted a telephone survey of a sample of about nineteen hundred residents throughout the state. From this, we have a wealth of data on how the citizens think about social, economic, and political matters. The NASIS material will

2. "Back to Conservatism?" *Economist*, Nov. 5, 1966, p. 565.

3. John Gunther, *Inside U.S.A.*, rev. ed. (New York: Harper and Row, 1951), p. 262.

4. James Reichley, *States In Crisis: Politics in Ten American States, 1950–1962* (Chapel Hill: University of North Carolina Press, 1964), p. 75.

5. Neal Peirce, *The Great Plains States of America: People, Politics, and Power in the Nine Great Plains States* (New York: W. W. Norton, 1973), p. 214.

be integrated with other data in an attempt to sketch a portrait of the Nebraskan as a political animal.

Orientations toward State Government

Do Nebraskans feel that their state government is very important? Do they know much about its major institutions? Do they trust the political system and feel that they can influence it? The answers to these questions can tell us how Nebraskans are likely to behave as citizens.

The Salience of State Government

No one can even try to pay attention to everything that intrudes on his or her daily life. All of us set priorities, attending selectively to what we find most important. This is also the case with political affairs, where certain aspects are more salient or more important than others. Some, for example, may be engrossed in foreign policy to the exclusion of domestic issues. Others may focus on the executive and ignore the legislature. One can assume that the areas of greatest salience are also the locus of most intense political activity.

A major question is how citizens rank the importance of the various levels of government—national, state, and local. Studies of other states show that state government generally trails national and local government in terms of citizen concern.[6] This pattern is often explained by size. States may be too large to stimulate much in the way of civic participation, yet not significant enough to be involved in the important affairs of the nation. According to the 1978 NASIS survey, when given the three alternatives, a majority of Nebraskans (51 percent) indicated that they follow the national government most closely. Fewer than one out of four responded that state government was most important to them. Compared to other states, state government in Nebraska is somewhat more salient to its citizens, but the

6. M. K. Jennings and L. H. Ziegler, "The Salience of State Politics among Attentive Publics," in E. Dryer and W. Rosenbaum, eds., *Political Opinion and Behavior* (Belmont, Calif.: Wadsworth, 1970), pp. 257–85.

national tendency is followed in that the state is seen as less interesting than the other two levels.

The 1981 survey contained questions for measuring issues of greatest concern to citizens. Respondents were asked to identify the level of their interest in a number of areas. The economy was the area of greatest concern, with 76.1 percent asserting that they were very interested. Presidential actions, at 69.7 percent, and energy and oil, at 63.4 percent, also ranked highly. The governor and the state legislature were named by 42.8 percent as an area of great interest, while only eight percent declared they were uninterested in these organs of state government. While state government may not be at the top of the list, then, it claims the attention of nearly a majority of the citizens.

From further analysis of the survey data, it is possible to isolate a group of citizens for whom state government is highly salient and whose attention level is high. These are the respondents who claim that they follow public affairs regularly and that they are most interested in state government. This group represents 18 percent of the state's population. Whether this figure, in terms of a theory that says an attentive and vigilant public is necessary for popular government to flourish, is too high or too low is impossible to determine.

Knowledge of State Government

If citizens are to play an active role in their government, they need to be informed. However, about what are they to be informed? One approach to identifying an adequate level of knowledge would be to specify some minimal standard. With respect to state government, for example, one might expect some awareness of its structure and operation. This would not involve a thorough knowledge of complex bureaucratic procedures or the processes involved in passing a bill, but simply some of the more obvious institutional features. It should include as well a knowledge of the names of major incumbent officeholders.

We can define a knowledgeable citizen as a person who is aware of some key elements in the structure of state government. Two important and basic features concern the state legislature of Nebraska: it is a unicameral body and it is elected and operated on a nonpartisan basis. Both features are unique to Nebraska and both have been part of the political process of the state since the 1930s. Both have received considerable publicity in the news media (the legislature is commonly referred to as the Unicameral), and public officials often express pride, particularly when these features are under attack, in the nature of the state's legislative system. It seems that anyone at all familiar with state government ought to be able to answer questions correctly about these features.

In response to a question whether Nebraska has a one- or a two-house legislature, 63 percent in a 1978 NASIS survey gave the correct answer. Nineteen percent answered incorrectly and 18 percent said they did not know. While it may strike some as remarkable that over one-third of Nebraskans do not know the state has a one-house legislature, this compares favorably to the level of public awareness regarding elements of the national government. For example, national surveys reveal that 68 percent know that the president is limited to two terms and 57 and 53 percent, respectively, can identify at least one of their state's United States senators and their United States representative.[7] Thus, Nebraskans appear to be somewhat more familiar with the unicameral aspect of their legislature than most Americans are with major elements of the national government.

Nebraskans are not as familiar, however, with the fact that candidates for the legislature are not identified on the ballot with a political party. Here only 20 percent responded correctly. This is a rather low level of awareness about a central feature of state politics. It is all the more unusual since, as discussed elsewhere in this book, party leaders have been suggesting more frequently than in the past that the state should restore partisanship in the legislature. However critical the party elites may feel this change is, they probably face a long educational campaign if they intend to convince the general public given that most Nebraskans are not even aware of the current situation.

Another test of political knowledge is whether citizens can identify prominent state officials. If citizens do not even know who their

7. R. Erickson, N. Luttbeg, and K. Tedin, *American Public Opinion* (New York: John Wiley and Sons, 1980), p. 19.

political leaders are, it is difficult to hold those leaders accountable for their performance in office. How well, then, do Nebraskans do in identifying who represents their district in the legislature? The citizens supposedly have an advantage over other Americans in this area since there is only one legislator per district. Even so, Nebraskans do not do well on this test; about one-third of them, according to the 1978 NASIS data, could correctly name the legislator elected from their district. Seventeen percent gave the wrong name and 52 percent simply did not know. Knowledge of the legislature, as measured by this simple test, seems low.

Support for State Government

If the institutions of popular government are to function properly, citizens need to support them. Ideally, public support should be high. This does not mean that citizens must agree with everything that government does, but rather that a sizable number of them must maintain respect for the institutions and the processes by which decisions are made.

The state legislature serves again as the focus of discussion. How well do Nebraskans support the institution and its performance? The 1978 NASIS survey asked citizens to agree or disagree with three statements designed to measure support for the legislature. These were: (1) "There are times when it would almost seem better for the governor to take the law into his own hands rather than wait for the legislature to act"; (2) "It would not make a difference if the power of the legislature were reduced"; and (3) "Even though one might strongly disagree with a state law, after it has been passed by the state legislature, one ought to obey it." The first statement concerns the inherent slowness of legislative deliberations as compared to the swifter actions of the executive; the second, the power and authority of the legislature; and the third, the matter of compliance with the law.

To the first question, 57 percent answered no, which supported the authority of the legislature; 67 percent agreed with the second; and 89 percent answered positively to the third. The third question is probably the most important since it shows the propensity of citizens to comply with the law; compliance is the absolute essential for any political system and Nebraskans score very high in this regard. The softest area of support of the legislative process, as measured by the first question, is for what can be called the deliberative nature of the legislative process.

Another feature of the legislature is its perceived performance. The 1978 survey probed this by asking citizens to evaluate how well they thought the legislature was doing its job. Forty-seven percent rated the legislature as good; 46 percent, fair; and seven percent, poor. Data from the 1979 and 1980 NASIS surveys, based on questions that asked respondents how satisfied they were with the job the legislature was doing, showed 62 and 57 percent, respectively, reporting satisfaction. Seventeen and 23 percent, respectively, reported being dissatisfied. These figures are in line with those for the executive branch; 64 percent in 1980 survey reported being satisfied with the job that the governor and state agencies were doing, while 13 percent were dissatisfied. It seems accurate to describe the political culture of the state as one that is reasonably supportive of its major governmental institutions.

Feelings of *political trust* reflect more general support for the political system. To trust the existing system is to express confidence that it is operating in an approved way. While the performance of the legislature and the governor would certainly be part of this, trust is more than the result of short-term evaluations of incumbent office holders; it includes also a more stable assessment of overall system performance. The 1981 NASIS survey contained two items that relate to political trust. Respondents were asked to agree or disagree with the following statements: (1) "State politicians represent the general interest more frequently than they represent special interests"; and (2) "A large number of politicians in Nebraska state government are incompetent." For the first statement, 59 percent gave what would be a high trust response, and 72 percent gave a high trust response to the second. These figures can be placed in sharper perspective by comparing them with the results of surveys on political trust at the national level. In a national poll in 1976, only 27 and 47 percent, respectively, gave the high trust response to similar items.[8] In terms of political

8. Ibid., p. 96.

trust, Nebraska state government fares much better than the national government. Of course, the national figures may reflect a decade of disillusionment after Vietnam and Watergate, but it is clear that Nebraskans do indeed support their state government.

Political efficacy refers to one's belief that the political process can be influenced. It is a concept related to political trust, but it focuses more on what is often labeled input into the system rather than output or how the system is performing. A high sense of efficacy contributes to involvement in political activity, while a person with a low feeling of efficacy believes there is little point in participating in politics. Scholars have found that the level of efficacy varies among the states; although efficacy is only one dimension, states high in efficacy might be considered high participation cultures. A preference for citizen participation nourishes a higher sense of efficacy. One item contained in the 1981 NASIS survey relates to feelings of political efficacy. It asked respondents to agree or disagree with the statement: "People like me don't have much to say about what Nebraska government does." Fifty-five percent gave the high efficacy response. Again, national figures place this in perspective. In a nationwide survey in 1976, about the same percent—58 percent—gave the high efficacy response to the same statement.[9] Further data relevant to the efficacy question are contained in the 1978 NASIS survey. Respondents were asked to judge the likelihood that they could personally influence the legislature to change an unfair law. Six percent said it was highly likely, 20 percent said somewhat likely, while 41 and 34 percent, respectively, answered not too likely or not at all likely.

From these studies, we conclude that Nebraskans are more trusting of their state government than all Americans are with respect to the national government. In terms of political efficacy, however, there is little difference. Moreover, Nebraskans do not have much confidence in their ability to influence the legislature, even when the cause is a just one. The imbalance between trust and efficacy may reflect a situation in which citizens have learned to be good subjects by supporting the political system, but have not fully developed a participant posture that enables them to use the system to satisfy their own ends.

9. Ibid.

This pattern has been found to be typical of many southern states.[10] It can have as a consequence the passive acceptance of political authority.

Electoral Participation in State Government

In a democracy, the act of voting remains the most important form of political participation. There are wide variations in the level of electoral participation among the fifty states which reflect differences in political culture. The political culture of a state, in turn, influences the legal context within which participation takes place.

Not all people within the state are eligible to vote. The constitution specifies that one must be a citizen of the United States, at least eighteen years of age, and a resident of the state. Statutes require that one must be registered to vote. To be registered, a voter's name, address, date of birth, and party affiliation (if any) must be recorded with the county clerk or election commissioner in the county where one resides. This is generally done in person but there are provisions for doing it by mail or by a designated agent. The information is recorded and becomes part of the registration record (poll book), which is used on election day to ensure that those who present themselves at the polls are entitled to vote and to prevent people from voting more than once in the same election.

For purposes of voting in state elections, one must be registered ten days before the election. Registration remains in effect unless the voter changes his or her name or address or fails to vote within a two-year period. If registration is canceled, the voter must register again. In 1981, there were 856,182 registered voters in Nebraska. The estimated adult population (eighteen years or older) was 1,138,000. Thus, about 75 percent of the potential electorate was eligible to vote. This compares favorably with the 74.4 percent in a 1981 nationwide Gallup poll who claimed to be registered voters.

How many of those registered actually show up on election day also varies from state to state. For example, 75 percent of registered

10. Daniel J. Elazar, *American Federalism: A View from the States,* 2d ed. (New York: Thomas Y. Crowell, 1972), pp. 84–126.

Nebraskans voted in the 1980 presidential election, compared to the highest turnout of 87 in Minnesota and to the low of 60 percent in Mississippi. Of course, presidential elections attract the most attention and the highest turnout. Other elections attract far fewer voters in most circumstances.

Nebraska clearly illustrates the dramatic dropoff in voter interest in nonpresidential election years. When the governor's term was two years, there was about a 20-percentage point difference between elections in presidential and nonpresidential election years. The highest turnout for a gubernatorial election was recorded in 1952, when an estimated 74 percent of the voting-age population went to the polls. Since the term of office was increased to four years and the election moved to the nonpresidential years, the decrease in participation has been notable. For the four elections between 1966 and 1978, the turnout rate of eligible voters held steady at between 44 and 46 percent. Thus, while Nebraskans, as we have seen, are reasonably supportive of their state government, only a minority is involved in the selection of its highest officials.

Parties in a Nonpartisan Context

Partisan attachments are an important part of the state's political culture. Political scientists have attempted to classify the great diversity in competitiveness among state parties. The one-party state is one classification, in which the minority party has no chance of winning election; the examples of this type have almost disappeared as Republicans now win in the once "Solid South" and Democrats control important offices in the GOP bastions of New England. Other states have what is called a competitive system, in which either party has an equal chance of winning elections and where partisan feelings normally run high. Another type is the one-party dominant state, in which the majority party will win most elections with the minority having some chance to capture an occasional office. Finally, some states can be described as nonpartisan or antipartisan, in that party labels are not as critical in determining the outcome of elections. Nebraska is something of a paradox in that it combines elements of the one-party dominant and nonpartisan types.

In most elections, the Republicans are solidly in the majority. Nebraska is one of six states that have supported Republican presidential candidates in every election since 1940, with the exception of the Johnson landslide of 1964.

Between 1946 and 1982, Democrats have won nine out of seventy-nine contests for seats in Congress and only two Democrats, Representative John Cavanaugh and Senator Edward Zorinsky, won reelection. With the exception of the governorship, Republicans have held a near monopoly of offices in state government. In general, it would seem to be a mistake to bet against the victory of a Nebraska Republican.

However, being a Nebraska Democrat is hardly an exercise in futility. When it comes to capturing the governor's office, the party is competitive, having beaten the Republicans in seven out of fifteen elections between 1946 and 1982. Between 1979 and 1981, the Democrats had a majority of the five-member delegation to the U.S. Congress. In January 1983, the governor, both U.S. senators, and the mayors of Omaha and Lincoln (although elected on a nonpartisan basis) were Democrats. Even though the odds may favor them, the Republicans can never afford to discount the threat of a serious Democratic challenge in the most important races.

On the surface, Republican dominance is a little hard to explain and the devotion to Republicanism may not be very intense. Party identification, in the American context, is largely the psychological attachment that one may feel toward a political party; that is, the individual person rather than any formal party organization determines his or her membership. Over 70 percent of Nebraskans in the NASIS survey of 1980 and 76 percent in the 1981 survey thought of themselves as Republicans or Democrats. Compared to the national percentage of self-identified partisans—59 percent in 1978—Nebraskans would seem to be more partisan than most other Americans.

There is also a reasonable balance between the two parties. Thirty-eight percent in the 1980 NASIS survey claimed to be Republicans and 33 percent said they were Democrats. In 1981, the percentage of Republicans had increased to 45, while the Democrats dropped a point, to 32 percent. The Republicans gains, perhaps attributable to

Table 7.1: Statewide Registration Totals

Year	Republican Number	%	Democratic Number	%	Nonpolitical Number	%
1968	346,705	52	300,387	45	20,289	3
1970	366,567	52	316,818	45	22,660	3
1972	401,409	50	370,993	46	34,865	4
1974	387,612	49	363,003	46	37,235	5
1976	404,861	48	388,279	46	47,296	6
1978	402,097	48	382,693	46	47,836	6
1980	424,963	50	376,534	44	54,471	6
1982	416,938	50	362,188	44	52,995	6

the resurgence of the party at the national level, were at the expense of independents and those declaring no party affiliation in 1980.

Party affiliations are even more balanced in the important area of registration. These are the people most likely to vote. Among this politically aware group, the Republicans have never claimed more than a small majority. Nebraska has a closed primary system, which means that a prospective voter is confronted at registration with the question of "joining" one of the legally recognized political parties. Those who become members are allowed to vote only for candidates of that party in the spring primary elections. Those who prefer to claim an independent status are recorded as nonpolitical. Independents may vote only in the nonpartisan segment of the primary for such offices as state senator, University regent, or natural resources director. The enrollment system for determining party membership started first in the cities and has been in operation throughout the state only since 1968. Table 7.1 contains the registration figures at the time of the general election since 1968.

These registration figures are not consistent with the Republican dominance in elections or, for that matter, with little else in Nebraska politics. The Republican edge, for example, was greatest in 1970, the year of Exon's election as governor. If registration statistics were valid predictors in a milieu of intense partisanship, elections should be highly competitive, with the outcome determined by the choices made by the independents. Since that is not an accurate description of recent elections, the only other explanation is that Nebraskans do not take very seriously the party labels they give themselves.

This is not to say that Nebraskans are frivolous in their party identifications. If nothing else, there is a practical reason for signing up with a party during registration. To claim independent status, even if that is one's natural inclination, is to choose disenfranchisement from several important primary contests, including that for president. Even taking that into account, however, it is probably true that party identification is not always a reasoned commitment to party goals.

We can at least speculate that there is a relationship between loose partisan attachments and fairly weak party structures on the one hand and the factor of nonpartisanship on the other hand. Nonpartisanship added to the weakened condition of the parties to the point that they can no longer enforce any sense of discipline among their nominal members. The absence of organized majority and minority groups in the legislature deprives the "outs" of an established base from which to stimulate interest in the next election. Nonpartisanship is also connected to two other features of the Nebraska political scene.

Partisans in Power

In Nebraska, crossing party lines is not the fatal step it might be in other states. That is, candidates, in many cases do not seem overly obsessed with niceties of party loyalty, while voters are seldom repelled by the campaign adventures of recently converted members of the opposition party. Terry Carpenter, for many years one of the most powerful members of the Unicameral, won the Democratic nomination for representative, senator, and governor between 1934 and 1972; this did not prevent him from trying his luck in the Republican primaries and, in 1956, he wound up as a delegate to the Republican National Convention, where he achieved notoriety by nominating "Joe Smith" for vice-president as an alternative to Richard Nixon. Senator Zorinsky was a registered Republican shortly before winning the Democratic nomination in 1976.

This independent frame of mind among politicians is no doubt influenced by the sort of behavior necessary to succeed in a nonpartisan situation. Personal considerations, instead of party discipline, will determine the offices one wishes to seek. In this hospitable environment for mavericks, cynical observers have suggested that Democratic candidates are, likely as not, Republicans who did not like their chances in their own party's primary. More seriously, it has been asserted that Democratic officeholders in Nebraska are more like Republicans than they are like Democrats from other states.

Since there are few standards of national party orthodoxy, such an assertation is hard to verify, beyond stating the truism that what sells in New York City may not go over in Benkelman. The best available test that we can apply, at least to members of Congress, is the party unity index published annually by the *Congressional Quarterly*. That score measures the number of times that a member of Congress has voted with the majority of his or her party.

From 1949 to the present, seven Nebraskans (five representatives and two senators) have served in Washington as elected Democrats. The party unity scores they compiled do not substantiate conclusively the claim that the state's Democrats are out of step with their fellow partisans. Eugene O'Sullivan (1949 and 1950) was nearly perfect in his party loyalty in Congress. Of the two Democrats in the Eighty-sixth Congress (1959 and 1960), Lawrence Brock tended to vote against his party while Donald McGinley was near the average; both were defeated for reelection. Clair Callan (1965 and 1966) was above average and John Cavanaugh (1969 through 1980) was near average in party loyalty among Democratic members of the House. The current senators, Zorinsky and Exon, are the most extreme cases. Exon has been below average in support of his party, and Zorinsky has been more likely to vote in opposition to rather than in support of the Democratic majority.

On the Republican side, there is more uniformity in party support and the levels of unity are consistently high, indicating closer congruence among Nebraska congressional Republicans and their national party leaders. But whatever variations in party unity scores exist, they may say more about the loosely constructed federation of state parties into national units than about the nature of Nebraska Democrats. Elected party members no doubt feel compelled to stand by their national leaders but they are not bound to do so. The same anarchy obtains within the state and, as long as one can convince the voters in the primary that one is a good Democrat or Republican, the incumbent is beyond punishment by the formal party structure.

Money and the Future of the Parties

If, as has been suggested in this and other chapters, a move toward eliminating nonpartisanship in state elections would improve the political process, is there much chance of the change occurring? It may be too late in the day to talk seriously about the reform of the party system in the United States. In April 1982, a distinguished group of citizens met under the auspices of the American Assembly at Columbia University. In their assessment, political parties have lost their dominant role in political life. The major reason for this was an expensive new technology. They concluded, "Television has become an even more powerful means for candidates and officeholders to reach the largest number of voters than political parties. The new technologies for campaigning and raising money have enabled a larger number of organizations other than parties to position themselves so as to influence the outcome of elections." [11]

It has seldom been truer that, in politics, money talks. Television, mailing lists, and the maintenance of a retinue of campaign consultants forces candidates to be concerned about finances. Federal and state campaign financing laws have, in only the past decade, been revised to deal with the problem, if not for the benefit of democracy, at least for the candidates and special interests. Laws now encourage the establishment of political action committees (PACs). The PACs are a vehicle by which corporations, unions, and other special interests can channel the contributions of their members to the "right" candidates. Nationally, PACs control several millions of desperately needed dollars. Candidates are encouraged to "shop around" among the PACs to put together a coalition with enough money, thus freeing them from dependence on the party structure. The American Assembly noted,

11. American Assembly, *The Future of American Political Parties* (New York: Columbia University, 1982), p. 3.

"Whereas in years past it was the party which usually had, or had access to, the money needed to run a campaign and the candidates who wanted it, today it is the candidate and the officeholder who have the money and the party which needs it."

Campaigning in Nebraska has become substantially more expensive in the past three decades. Many candidates for statewide office retain public relations firms to help in their campaigns. These specialists employ television and radio heavily and hire pollsters to sound out voters on issues and candidates. This technology takes money. Robert Crosby estimated that his expenditure for the governor's race in 1952 was $25,000. Thirty years later, both candidates for the same job spent nearly $2,000,000; the 1982 election cost Charles Thone $1,028,531 while the winner, Robert Kerrey, spent $867,701. Even running for lesser offices may require a healthy bankroll. In 1982, Senator John DeCamp and his opponent, contesting a seat in a rural legislative district, set a spending record of $124,118 for the primary and general elections. If the past is any guide, these records will be broken at the next election.

The possibility for abuses in campaign financing led Nebraska to pass a law regulating the process. In 1977, the Political Accountability and Disclosure Commission began the controversial business of policing campaigns, as well as overseeing lobbying and watching for potential conflicts of interest by public officials. The Commission requires information about receipts and expenditures from political parties, political action committees, and individual contributors to state and local candidates.

The data compiled by the Commission for the primary and general elections of 1980 are instructive since, at all levels, this was an almost wholly nonpartisan election (candidates for national office are governed by the Federal Election Commission). In both elections, 114 candidates raised more than $1,000 for a total of $1,061,347.09. Of contributions of more than $100 to these candidates, only seven percent came from the political party committees. Thirty-seven percent was donated by PACS, 26 percent by business, and 30 percent by individual citizens. The parties, therefore, were on the sidelines in this election when it came to providing the "vital stuff" of modern politics.

PACS in Nebraska will probably become even more important as a source of revenue for candidates. Inasmuch as campaigns are not likely to become any cheaper, this may not be a deplorable development. The money will have to come from somewhere and, under current regulations, the process may be more visible than in the "good old days" when "fat cats" bought and sold candidates. The major question is how representative the PACS are of the broad spectrum of interests within the state. In 1980, there was a bias in favor of professional and business groups; PACS raising more than twenty thousand dollars included the Committee on Responsibility and Truth (attorneys), the Dealer Political Action Committee (auto dealers), Inter Mutual of Omaha Companies PAC, the Nebraska Bankers State PAC, and the Nebraska Medical PAC. The Nebraska State Education Association, while not officially a PAC, was another major contributor to legislative races.

Whatever the future of the PACS, the point remains that they are one more challenge to the parties. However, are Nebraska political parties terminal cases? They are losing control of the all-important financial side of campaigning, they have a weak hold on the loyalty of both their voters and their candidates, and their sphere of operation has been limited by nonpartisanship. Feasible first aid measures do not come immediately to mind. For example, the parties were once authorized by state law to endorse candidates in the primary (called preprimary endorsement). The parties enjoyed only limited success in controlling nomination by this device and the law was revoked in 1953. Nebraska will continue to reflect the nationwide trend regarding the position of parties. They will not die and we can expect to find Republicans battling Democrats well into the next century. But they will not regain their dominant position in the political life of the state or the nation.

Ideological Orientation

Ideological orientation may be more important than party considerations for understanding politics in the state. Nebraska has often been regarded as one of the more conservative states in the union. But just what does this conservatism consist of? In the American political spectrum, a conservative basically prefers less government activity while liberals endorse a more active role for the public sphere in solving social and economic problems. On the national scene, the Republican Party has been identified as the conservative party while the Democrats are thought of as more liberal. Nebraska's electoral Republicanism may account for much of its reputation for conservatism.

Public attitudes toward government spending provide another measure of the conservative-liberal continuum. A statewide survey conducted by Selection Research of Lincoln in 1979 found that 63 percent of Nebraskans polled favored limiting increases in state spending to seven percent per year. Another Selection Research survey in 1981 reported that 86 percent of those asked supported President Reagan's spending and tax cuts. At least in the abstract, Nebraskans are sensitive to issues of government expenditure; when it comes to money, Nebraskans are conservative.

There is, however, another side to this dimension of ideology. The NASIS survey in 1978 asked whether state government should be doing more to solve a number of problems. The results are contained in Table 7.2. If the degree of conservatism in the state is measured by the percentage of those who are ready to identify specific areas in which state government should be doing less, Nebraska may be more liberal than expected. Only an insignificant minority in each instance felt that the government should do less. In four areas, a majority indicated a preference for a more active government. Nebraskans, in other words, are certainly not opposed to government's involvement in a number of sensitive policy areas, nor does there seem to be any clear indication of where government can be reduced. Of course, these data may only be a reflection of the poverty of American ideology; while in principle one may be in favor of a reduced role for government, it is not easy to identify actual programs to cut back. Like that of other Americans, the conservative bark of Nebraskans may be worse than the bite.

Conclusion

While we must be cautious about making too much of two or three questions contained in several surveys, some tentative conclusions about the political culture of Nebraska can be integrated into a broader theoretical perspective. A number of years ago, two political scientists

Table 7.2: Support for Govt. Involvement in Problem Solving

Problem	Govt. should do more	Govt. should do less	Govt. doing about right	Don't know
Energy resources	52%	1%	37%	10%
Crime prevention	57	1	37	5
Drug abuse	69	2	21	8
Public education (primary and secondary)	39	4	49	8
Water resources	39	3	45	13
Condition of elderly	52	1	39	7
Condition of farmers	58	3	36	13
Health	24	2	67	7

SOURCE: Alan Booth and Susan Welch, *More for Less: Nebraskans and State Government Programs,* NASIS Report no. 78.

offered a three-category typology of political culture. While it was designed for the comparison of nations, the broad outlines of each type may be relevant to the study of American states.[12] A parochial political culture is one in which citizens have developed no orientation toward the political system. The citizens expect nothing of the system; in fact, they may be unaware of its existence. A subject culture is one in which citizens are aware of the political system and are able to evaluate its performance in terms of policy outputs, but they are at the

12. Gabriel Almond and Sidney Verba, *Civic Culture* (Boston: Little, Brown, 1965), pp. 16–18.

same time not sensitive to their potential role in shaping government policy as a participant. That is, citizens know government is there, doing important work, but, like the weather, it is something that "just happens." Finally, the participant culture is one in which citizens not only pay attention to policy output but are also conscious of the structure and processes whereby they can shape those policies. Although no one of these three types exists in a pure form in the modern world, the categories may be applicable to political life in Nebraska.

Our examination of some admittedly sketchy evidence about the state's political culture suggests that it conforms most closely to the subject category; since political systems are always developing, Nebraska is probably moving in the direction of the participant type. Nebraskans are reasonably satisfied with their political system and levels of trust in it are fairly high. They were able to articulate preferences for more or less government activity in a number of policy areas. In other words, Nebraskans appear to be oriented to the output side of politics. On the other side of the coin, in what we called political efficacy, perceptions that one can influence the inputs into the system are somewhat less developed. A rate of electoral participation in major state races of less than 50 percent is one manifestation of this. The underdeveloped condition of the parties, major vehicles for bringing citizen inputs before government, is another. State government is the least salient level and less than 20 percent of the citizens can be considered highly concerned with state issues. Low levels of knowledge about the identity of state senators also serves to inhibit participation.

If these data indicate a subject political culture, opinion leaders in the state may want to reconsider the agenda of reform. Presumably, greater citizen involvement in the input side of government is desireable, but if citizens lack a fully developed participant orientation, then institutions should be altered to facilitate participation. There are a number of aspects of the Nebraska political system that could be altered to accomplish this goal.

Clearly, the nonpartisan legislature is an obstacle to participation. A return to partisanship, a relatively simple change and one that the political parties already endorse, might be considered. The number of elected officials could safely be reduced, thus lessening the complexity of the ballot. Ways of increasing electoral turnout are not immediately obvious, although a return to combining gubernatorial with presidential elections would, as pre-1966 statistics prove, draw more people to the polls. The resuscitation of the political parties, perhaps by giving the party leadership more control over nominations and contributions, is another area for investigation.

A call for reform, of course, is not an implication that the state is in desperate shape. The Nebraska political system appears to work, perhaps as well as any in the nation. The point is that the components of a political culture are always in flux, always changing, as the composition of the citizenry changes. The institutions that reflect that culture, therefore, must also continue to grow.

JOHN G. PETERS

EIGHT

Trends in
State Expenditures
and Revenue

In the view of some scholars, all countries face a basic and perhaps fatal crisis. In the not-too-distant past, there was a period of human history in which expanding economic production provided governments with enough revenue to meet increased public demands for services. But in this modern "age of limits," the inevitable crunch has come, and policy makers are having difficulty in finding the money to support services at the level to which citizens have become accustomed. Taxpayers resist giving more of their personal resources to the state while the recipients of benefits keep asking for more — or at least regard proposed reductions as threats to their very existence.

As a matter of survival, everyone is forced to reconsider the principles of the dismal science of economics and to become familiar with the generally arid topic of public finance. Public discussions today concentrate on balanced budgets, interest rates, supply-side economics, or the impact of various taxes on the money market. Nor is the subject of government revenue purely a matter of idle talk. Beginning in California in 1978, beleaguered citizens have taken to the polls, in the view of many, to protect themselves from their own government. The election of Ronald Reagan and his strenuous efforts to reshape American public finance may be the most critical signs of a profound change in the nature of government.

The immediate significance for Nebraskans of all these currents of change is hard to describe. In many areas of public finance, the state was the anomalous case. Perhaps readjustments to present reality will be less painful since Nebraskans have not been living as "high on the hog" as other Americans. Or it may be that since the state made a late, and still incomplete, entry into that postwar era of massive expansions in government spending, it will have to buck the trend toward fiscal cutbacks just to maintain nationally established standards of service. Whatever the case, we can be assured that the choices will not come easily, given that long Nebraskan tradition of questioning the wisdom of any but the most basic of state expenditures. The descendents of those early pioneers who resisted statehood itself because it was a needless expense are still around.

This chapter will not resolve any of the fundamental issues. The best we can do here is sketch the growth in state expenditures for public programs and services and the corresponding increase in the revenues needed to finance this expansion. Wherever possible, statistics that compare the record of Nebraska with the rest of the nation will be used.

Trends in Expenditure Patterns

Which comes first, the raising of money or the need to spend it? In 1950, Professor C. S. Miller of the University of Nebraska asked, "How does Nebraska do it?" How did the state get by without a sales or income tax? By comparing the state with eight of its neighbors, he concluded that a major reason was that "Nebraska's state government generally has spent less per capita than its neighbors on state services and assistance."[1] In particular, Nebraska was unlike its neighbors because it gave so little in aid to local schools.

Nebraskans held dearly to this fiscal policy, but there was no way to withstand the tremendous upsurge in the demand for increasing the size and scope of governmental activity at all levels. The property tax could not support state government and so newer taxes were imposed in the 1960s, causing an escalation in government expenditures. Has

1. C. S. Miller, *Nebraska State Finances* (Chicago: Council of State Governments, 1950), p. 41.

the state caught up with the rest of the country? One observer in the 1970s doubted it, suggesting that the state might be called the "Mississippi of the North."[2] Questions of too much or too little in public finance make for interesting politics but poor scholarship. The most we can do here is point out the dramatic increases that have taken place in the past few years.

The rate of growth, it must first be noted, has not been the same in all areas of government activity. The differential rates show up clearly in the functional categories used by the state in the preparation and presentation of the executive budget. Every activity supported in any way by state funds is included in one of six groups: (1) education; (2) general government and administration; (3) human resources; (4) public safety; (5) natural resources, and (6) transportation. Figure 8.1 shows the pattern of acceleration in these six categories.

Education, general government, and human resources were the major growth areas; the others show a slow but steady increase. To be more precise about the categories, education covers all state support for public education, through the colleges and the university, as well as libraries and the arts; a substantial portion includes state aid to local public schools. General government refers to the activities of the executive, legislative, and judicial branches which relate to the management and control of state agencies. Human resources are all social services such as welfare, public health, the state hospitals, correctional institutions, and civil rights agencies. Public safety refers to the statewide protection of the public, including enforcement of motor vehicle laws, public defense, and the regulation and supervision of trades and professions. Natural resources covers all activities pertaining to the preservation, development, and utilization of the state's natural assets, including agriculture. Transportation refers to state activity related to public roads and the regulation of motor vehicles and aviation.

The state budget is also displayed in terms of objects of expenditures. The trends are shown in Figure 8.2. The largest and fastest growing budget outlay is for governmental aid—grants of money to

2. Neal Peirce, *The Great Plains States of America: People, Politics, and Power in the Nine Great Plains States* (New York: W. W. Norton, 1973), p. 203.

Figure 8.1: General Fund Expenditures By Government Function, 1966–80

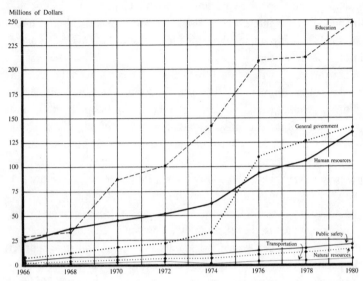

SOURCE: Compiled from *State of Nebraska: Annual Fiscal Reports 1966–1980.*

both local governments and individual citizens. Personal services, largely the salaries paid to state employees, has also shown a dramatic increase. Over 80 percent in the growth of Nebraska government is accounted for by these two categories.

Perhaps the best way to understand the growth of public programs in Nebraska is to compare the state with the rest of the nation. In Table 8.1, the amount of money spent per capita for selected government programs in Nebraska is compared to the national averages (all state governments combined) for the years 1970 and 1980. The table indicates that in general during these years, for both Nebraska and the nation, per capita expenditures for every major government activity have increased. Even though Nebraska's $854 per capita expenditure for all programs was below the national average of $1,010, since 1970 the Nebraska average has increased 188 percent, compared to 165 percent for the nation. Moreover, Nebraska spends above the national

Figure 8.2: State Expenditures by Major Object, 1966–80

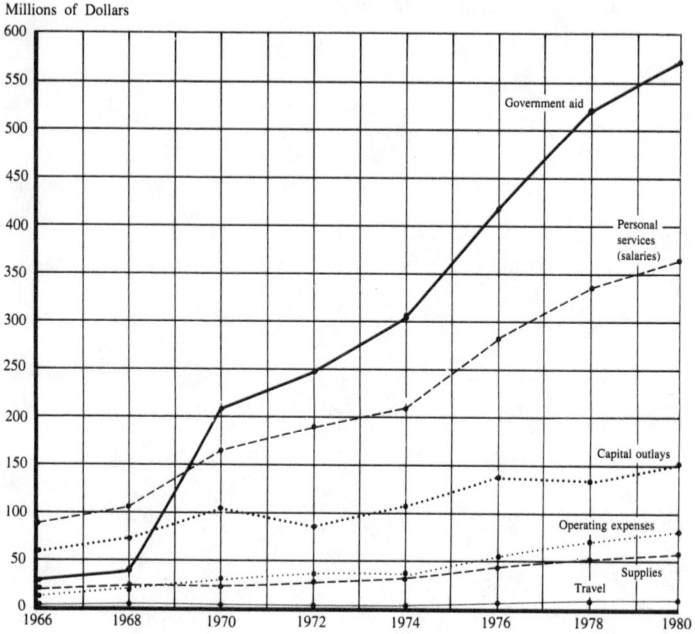

Millions of Dollars

SOURCE: Compiled from *State of Nebraska: Annual Fiscal Reports 1966–1980*.

average for some programs. This is the case, for example, in education, for which Nebraska spends more money per capita for direct expenditures to public schools and for aid to higher education (although dramatically less in state aid to local schools). Two other areas in which the state spends considerably more than the national average are highways and natural resources.

Overall, the conclusion emerges that from an analysis of the growth of state expenditure and comparisons with other states is that Nebraska has started to build its public programs later than most states and consequently has had to increase its effort substantially within a short period of time to provide services on a par with other states. Officials and citizens may feel that they have made heroic efforts, but the truth is that the state remains behind the rest of the nation in terms of its

Table 8.1: Per Capita Amounts for
Selected State Government Activities

Activity	1970 National average for all states	1970 Nebraska	1980 National average for all states	1980 Nebraska
Total general expenditures	$384	$297	$1,010	$854
Education, total	152	117	389	265
Intergovernmental	84	40	233	93
Direct education expenditure	68	77	156	172
Higher education	54	66	123	150
Highways	66	70	110	169
Public welfare	65	39	196	122
Hospitals	21	21	50	52
Health	6	2	29	24
Corrections	5	4	20	21
Natural resources	11	16	19	34

SOURCE: Adapted from U.S. Bureau of the Census, *State Government Finances: 1970, 1980*.

contribution to total government activity. In fact, Nebraska ranks forty-eighth in terms of state government's share of total state-local expenditure.[3]

Beyond the fact that Nebraska started late in developing its public programs, what general explanation can we offer for this rapid growth? One reason is the change in population between 1960 and 1980 and the resulting change in the needs and desires of the citizens. During the 1970s, the population of the state increased by 6 percent to 1,574,000 persons. While this was below the national average of 8.3 percent, it was higher than the 4.8 percent for the plains states. The recent increase reflects a turnaround in the outmigration of people. For the first time in several decades, the net inmigration and outmigration were about equal. The percentage of people in the sixty-five-and-over age group increased to 13 percent of the population while those under eighteen dropped from 34 to 28.5 percent. The size of the rural population (both farm and nonfarm) has steadily declined until, by 1980, it represented a little more than one-third of the total population of the state.

Changes in the size and composition of the population bring new demands on government for social services. The health needs of an aging population, and the differences in the priorities of urban dwellers compared to rural citizens, including a shift in beliefs about the proper role of government, surely have an impact on the growth of state activity. With about 10 percent of the population below the official poverty income level, traditional ways of caring for the needy have been replaced by major components of the welfare state.

Similarly, changes in the labor force and employment patterns have contributed to demands for government help in terms of unemployment compensation, vocational training, job placement, and labor-management relations. The nature of employment in Nebraska has changed to the extent that by 1980 only 10 percent of all workers were engaged in agriculture. Between 1960 and 1980, the largest increase within the state's labor force occurred in the areas of wholesale and

3. Advisory Commission on Intergovernmental Relations, *Significant Features of Fiscal Federalism; 1980–81 Edition* (Washington, D.C.: Government Printing Office, 1981), p. 24.

retail trade, services, and government employment. The movement from an agricultural to a service economy has caused a shift in the sorts of demands made on government.

It left to its own devices, Nebraska might have responded to each new problem in a distinctive way, but today no state is an island. Government activity has been "nationalized," with services becoming more uniform across the country. Part of this has been caused by the role of professionals—educators, engineers, welfare workers, mental health specialists—who tend to look to their national organization for information about adequate levels of performance. Of course, the major reason for the homogenization of activity has been the federal government. At the beginning of the 1980s, about 20 percent of total state-local revenue came from the federal government. While that is a sizable piece of cash by itself, the real leverage comes from the guidelines that affect a whole area of activity. One of the great confrontations over the power of the state occurred when Governor Exon was told by the federal highway administrator to remove signs announcing the state's tourist attractions from the right-of-way of the interstate. The state could have kept the signs, but at the risk of losing all federal money for road construction. Similarly, the University of Nebraska has developed a program of women's sports, not so much because of a dedication to equality but rather because of a concern over losing millions of dollars in federal grants and contracts.

The Revenue Side

The growth in the demand for public programs throughout the postwar period strained the revenue-raising capacity of Nebraska state government. For a century the major source of state revenue was the property tax, both real and personal. Over the years, public officials and citizens began to recognize the necessity of relieving property owners from the burden of a fairly primitive tax system and replacing it with a fair and dependable revenue source to provide for expanding government services. In the reforms brought on by the abolition of the property tax for state revenue and the passage of the Revenue Act of 1967, the income and general sales taxes became the backbone of the state's revenue system, with the property tax, as a percentage of total state-local revenue, dropping from 72.3 percent (by far the highest in the nation) to 41.6 percent in 1980.

The dramatic impact of these tax measures cannot be underestimated. One can argue that, because of the new revenue raising capacity, it was now possible to pay for current services while adopting new programs. The revenue raised from all tax sources increased from a little over $100 million in 1969 to $751 million in 1978, and by 1980 to $816 million. A little over 69 percent of current tax receipts comes from the income and general sales taxes, with most of the remainder from petroleum and excise taxes. The other major source of state revenue is intergovernmental aid.

The passage of the Revenue Act must be viewed as a far-sighted political act on the part of Governor Tiemann and the legislative majority who voted for it, since both the income and sales taxes were new experiences for Nebraskans. Unlike legislators in other states, where the two taxes had been introduced at different times, Nebraska senators attending the birth of these taxes insisted on regarding them as twins and turned over their care to a special nurse, the State Board of Equalization and Assessment.

Setting the Tax Rates

Since the state is prohibited by its constitution from borrowing to meet general fund obligations, special care must be taken to ensure that a combination of income and sales taxes will provide enough revenue to fund the programs authorized by the legislature and the governor. By statute, there must also be a 3 percent reserve in excess of anticipated expenditures. Another basic statutory requirement reads as follows: "The rates of the sales and income taxes shall be fixed so that the total sales and use taxes levied will as nearly as possible equal the total individual income tax levied for the calendar year for which the rates so fixed will be effective." That is, the liability for the taxpayer for each tax shall be as equal as possible. The amount by which either tax can be adjusted is also restricted; the sales tax rate can be changed in half-percent increments and the income tax can be raised or lowered by a full percentage point.

Nebraska has gone as far as any state in piggybacking its income tax system on the federal internal revenue code. With the state tax liability set as a percentage of the federal levy, taxpayer compliance and general administration are fairly convenient. State lawmakers, not so incidentally, are also relieved of the necessity of defining taxable income. The negative side is that when Washington sneezes, Nebraska catches pneumonia. After Congress adjusts the federal rate or redefines what can be taxed, state revenues automatically go up or down. The fiscal crisis of the early 1980s resulted largely from the instability introduced by President Reagan's tax reduction program. Legislative leaders have suggested that the state divorce its rates from the federal structure and uncouple the state income and sales taxes. This would, it is felt, give the state greater flexibility and independence in state financing, an important consideration in light of the stringent constitutional requirements prohibiting indebtedness.

The business of setting rates is facilitated by predictions of revenues to be raised by various rates, based on estimates of the state's economic prosperity in the coming year and a review of previous surpluses in the state treasury. Economic forecasting is still an uncertain art, often resulting in excessive surpluses or impending deficits. Anything short of a bull's-eye hit will cause political reverberations. State Tax Commissioner Donald Leuenberger noted the effect of inaccurate predictions about the economy and federal tax changes:

> Even if the department were accurate 18 months, 12 months or whatever in advance at the 97, 98, 99 percent level — which would be phenomenal skill or blind luck — you must bear in mind the budgetary damage each 1 percent error results in. A 1 percent error this year in total amounts to slightly over $9 million. Few entire state agencies approach this amount. Fiscal planning becomes a fearsome enterprise indeed.[4]

From 1967 through 1983, Nebraska was the only state in which the major tax rates were set by an executive body instead of by the legislature. Four elected officials—the governor, secretary of state, auditor, and treasurer—together with the state tax commissioner, a gubernatorial appointee, made up the Board of Equalization and Assessment. In the transition from the property tax to the sales and

4. Donald Leuenberger, "State Tax Policy Prey to Uncertainty," *Lincoln Sunday Journal and Star*, November 21, 1982.

income tax system, the Board retained its major function of setting the rates at the end of each legislative session and between sessions if conditions demanded. The legislature, in April 1983, voted to take back the rate-setting power.

In its obituary of this "prudent, high-minded" system, the *Lincoln Journal* lamented that "Nebraska simply found living with a sophisticated, rational system of tax-rate setting too stressful. Which ultimately says more about the cut of our political establishment than anything else." This editorialist was probably unduly dismayed by the gubernatorial machinations, especially by Exon and Thone, which accompanied the decline of the Board. Any student of politics should not be surprised to learn that tax policy is a highly controversial matter and will remain so whether it is shaped by the legislature or the governor. To take taxation out of politics or politics out of taxation is to attempt the impossible.

The Board of Equalization and Assessment retains its other major function, namely, the equalization of the assessments of property among counties so that, for example, owners of property worth fifty thousand dollars in Douglas County will have approximately the same tax liability of someone with fifty thousand dollars worth of property in Scotts Bluff County. Although the Board has the power to raise or lower assessed valuation in any county, it rarely does so, given the political risks in taking such action. Recent tax commissioners have played a more aggressive role in property tax assessment and the state has been more active in the equalization of local property tax assessments.

The Tax Structure

The state income tax includes taxes on individual, fiduciary, and corporate income. The tax on personal income is based on a percentage of the citizen's federal income tax liability. Rates for fiduciary income from trusts and estates are calculated in the same manner. The personal rates have varied from an original low of ten percent of federal liability in 1968 to 20 percent in 1983. The tax on corporate income is calculated as a percent of that earned in Nebraska; the rate is set as a percentage of the individual tax rate.

Table 8.2: State Government Revenue (In thousands of dollars)

	Amount		
Source	1960	1970	1980
Total Revenue (all sources)	$182,125	$486,473	$1,505,994
Total general revenue	172,052	470,748	1,419,516
Tax revenue	91,058	261,307	816,767
Sales and gross receipts	50,679	171,008	446,856
License taxes	11,283	33,185	67,038
Individual income	——	44,444	235,821
Corporation income	——	8,550	57,579
Property	27,173	2,006	2,502
Death and gift	374	816	2,277
Severence	1,354	766	2,948
Document and stock transfer	——	532	1,746
Intergovernmental revenue	59,169	135,239	389,420
From federal government	50,033	113,629	361,420
From local government	9,136	21,610	28,235
Charges and miscellaneous revenue	21,825	74,202	213,329
Insurance trust revenue	10,073	15,725	86,478

SOURCE: Adapted from U.S. Bureau of the Census, *State Government Finances, 1960, 1970, 1980.*

The position of the income tax in the total tax structure is indicated in Table 8.2. The individual and corporate tax yield has increased steadily since 1967 to over $290 million in 1980. The personal income tax annually yields approximately four times the revenue from the corporate tax.

The other major source of revenue since 1967 has been the general sales tax. Under provisions of the Revenue Act, a tax is levied on retail sales within the state. A general use tax applies to goods purchased outside of Nebraska for use within the state. The tax is applied to food, although people who file a state income tax return receive a tax credit for food.

State law provides that a municipality may impose a local sales and use tax to be collected and administered by the state department of revenue and returned to the local government (less a percentage for an administrative fee). The rate of the local tax can be set at either .5 or 1 percent of retail sales within the municipality. By a special act of the legislature in 1978, the city of Omaha was permitted to raise its rate to 1.5 percent. The local sales tax, as of 1982, has been adopted by seven cities and is an important supplement to the revenues of Omaha and Lincoln.

In addition to the income and sales taxes, Nebraska derives revenue from over thirty classes of miscellaneous taxes. These lesser taxes accounted for over $76 million of the tax receipts in 1980. In Table 8.3, some of the more important miscellaneous taxes are described. Legislators in all states like to earmark or reserve for specific purposes certain miscellaneous taxes. For example, in Nebraska, receipts from the motor fuels tax go into a trust fund for highway construction and maintenance. In this regard, one of the more controversial taxes is that on cigarettes. In the early 1970s, a nickel tax was added to the existing rate, with the proceeds dedicated to special projects, including the erection of a sports center in Lincoln. Senators have gone on to find other more or less worthy uses for this source of revenue, while smokers argue that their little vice is being exploited too heavily by the state.

The Tax Burden

It is hard to answer the basic question whether Nebraska's taxes are too high or too low. The taxpayers themselves probably are not good witnesses on this point. A 1980 NASIS survey found that 20 percent of Nebraskans felt their taxes are higher than in other states while 56 percent believed they were about the same as other states. In fact, however, the total state-local tax burden in Nebraska is less than the national average. In Table 8.4, a comparison is made of per capita revenues for Nebraska and the national average for 1970 and 1980. In

Table 8.3: Nebraska Miscellaneous Taxes

Tax	Basis/Rate, 1980	Administered by	Distribution	1980 yield
Liquor taxes	Licenses, $5–$1,000 Excise: Beer, 12¢/gal. Wine, 55¢/gal. Alcohol & spirits, $2.50/gal.	State Liquor Commission	Excise: General Fund License: School fund of relevant county or city	$13,103,618
Cigarette tax	13¢ per pack	Department of Revenue	General Fund, 8¢ Outdoor Recreation Fund, 1¢ Capital Construction, 3¢	$13,951,891
Pari-mutuel wagering tax	5% of sum wagered in excess of $1,000,000	State Racing Commission	General Fund State Fairground Building Fund	$7,443,681
Motor fuels	11½¢ per gal. 6½¢ gasahol	Dept. of Revenue	Highway Trust Fund	$104,175,555

SOURCE: Compiled from Nebraska Department of Revenue, *1980 Annual Report.*

Table 8.4: Average Per Capita Contributions to State Revenues

Item	1970		1980	
	National average	Nebraska	National average	Nebraska
Total general revenue	$384	$317	$1,034	$904
All taxes	237	176	607	520
Individual income taxes	45	56	164	150
Corporate income taxes	18	14	59	37
Sales taxes & gross receipts Total	135	115	300	285
General sales	70	50	191	176
Motor fuels	31	46	43	66
Alcoholic beverages	7	4	11	8
Motor vehicle licenses	13	16	22	29
Property taxes	5	1	13	2
Death and gift taxes	5	1	9	1

SOURCE: Adapted from U.S. Bureau of the Census, *State Government Finances, 1970, 1980.*

general, the revenues raised by state governments from most sources almost tripled during the 1970s. The per capita national average for all revenue regardless of source increased from $384 to $1,034. The Nebraska per capita average also rose rapidly during the decade, but for most revenue sources, the state average is below the national average. The Nebraska average income tax is $150, compared to $164 for all states; and the corporate income tax was $37 per capita, compared to the national average of $59. A few Nebraska taxes are higher than the national average. These include the motor fuels tax ($66 to $43), and motor vehicle license charges ($29 to $22).

The situation can also be viewed in terms of tax capacity and tax effort. According to the Advisory Commission on Intergovernmental Relations (ACIR), which has been striving to improve the accuracy of the measures used in this area, tax capacity refers to the ability to raise revenue using the same taxes as other states. The ACIR's rather complicated formula finds that Nebraska's capacity is 97 percent of the national average. That is, if the state levied exactly the same taxes as every other state, it would collect only 97 percent of the average. The tax effort is the ratio of the total tax collections to tax capacity. In this measure, Nebraska was at 98 percent. Taken together, these figures mean that Nebraska could raise its taxes to bring it up to the national average, but even if it did it would take in less money than the average state, since its composite tax base is not as lucrative as those of the wealthier states.[5]

Such gross comparisons must be used carefully because of the wide variations in the condition of individual taxpayers. With that caveat in mind, some further computations by the ACIR show that the typical Nebraskan receives a somewhat smaller tax bill than other Americans. Specifically, in 1980, a urban Nebraska family with an average income of $21,583 paid 97 percent of the national average of combined federal, state, and local taxes. That same family paid 4.5 percent of its income for property taxes, one percent for state income tax, and 1.5 percent for state and local sales taxes. Overall, Nebraskans pay considerably below the national average in state income and sales taxes while their property taxes are nearly a third higher than the national average. Property tax rates are notoriously hard to compare, but the ACIR estimated that the average effective rate on a single family home was 2.37 percent; only Massachusetts, New York, New Jersey, and Michigan, in 1980, had higher rates.[6]

One can manage a little more sympathy for Nebraskans if the rate of growth in taxation is considered. There, the taxpayer's tax burden increased faster than the national average; for the years between 1967 and 1974, Nebraska's growth placed it thirteenth among all states. The shock of the change in the tax system was more than a figment of the citizen's imagination. The 1970s were a period of even more rapid growth, with state taxes increasing by 195 percent. This rate put

5. Advisory Commission on Intergovernmental Relations, *Tax Capacity of the Fifty States: Methodology and Estimates* (Washington, D.C.: Government Printing Office, 1982).

6. ACIR, *Significant Features,* p. 152.

Nebraska seventh on the list of states arranged according to increases in tax burdens.[7]

The most urgent question in taxation policy facing Nebraskans would appear to be the property tax. Since that tax supports almost all of local government, two options appear possible. First, the state could increase the taxation options for local government, although ways of doing that without cutting into the state's revenue are not clear. Second, the state could try to approach the national average in terms of state aid to localities. The attractiveness of that option will depend on how reliable state leaders feel federal aid will be in the future.

Conclusion

Nebraska promoters have pushed the theme that their state is a source of the "good life." The words fit neatly on bumper stickers, but as philosophers since the ancient Greeks have known, government is a confusing ingredient in life, good or bad. Some people believe that they are the best judges of what to do with their money; others insist that the good life is possible only if government promotes the public welfare over selfish interests. Most of us would probably prefer to have it both ways—low taxes and a wide variety of public services. As noted at the beginning of this chapter, there was a time when it appeared that an expanding economy might make the paradoxical a possibility. Now, in an economy that seems to be stable if not shrinking, individual and collective choices are much harder.

Public attitudes about the future are highly volatile but an attempt was made in March 1981 to assess the views of Nebraskans. Some 1,890 adults were asked questions measuring feelings of optimism or pessimism about the future. The authors concluded, "Significant proportions of Nebraskans are pessimistic about future progress. While a majority feel that new discoveries and advances in technology are likely to alleviate these hard times, the more pressing reality is that

7. Advisory Commission on Intergovernmental Relations, *Regional Growth: Interstate Tax Competition* (Washington, D.C.: Government Printing Office, 1981), p. 56; *Public Administration Times,* December 1, 1981, p. 3.

many Nebraskans report that they have already suffered decreases in their standard of living and that their economic prospects are worse.'' In relating these attitudes to the respondents' feelings of political trust, tolerance of inequality, propensity for collective action, and political involvement, the authors speculated that the political lines are bound to harden and that conflict over the sharing of resources will become more intense.[8] If this is so, then it will take all the wisdom at the command of the political leadership of the state to keep the struggle over expenditure and taxation policy within the confines of existing institutions. The preservation of the good life, if that is what Nebraskans have, will be a great challenge.

8. Lynn White and David Brinkerhoff, *The Political Consequences of the "Age of Limits,"* NASIS–81. no. 3 (Lincoln: University of Nebraska, Bureau of Sociological Research, 1981).

NINE

Local Government

The bare statistics show that Nebraskans prefer quantity and variety in their local government. Whether they are thus well governed is quite another matter, the dimensions of which this chapter will illuminate.

Every five years, the Census Bureau tries to count all units of government in the United States. A unit of government, according to the Bureau, "is an organized entity which, in addition to having governmental character, has sufficient discretion in the management of its own affairs to distinguish it as separate from the administrative structure of any other governmental unit." This definition covers counties, municipalities, townships, school districts, and special districts. Specifically excluded in Nebraska are such local bodies as county hospital boards, railroad transportation safety districts, urban renewal authorities, and street improvement districts.

The latest tabulation was in 1977. At that time, Nebraska contained 3,485 units of local government. Only five states have more and, on a per capita basis, Nebraska outranks all the others. The statistics for the state are summarized in Table 9.1.

The Census Bureau also found, in 1977, that 15,614 elected officials were supervising the work of 62,124 employees. There were 400.8 local government employees per 10,000 of population, which is considerably higher than the national average of 355.3. These governments spent $2,756,000,000 in the 1979–80 fiscal year and were

Table 9.1: Units of Government

Year	County	Munici-pality	Town-ships	School district	Special district	Total
1942	93	530	476	7,009	198	8,306
1952	93	534	477	6,392	485	7,981
1957	93	534	478	4,942	610	6,657
1962	93	537	478	3,264	752	5,124
1967	93	538	486	2,322	952	4,391
1972	93	537	476	1,374	1,081	3,561
1977	93	534	471	1,195	1,192	3,485

carrying $4,405,000,000 of bonded indebtedness. Local government in Nebraska, as a composite, is no small thing.

As in other states, local governments are major components in the conduct of the policy of state government and in law are referred to as "political subdivisions of the state." That is, local governments are created and directed by state law but, with varying degrees of independence, administer their own affairs. Since these governments possess greater or lesser amounts of discretion, the relationship between the state and local governments is not always clear-cut. A recent study by the Advisory Commission on Intergovernmental Relations, however, indicates that the discretion of Nebraska local government may be more apparent than real. On a composite ranking of local discretion, the state ranked forty-first; Nebraska counties had more freedom of action than those in only seven other states.[1] The relationship is still an ambiguous one, and the confusion is often exploited by politicians at either level. In recent years, the legislature mandated the method by which Omaha must elect its council members, yet begged off the controversial issue of the teaching of creationism by insisting that the determination of the elementary school curriculum was purely a local matter. In short, it is not always easy to tell exactly

1. *Public Administration Times,* July 15, 1982, p. 3.

who may do what to whom, but one must begin the search for responsibility within the state capitol.

Local governments were not slow to learn this lesson. Many of them are associated in statewide organizations that conduct strong lobbying efforts each session of the legislature. These groups include the League of Nebraska Municipalities, the Nebraska Association of County Officials, and the Nebraska Association of Resources Districts. A recent trend, at least among larger units, is the employment of a lobbyist to represent their interests before the Unicameral.

County Government

In several states, counties have outgrown their traditional role as predominantly rural administrative subdivisions of state government; county home rule and the county-manager plan as well as other moves toward modernization are not uncommon elsewhere. But not in Nebraska, and Buffalo Bill or Old Jules could probably still find their way around most of the state's courthouses. Certainly little has changed since 1954, when Professor Breckenridge found a great deal of stability in the first hundred years of the counties.[2]

Since Arthur County was organized in 1913, the state has had 93 counties. Over the years, scholars have suggested that the number could be reduced and even a casual observer must wonder whether the nine counties with less than a thousand people could not be eliminated. But there has been little popular support for any change. If it was good enough for William Jennings Bryan, one supposes, it is good enough for us.

Nebraska counties are headed, in theory at least, by a board exercising both legislative and executive powers. Governing boards come in two varieties: the board of commissioners in precinct counties and the board of supervisors in township counties, depending on whether the county has organized townships. Except for some differences in the number of board members and their method of election, there is little

2. A. C. Breckenridge, "Nebraska County Government: 100 Years," *County Officer* 19 (1954): 80–88.

to distinguish between the two types. The *Nebraska Blue Book* contains a succinct description: "The distinction between the supervisor and commissioner forms of county government is relatively unimportant, since the county boards under the two systems have precisely the same powers and tenure, and the other officers are the same for counties of the same population class."

The insinuation that the board's supremacy in county government is largely theoretical arises from the fact that many other county officials are elected and therefore not directly subordinate to the board. All counties elect their clerk (ex officio comptroller in Douglas County), treasurer, sheriff, and county attorney (ex officio county coroner) on a partisan basis. The assessor, clerk of the district court, register of deeds, surveyor (ex officio county engineer in some counties), and public defender are also elected, depending on the population of the county, on a partisan ballot; the office of superintendent of schools, where still filled, is nonpartisan. All local judges, as described in chapter 5, are chosen by a special appointment-election system. Nebraska counties represent Jacksonian democracy at its best (or worst) and the courthouse is the scene of much politicking as local officials, nearly independent within their little fiefdoms, carry out the business largely mandated by state law. Because of their formal authority granted by the state and their informal power based on vote-getting ability, it is never a foregone conclusion that these officers will tolerate much direction from the board.

The elected officials share among themselves the responsibility for the conduct of most of the traditional functions of county government. There are in many counties, again depending on population, a number of appointed officials who represent the involvement of county government in more modern functions. These include the election commissioner, the welfare director, the health director, weed control superintendent, veterans' services officer, and civil defense director.

What does the county do? In fiscal year 1979–80, Nebraska counties spent $275.4 million. Of that amount, 32 percent went to highways and roads, 21.5 percent to health and hospitals, and 5.6 percent to public welfare. The largest category of expenditure—"all others"—was 34 percent and includes functions associated with general administration; for example, record keeping, issuing licenses, and enforcing laws. As an administrative arm of the state, the county supervises the machinery for all federal, state, and local elections. The assessor and the treasurer provide basic financial services for all other units of government within the county.

County government, in general, has not been on the frontier of creative change. Its parent, the legislature, has from time to time rather absentmindedly assigned new functions to a variety of offices. The public itself has never been so put out with the county that it has demanded radical changes in structure or function. County officials have seldom demonstrated much interest in modernizing the structure under which they must work. We have little reliable information about the typical county official other than the work of Carroll McKibbin and Peter Shocket in their study of twelve counties in the central part of the state. After interviewing nearly all of the officials in that area, the authors concluded that most of them were locally oriented in their outlook on government, convinced of the benefits of small government, and generally uninterested in pursuing a political career beyond their current position.[3] If this group can be called typical of the rest of the state, we should not look for reform of county government to come from within.

Municipal Government

Nebraska has more incorporated municipalities than California and nearly as many as New York. Even though regarded as a rural state, 75 percent of its population lives within the boundaries of a municipality. The real heart of local government in Nebraska is in its villages and cities. Although these many potential political laboratories have yet to produce any revolutionary breakthroughs in the art of government, they have demonstrated far more adaptability to modern conditions than have the counties.

3. Carroll McKibbin and Peter Shocket, *County Officials of Central Nebraska: Attitudes and Attributes* (Lincoln, Nebr.: State Department of Economic Development, 1974).

The charter is the constitution of the village or city. In Nebraska, as in most states, the specific structure and powers available to any municipality are largely determined by the legislature. Nebraska follows a system of classification that determines the charter options. The metropolitan class is any city of more than three hundred thousand people; the primary class, between one hundred thousand and three hundred thousand; the first class, between five thousand and one hundred thousand; the second class, between eight hundred and five thousand; and villages, between one hundred and eight hundred. The minimum number of people who can incorporate is one hundred, but an incorporated place does not lose that status if it drops below the minimum, so there are municipalities in the state with fewer than one hundred people. At present, there is one city each in the two largest classes.[4] Before the adjustments resulting from the 1980 census, there were 28 cities in the first class, 188 in the second class, and 403 villages.

State laws addressed to specific classes of cities as well as statutes concerning all municipalities determine the bounds within which the government can operate. In an attempt to give cities a little greater freedom from state control, citizens approved in 1912 a constitutional amendment allowing cities with five thousand or more in population to exercise the right of "municipal home rule." Since Grand Island abandoned its home rule charter in 1963, only Omaha and Lincoln enjoy this option. Home rule supposedly allows the city to write its own charter and thus to determine a unique approach to matters of purely local concern. But what is local and what is statewide? The system requires some sort of referee and, according to Professor A. B. Winter's thorough history of home rule, the courts have willingly filled the role, usually to the disadvantage of the city. Winter concludes, "The net result of home rule status . . . is to increase the lobbying workload and expense of Lincoln and Omaha as compared with other state municipalities. Unfortunately, the record does not reveal any advantage to this system with the possible exception of

4. The courts have held that such classifications are not in violation of constitutional prohibitions on special legislation. See A. C. Breckenridge, "The Mockery of Classification," *National Municipal Review* 36 (1947): 571–73.

some intangible prestige stemming from the possession of the home rule label.''[5]

For most villages and cities, the form of municipal government is spelled out in the appropriate legislation. The legislative and executive power of villages is vested in a five-member board of trustees. The board appoints other village officials, the most important of whom is the clerk, for most of the day-to-day operation of the village is in his or her hands. In larger cities, state law permits some variety. The commission form of city government is available to cities with two thousand or more in population. This rather awkward system, in which elected commissioners fill both the legislative and executive roles, has been retained only by Nebraska City. The great majority of cities in the state use some version of the mayor-council form. Omaha and Lincoln have the most fully developed versions of the strong-mayor form, with a full-time elected executive in charge of city administration. Smaller cities have adapted the role of the mayor in a number of ways.

The increasing complexity of providing municipal services has led many Nebraska cities to explore systems that permit the combination of professional administration with electoral accountability. The council-manager, or city manager, form of municipal government is available to cities in the one thousand to three hundred thousand population range. The form has been popular in other states, particularly among smaller communities with a homogeneous population, but it has not been widely adopted in Nebraska. Only ten cities now have a charter dividing governmental authority between an elected council and an appointed manager. Oddly enough, all of the manager cities are in the western part of the state. More common is the ''modified'' mayor-council, or city administrator, system. The major difference between the city manager and city administrator is in the source of authority. The duties of the city manager are spelled out in the statutes and are part of the city charter. Administrators are added to a mayoral system through local ordinances and their authority is

5. A. B. Winter, ''Nebraska Home Rule: The Record and Some Recommendations,'' *Nebraska Law Review* 59 (1980): 614.

determined by local action, including many informal understandings. Nearly forty cities have some version of the city administrator, with sixteen of them recognized by the International City Management Association as meeting the standards of the city management profession. Most of the city administrator municipalities adopted their plans in the 1960s and 1970s.

Lincoln and Omaha developed their governments in somewhat different ways. At the turn of the century, Omaha politically resembled an eastern industrial city. City politics until 1933 was dominated by boss Tom Dennison and his machine. Power today is distributed among a number of familial and ethnic coalitions. Lincoln was shaped in the "good government" mode; that is, it was dominated by a middle-class ethos under the benevolent leadership of business elites. It was only slowly recognized in both cities that there were new elements in the community who were demanding a system more open to a variety of participation. Although shaken by racial tensions in the 1960s, Omaha refused to change its method of electing council members at large and it was only after the legislature imposed district elections that the first black council member was elected in 1981. Lincoln has opened up more avenues for citizen participation and in recent years there has been considerable emphasis on the development of neighborhood associations. Lincoln is now one of the few cities in the nation with an office of neighborhood assistance. In 1978, neighborhood-based activists led a successful campaign for the election of a majority of the council by districts.

Townships

The last, and by any measure least, form of "general purpose" local government is the township. Remnants of a rural past, these units exist in twenty-eight counties and include 14 percent of the state's population. The major function of the township is rural road maintenance, although some operate libraries and cemeteries. State law does permit townships to provide "a fund for the maintenance of a band organization to render free public concerts, musical festivals, and entertainment within the township limits," but I am unaware of any township exercising this power.

Of the 471 townships, 428 have fewer than one thousand people. Interest in township affairs appears to be waning (if it was ever high) and many of the units report difficulties in finding people willing to run for the elected positions. Three elected members—clerk, treasurer, and chairman of the board—make up the board of trustees and handle most of the routine business. Townships, as well as Class I and II school districts, have one interesting feature: in an annual meeting similar to the New England town meeting, the voters can convene in order to decide certain policy matters.

Perhaps the townships would have continued to slowly fade away had not the federal government determined in 1972 that they were general purpose governments and therefore eligible for General Revenue Sharing funds. Since then, townships in Nebraska, if otherwise eligible, have received regular checks from Washington. For example, between 1972 and 1981, Arnold Township in Custer County received $72,206 just by existing. This is undoubtedly a major disincentive to closing up shop.

School Districts

Writing in 1957, John Bollens stated, "Nebraska has approximately 6,000 school districts, the largest number in any state; Minnesota, in second place, has about 1,100 less. Nebraska's school districts, almost as numerous as they were in 1890, together have more governing board members than teachers."[6] By 1983, the number of independent districts had been cut to 1,014 and estimates indicated that both Texas and California had passed Nebraska in this category. Even with a reduction of 83 percent since 1942, some educational leaders feel that the state has not gone far enough and, as Keith Mueller writes in chapter 10, the issue of school consolidation is very much alive.

Under current law, districts are classified on the basis of facilities and population. Class I schools are K-8; in other words, they maintain grades kindergarten through eight. Class II schools are K-12 in areas of a population of one thousand or less. Class III, IV, and V schools

6. John C. Bollens, *Special District Governments in the United States* (Berkeley: University of California Press, 1961): 219.

are also K-12, in areas with populations of one thousand to fifty thousand; fifty thousand to two hundred thousand; and over two hundred thousand, respectively. Class VI districts provide only high school education. Each district is governed by a board elected on a nonpartisan basis which has the power to levy a property tax.

The county superintendent of schools is the chief educational officer within a county and serves as a link between the districts and the State Department of Education. The activity of the superintendent has decreased with the consolidation of districts and so the legislature has abolished the office for single-district counties containing a population of less than three thousand. Since 1973, the county boards have the power to discontinue the office of superintendent.

Some of the former functions of the superintendent have been taken over by educational service units (ESUs), which, strictly speaking, are special rather than school districts. These multicounty organizations provide supplemental educational services to local districts. Such services include data collection and research, special educational programs, media centers, and liaison between the state and local school districts. ESUs are governed by an elected board, with one member elected from each member county and four members elected at large. The ESU levies a tax and receives money from state and federal sources.

The most recent addition to the educational scene is a system of locally governed technical community colleges. A state law passed in 1971 brought within one statewide system the then-existing junior colleges and vocational technical schools. The state is divided into six technical community college areas, with each having an elected board of governors. Each of the boards is autonomous and operates with minimal control from the state. The boards have the authority to levy a tax for the partial support of the schools, with another large grant of money coming from the state. The institutions associated with this system have experienced rapid growth since they began operation in 1973.

The education profession in Nebraska is a formidable political force, often insulated within a system of organizations from the state down through the regional level to the local district. Its most vulnerable point is its dependence on the increasingly unpopular property tax. The establishment was stung in 1978 when voters in Omaha and Nebraska City imposed very stringent lids on school spending. Moreover, the consolidationist principles of the profession still meet with strong resistence, not only by rustic defenders of the "little red schoolhouse" but by sceptical academics who feel consolidation is more a boon to teachers than to students. We may expect that the struggle over the direction of public education in Nebraska and particularly the fate of the remaining Class I schools will continue into the next century.

Special Districts

A special district is a unit of government which performs (in most cases) only a single function. In a strict sense, schools are also special districts, but they are generally counted separately because of their long history and large numbers and the unique political role of public education. Concerned governmental reformers might add another reason for distinguishing between the two types of districts: while the number of school districts is steadily decreasing, the special districts continue to proliferate. In this, Nebraska is typical of the rest of the country.

The identification of the number and location of all special districts is a nearly hopeless task, since there is often no central authority to which they must report. Each type of district has been authorized by a separate law (and in some cases by more than one statute). The Census Bureau has identified statutory authorization for the following types of districts in Nebraska: airport, cemetery, drainage, groundwater conservation, health, hospital, housing, irrigation, mosquito abatement, natural resources, public power, reclamation, road improvement, rural and suburban fire protection, rural water, sanitary and improvement, weather control, and weed control, as well as Omaha's Metropolitan Transit Authority (MTA) and Metropolitan Utilities District (MUD).

Critics of special districts, including most political scientists and a good many federal policy makers, argue that this form increases governmental fragmentation, inhibits the coordinated solution of large-scale problems, and turns over to narrowly oriented special interests some of the power of government. Furthermore, because of the limited nature of their functions and their lack of visibility, districts make a mockery of democracy. It is hard to believe, for example, that many Lincolnites have much idea about the business of the Lancaster Noxious Weed Control Authority, although they are periodically asked to vote for members of the board. Civic virtue is not promoted by asking people to be informed about what, for most of them, are trivial matters.

Other writers suggest that the criticisms of special districts are overdrawn. Most districts are useful tools with which small groups of people solve common problems. While in theory the sheer numbers may seem worrisome, in practice most districts probably provide a needed service to their members. It seems unlikely, to take one example, that the maintenance of rural cemeteries would be greatly improved if they were turned over to the county or state; a small cemetery district is certainly a reasonable way to handle this function. To be sure, rigorous analysis might reveal more efficient ways of performing many district functions, but to date we have no absolutely compelling evidence to support a blanket indictment of the district form.

Natural Resources Districts

In 1974, the National Governor's Conference asked each governor to identify the state's most significant innovation in government. Governor Exon submitted the creation of the Natural Resources Districts (NRDS).[7] The NRDS were a logical development for a state highly dependent on the wise management of its most important resource— water. When the NRD law was passed in 1969, several hundred small water-related districts had already sprung up to chase this fugitive resource. At the time, some 506 independent units of government were concerned with water in some way, including watershed, watershed conservancy, watershed planning, soil conservation, rural water,

7. J. James Exon, "Better Geographic Units for Government Service," in *Innovations in State Government* (Washington, D.C.: National Governor's Conference, 1974).

groundwater conservation, drainage, sanitary drainage, sanitary and improvement, irrigation, reclamation, public power, and flood control districts. Seven kinds of districts were statutorily empowered to deal with drainage problems, six with flood control, six with water supply, four with recreation, four with erosion control, and three with hydroelectric power. It was governmental anarchy.

Out of this tangle of districts the Natural Resources Districts emerged. NRDs were formed by the consolidation of soil and water conservation, watershed conservancy, watershed districts, and advisory watershed conservancy and watershed planning boards. The law also prohibits the further formation of drainage, groundwater conservation, and rural water districts. These districts, along with the reclamation and irrigation districts, are encouraged by the law to cooperate with the NRDs and, where appropriate, to merge with them. Approximately 140 special districts were replaced by 24 NRDs on July 1, 1972.

The NRDs cover the entire state and the boundaries are drawn according to hydrologic patterns as indicated by the major river basins. Each district is governed by an elected board of directors, which in turn hires a general manager for the district. The statute provides authority for a number of resource-related activities, from erosion prevention and flood control to park facilities and forestry management. The most sensitive matter handled by NRDs concerns restrictions on the pumping of groundwater and the drilling of new wells.

A state agency, the Natural Resources Commission, provides general supervision of the NRDs and coordinates their activities to prevent conflicts in operations. One major function of the Commission is to review the comprehensive plans of the districts to ensure their consistency with the state water plan. The commission also administers the Nebraska Resources Development Fund, a source of money for political subdivisions of the state for the development of water and associated land resources.

The NRDs were an ambitious attempt to implement a multiple-purpose approach to resources management, and because of their broad range of powers they are considerably more than the traditional special district. After ten years, NRDs are well beyond the threshold of survival for new institutions, but we still lack a thorough evaluation of their effectiveness. I am not qualified to speak to their performance in solving the state's water problems; any lack of success in that area, however, may have to be attributed to the continued avoidance of the whole issue by the legislature and governor.

As a political scientist, however, I can express some disappointment at the failure of NRDs to revitalize local government. Because of their size and importance, it was hoped by many that NRDs would have greater visibility and serve as a vehicle for greater political participation by a variety of citizens. A survey conducted after the first year of operation found that 39 percent of Nebraskans had never heard of NRDs, while in 1980 a similar poll revealed that 41 percent were unaware of their existence. In a 1979 poll, 73 percent of Nebraskans could not remember ever having voted in an NRD election; and in 1980, 89 percent could not name a current NRD board member.[8] There was a burst of interest in the first elections held in 1974, but since then participation by voters and candidates has fallen off and most board seats are not contested. In short, for most Nebraskans, the NRDs are not a topic of constant concern.

Public Power Districts

It is rather curious that, in Nebraska, all electric power is provided by local governments. Just how did this bit of socialism come about in what must be one of the most conservative states? Probably the only "ism" involved was prairie pragmatism. For a number of reasons, it seemed like a good idea at the time — the 1930s — and so one thing led to another until eventually the last investor-owned utility was bought out in 1945.

There are four public power districts in the state — Nebraska Public Power (NPPD), Loup River Public Power, Central Nebraska Public Power, and Omaha Public Power. In addition, thirty-two rural electric systems exist, either as membership cooperatives or as rural public power districts. Many municipalities also operate their own generat-

8. Susan Welch, *Nebraskans and State Water Policy: An Update,* NASIS – 80, no. 8. (Lincoln: University of Nebraska, Bureau of Sociological Research, 1980).

ing and distribution facilities. The public power districts are governed by an elected board of directors. The districts have certain governmental powers, but they are not authorized to levy taxes or to issue bonds secured by tax funds.

Very well, the Nebraska system is rather novel and all that, but to put it bluntly, so what? Do Nebraskans get a better deal than citizens in other states? A consultant's report to the legislature summarized the confusion on this question: "This leads to the bottom question of any analysis of the Public Utility Industry. . . . Do the citizen-customers receive an adequate return on their investment in the electric utilities by way of reduced rates? Unfortunately, the answer to this question is unknown and the reason that it is unknown at this time is the difficulties which characterize the industry today."[9] As any customer knows, these are not happy times in which to contemplate the whys and wherefores of the energy industry. Many citizens right now are undoubtedly upset with their utility bills, no matter whether the operations are owned by the state or a private firm.

One can make the argument, however, that public ownership is not a decisive feature of the energy structure of the state. If Nebraska were capable of going it alone, the case might be different, but the state is only one small part of a national and international power network. As citizens of Lincoln learned in 1981, when they submitted a petition to put a lid on the rates charged by their municipally owned utility, such popular efforts are just too feeble to make an impact on the complicated system by which electric power is financed, produced, and distributed. Public power is certainly not the darling of environmentalists and consumer advocates. They contend that NPPD is dominated by big business and that this influence is reflected in its involvement in nuclear power and its rate structure: "Special low rates are offered to large customers, while small residential users pay several times more for their electricity."[10] The retort to such a charge, of course, is that if

9. Drees Dunn Lubow and Company, *Final Report: Preliminary Evaluation of Public Power Pursuant to Legislative Resolution No. 34* (Overland Park, Kans.: Drees Dunn Lubow, January 9, 1978), p. 4.

10. Richard Morgan, Tom Tiesenberg, and Michael Troutman, *Taking Charge: A New Look at Public Policy* (Washington, D.C.: Environmental Action Foundation, 1976), p. 41.

it is true, at least the consumers have a clearer means of redress than they would with a private utility.

Participation in Local Government

If there are serious problems with all or any of the forms of government described above, perhaps we can at least identify where the fault must lie—namely, with the voters. All the governments are based on the assumption that citizens shall have the right to participate freely in the making of public policy. If citizens are outraged by their local governments, they can probably find the means in state statutes or other authorizations to seek redress. Not surprisingly, only a minority of Nebraskans take advantage of all the means for participating. Voting turnout for local elections tends to be nearly as low as in the rest of the nation. A 1980 survey attempted to measure other forms of participation by asking respondents if they had ever attended a city council or school board meeting; the statewide response for both questions was 13 percent, although involvement in community affairs was highest in smaller communities and lowest in Lincoln and Omaha.[11]

All elections in municipalities, school districts, and special districts are nonpartisan, which means the party affiliation of the candidates does not appear on the ballot. Some politicians argue that voter turnout would be higher in local elections if they were partisan. To make that case, however, one would have to prove that Nebraska political parties are powerful enough to draw large numbers of their members to the many elections for minor local offices.

A major legacy of the Progressive Era is the availability to citizens of the initiative, referendum, and recall. The federal Advisory Commission on Intergovernmental Relations recently classified Nebraska as one of the "fully participatory" states in this regard. Through the initiative and referendum, voters can require charter changes and ordinances to be voted on by the public. Many proposals, especially

---

11. Susan Welch and Alan Booth, *Nebraskans and Their Local Government,* NASIS–80, no. 4. (Lincoln: University of Nebraska, Bureau of Sociological Research, 1980).

those involving bond issues, must be automatically referred to the people for their approval.

The recall is perhaps the most controversial of the Progressive trio, and some observers have noted an increase in the use of this method for removing county, city, and school board officials before the regular expiration of their terms. If a petition containing a certain percentage of signatures (usually 25 percent of those voting in the last election for the office in question), the matter of retaining a public official must be put to the voters. Friends of this provision call it the "gun behind the door" for emergency use against dishonest or arbitrary officials. Its critics say its overuse inhibits officials while promoting continuing bitterness in the community.

Statutes also provide two powerful instruments whereby citizens can exercise that "watchfulness" which all Nebraskans know is the salvation of the state. Nebraska has an open meetings, or sunshine, law that applies to all governing bodies of all political subdivisions, as well as permanent or ad hoc study and advisory committees associated with any subdivisions (for example, a city planning commission). Citizens must be notified of any meetings of these bodies and must be allowed to attend them. Decisions made secretly in violation of the law can, the law states, be declared void and "any member of a public body knowingly violating any provision. . . . shall be guilty of a misdemeanor and shall, upon conviction thereof, be fined not more than fifty dollars."

The state's open records law makes available to citizens a wide range of public documents. The law says, "Except where any other statutes expressly provide that particular information or records shall not be made public, public records shall include all records and documents, regardless of physical form, of or belonging to this state, any county, city, village, political subdivision, or tax-supported district in this state, or any agency, branch, department, board, bureau, commission, council, subunit, or committee of any of the foregoing." The law does not provide criminal penalties for violations, but anyone feeling that a document has been wrongly withheld can request the attorney general to bring suit for the document's release.

Nebraska is one of the few states to have a separate office to handle complaints about government actions. The jurisdiction of the state ombudsman, however, does not extend to local governments. This has not prevented a large number of complaints about local government being directed to this "grievance office." Despite an apparent need, there does not seem to be any inclination on the part of the legislature to extend the authority of the ombudsman to the subdivisions of the state.

Local Finance

The best things in life are anything but free, most Nebraska local officials would agree. Their electorate is as ambiguous as other Americans are about public finance. While complaining mightily about taxes, they expect more and better public services. It was hardly surprising that a 1979 NASIS survey found that very few Nebraskans wanted less activity by government in a number of policy areas such as education, crime prevention, and water resources development.[12]

The structure of public finance in Nebraska does not permit a large number of options for beleaguered decision makers. In 1977–78, local governments raised $1,254,500,000, or $799.55 per capita. Over a quarter of local revenue was derived through intergovernmental grants—8.4 percent from the federal government and 19.2 percent from the state. With 72.4 percent, in 1978, raised from their own sources, Nebraska's local governments were second in the nation only to New Hampshire in the reliance on "own-source revenue." That is, local governments are relatively independent of state and federal grants.

This situation is likely to change. The general purpose governments—counties at 30 percent and cities at 36 percent—are the most dependent on outside grants. Federal revenue sharing has been a particular boon to these units, and local governments in the state have divided among themselves $264,690,710 in the ten years ending in 1981. In the long run, however, state aid is likely to be more important. Since 1967, when state government abandoned the property tax,

12. Alan Booth and Susan Welch, *Nebraskans' Evaluations of Their State Government,* NASIS–79, no. 4. (Lincoln: University of Nebraska, Bureau of Sociological Research, 1979).

the legislature has been slowly adjusting the state's role in local finance. The extent to which these moves are aimed at relieving the pressure of the personal property tax for agricultural and business interest is often debated. Whatever the reason, the state has lurched toward placing more of the burden of financing local government on the state income and sales taxes.

Left to its own devices, local government must rely on the property tax. Any alert politician might not need such empirical proof, but a recent survey of Nebraskans found that 50 percent of them viewed the property tax as the least fair of all state and local taxes.[13] This is especially bad news for local officials since their governments, as of 1978, received 91.6 percent of their total tax receipts from the tax. Only seven cities use the sales tax, and local income taxes are nonexistent.

So local government has citizens who want more for less. Perhaps this ambivalent attitude accounts for Nebraska's reluctant enlistment in the "great tax revolt" in the 1970s. Contrary to what many predicted, the spirit of California's Proposition 13 did not sweep the state. The real showdown came in 1978, when voters rejected a 5 percent constitutional lid on local government spending, a victory, many observers claim, for the Nebraska State Education Association. Subsequently, after a campaign year when all candidates wanted to prove their commitment to stopping government growth, there was enacted in 1979 a statutory 7 percent lid on local governments. No subdivision of the state may approve a budget that exceeds the previous receipts from state and local taxes by more than 7 percent. The localities may hold a special election to authorize a higher level of spending. With inflation running above 7 percent, the lid has meant that local governments have had to retrench just in order to maintain existing levels of services.

Local government, therefore, has few options. Since it is unlikely that many of them can continue to trim their budgets for a prolonged period and still meet citizen demands, it seems clear that the legislature will eventually be faced with a total revision of the structure of

13. Susan Welch and Alan Booth, *Taxes: Are They Fair?* NASIS–79, no. 2. (Lincoln: University of Nebraska, Bureau of Sociological Research, 1979).

local finance. In the 1930s, Nebraska boosters launched a campaign to attract industry by claiming to be the "white spot" on national maps that showed state sales or income taxes and public indebtedness. Because it was free of those modern evils, it was thought, business would be attracted to the state. Outsiders do not seem to have been impressed by this attempt to make a virtue out of backwardness.[14] But the idea has assumed a place in the state's political folklore and the loss of financial paradise in 1967 was traumatic enough that state and local officials have not been overbold in their attempts to further modernize the system. In the meantime, local governments will have to scrimp and save, make do, and hope that the federal spigot is not turned off completely because of the increasing frugality of Washington.

The Future of Local Government

There are several criteria by which one might evaluate the performance of local government in Nebraska. I will sketch here two that come immediately to mind about such a state. First, Nebraska certainly qualifies as a haven of grassroots government. In fact, the term *grassroots* is a key part of the vocabulary of the state's politicians. In reviewing the debates about methods of groundwater control, for example, one often gets the impression that any government larger than a single farmer and a couple of neighbors is a tyranny worse than anything ever contemplated by King George III. And in a state with fewer people than some American cities and counties, the capital city is often regarded as the home of an alien power.

But just how beneficial is government at the grassroots level? A quarter of a century ago, in his book *Grass Roots: Rural Democracy in America,* Roscoe Martin found little to admire in small government.[15] On two counts, small rural governments were deficient. They provided poor government; grassroots government is government by amateurs, by part-timers, by "good old boys" at the courthouse.

14. Farnsworth Crowder, "Tattle-Tale Gray on America's White Spot," *Survey Graphic* 27 (1938): 495–501, 521, 523–25.
15. Roscoe Martin, *Grass Roots: Rural Democracy in America* (University: University of Alabama Press, 1957).

Furthermore, small governments do not provide that diversity of opinion that makes democracy workable. Instead of stimulating free political action, the closeness of the small community punishes any unorthodox ideas.

I have no hard evidence to prove either the contention that Nebraska governments continue as the backbone of democracy or Martin's indictment of small government as both inefficient or illiberal. I am only suggesting that smallness is not an unquestioned virtue. And whatever virtues are attached to small government may very well be protected even if some centralization were to take place. After all, the whole state, compared to many other political jurisdictions, probably qualifies as grassroots itself.

The question of further consolidation leads us to the second criterion for evaluating government. Among students of local government reorganization, there are two schools of thought. The conventional wisdom holds that there are too many local governments. Nebraska might serve as Exhibit A in support of this argument. There are probably too many counties, municipalities, and school districts; and, without a doubt, 471 too many townships. Special districts, the consolidationists assert, have no justification at all and should be combined with general purpose governments. It would appear, then, that Nebraska is ready for a severe pruning of its local government thicket.

A more recent body of thought supports what we can call the "just about right" school (thankfully, no one is arguing the "not enough" theory of local government). These scholars declare that the variety and number of local governments illustrate the genius of American politics. The people, after all, are not being put upon by invaders from outer space. They did create all these governments and by their actions they keep them in operation. There are reasons behind the pattern of local government: the units are providing desired services to some group while not inconveniencing other groups. To be sure, fussy reformers might tidy up the map by eliminating many units, but would the status of the citizen be any better? Voters, we must assume, are not convinced that they would be. Government will change, but only when the people see some advantage in reform.

If Nebraska is a good case, the second school would seem to have the better argument. Changes in the pattern of local government will not come quickly. Major reorganizations affecting counties and cities appear now to be highly unlikely. In the 1970s, there was a brief spasm of interest in merging Lincoln and Lancaster County but within a few years the idea was a dead issue. Consolidation may have failed in this instance because very gradually city and county officials arrived at a series of accommodations whereby intergovernmental cooperation was taking place without drastic structural change. Peter Shocket and Barbara Smith found a similar style of functional consolidation occurring in rural Nebraska; while citizens and officials could see the benefits of increased cooperation within specific functional areas, there was little desire to surrender their political identity.[16] This pattern of mutual accommodation without consolidation will continue. So while the massive reorganization of local government does not seem to be a possibility, changes will take place as officials strive to satisfy the demands of their citizens.

16. Peter Shocket and Barbara Leigh Smith, *Regional Integration: A Guide for Community Development Specialists* (Lincoln, Nebr.: State Department of Economic Development, 1975).

KEITH J. MUELLER

TEN

Intergovernmental Relations

No description of Nebraska government and politics would be complete without a consideration of the state's complex connections to other governmental actors. Unfortunately, one must add, no description of intergovernmental relations could be complete within the confines of a short chapter, for this remains one of the murkiest areas of American political science. When speaking of the state or its subdivisions, we do not have totally self-contained units. Rather, these are the players, great and small, in the drama of federalism and there is no definitive script for any of them to follow. The day-to-day operation of federalism is largely a matter of improvisation.

The Dimensions of Intergovernmental Relations

The study of intergovernmental relations can be broken down into a number of groups of governmental actors: federal-state, state-state, federal-local, and so forth. As a member of the federal union, the state of Nebraska is constrained by the national and other state governments. The issue of water, for example, is one area in which a number of actors are trying to control the same resource. Nebraskans like to think of the state's streams as containing "their" water, but water is a notorious interstate fugitive, coveted by a number of users. The federal government claims the right, through its constitutional power to regulate navigable streams or its statutory authority over migratory waterfowl, to its share of water within the state. Upstream and downstream states view water moving in and out of Nebraska as belonging to them and so controversies spring up all the time. Many of the older issues about water use have been resolved through the device known as an interstate compact. The Big Blue River Compact Administration, with the membership of Kansas and Nebraska, and the Republican River Compact Administration, set up by Kansas, Nebraska and Colorado, handle mutual problems within those two river basins. But new problems are always emerging and currently Nebraskans are watching nervously the plans of South Dakota to sell Missouri River water to coal slurry pipeline developers.

As numerous Supreme Court cases have shown, the relations between the federal and state governments or among the states are complicated and in a state of flux. Matters become still more confusing when the local units are thrown into the equation. Even ignoring the relatively new field of federal-local relations, in which the national government bypasses the state to deal directly with cities and counties, the intergovernmental status of local units is invariably perplexing. As stated in chapter 9, local governments are creatures of the state, but the nature of state involvement depends on a number of variables—the unit of local government in question, the nature of the program, the practices of various state agencies, the amount of federal or state aid, and many other considerations.

The most pervasive type of state involvement in local affairs derives from the authority, constitutional or statutory, of state officers to oversee or direct the activity of the local units. A brief inventory of some agencies will show this: The secretary of state receives the abstracts of votes from county officials; the attorney general consults with and advises county attorneys; the state auditor receives annual audit reports from all municipalities; the Department of Economic Development provides planning and technical assistance to cities and counties; the Department of Environmental Control inspects local landfills; the Department of Welfare supervises the county welfare services; the state adjutant general coordinates civil defense and disaster plans of local communities; the Department of Education administers various types of financial aid to school districts. These examples are in no way exhaustive, but they may indicate the scope of the state role in local affairs.

The foregoing is mentioned as evidence of the many dimensions of intergovernmental relations and the impossibility of covering the whole field in adequate detail. The remainder of this chapter will concentrate on some problems of special concern to a state like Nebraska. Intergovernmental relations are very often thought to be a topic for large cities, the states, and the national government. After all, the big cities are the experts in grantsmanship, and the states are always demanding more rights and power in the federal system. While these aspects are certainly important, we must not overlook the role of small cities and other units of government in the intergovernmental system. The focus here is on the small local governments.

G. Ross Stephens, a political scientist, developed a composite centralization index for all states; he found that between 1957 and 1969, all state governments tended to centralize more services, personnel, and finances.[1] Nebraska was identified in both years as one of the most decentralized; in 1957, it was one of the five most decentralized and one of the two most decentralized in 1969. Nebraska was particularly out of step with similar states since it was the only smaller, rural-oriented state so decentralized. Thus, we can conclude that there is a strong tradition of local autonomy in public policy making and execution.

Nebraska is involved in that network of exchanges of money known as fiscal federalism to a lesser extent than the average state. The state, county, and township governments receive less than the national average for their classes from the federal government. Municipalities are the exception to the general pattern, although they take in only less than one-half of one percent than the national average for all cities. The pattern of lesser dependency holds for the largest units of local government. Douglas County received 44.8 percent of its 1978–79 revenue from intergovernmental sources and Lancaster County received 26.3 percent; nationally, counties with populations over one hundred thousand received 47.6 percent of their revenue from grants

1. G. Ross Stephens, "State Centralization and the Erosion of Local Autonomy," *Journal of Politics* 36 (1974): 44–76.

during the same period. Omaha received above and Lincoln below the national average for cities in their population range.

The pattern of intergovernmental relations in Nebraska indicates an exchange of large sums of money but in lower proportions than the national average. One can conclude that local governments in Nebraska do receive a large proportion of their revenue from state and federal sources. However, these governments, for the most part, are less dependent on the outside sources of money than are their typical counterparts throughout the nation.

Despite the tradition of local autonomy and the relative independence from the grants system, modern conditions are placing great strains on the state's intergovernmental system and it may be moving, sometimes erratically, toward the national average in centralization and financial dependence found in other states. This chapter will illustrate this movement by reviewing some ongoing changes in the structure of local government. As noted in chapter 9, Nebraska is characterized by a multitude of small local governments. Most intergovernmental interaction, then, is among small units or between the local unit and the state or federal government. Three major concerns dominate these interactions from the local perspective: continued existence, planning and coordinating, and financing. Three policy developments that illustrate these concerns are school district consolidation, the move towards substate regionalism, and state revenue sharing.

School Redistricting

The issue of school consolidation, which has been fought over several decades, indicates the major elements in the struggle for and against greater state centralization. The reformers in this case, the education profession, have had a strong base of operations in the State Department of Education, and their claim to expertise on the benefits of larger schools have impressed many. The defenders of the small districts have an advantage in that the districts do exist and it takes special effort to eliminate them. The reformers have had varying degrees of success in convincing citizens to endorse full-scale reorganization. The controversy springs to life each time the legislature attempts to pass laws speeding up the process of consolidation.

Advocates of school district consolidation have espoused the views of the Great Plains School District Organization Project (submitted to the State Department of Education in 1968) that larger school districts will improve the quality of education. The project report, *Guidelines for School District Organization,* declared that favorable relationships existed between school size and the following variables: cost per pupil, pupil achievement, program breadth and quality, teacher preparation and certification, supporting educational services, and educational leadership. The report concluded, "Larger schools, with greater pupil numbers can and do offer greater program breadth than their smaller counterparts."[2]

Opponents of school consolidation have argued that small districts encouraged closer control of the schools by parents, thus ensuring more citizen input in the important area of education. The opponents also rely heavily on those supposed virtues of the small schools which may outweigh their educational deficiencies. Parents assert that they are saving their children from the "blackboard jungles" in the city (although, one hastens to add, they seldom present evidence that "big cities" such as Cozad or Broken Bow are centers of sin or, for that matter, that rural youths are any less inclined to juvenile delinquency than their city counterparts). The inconvenience of transporting children long distances or boarding them in the city are also mentioned as drawbacks of further consolidation.

Until recently, the reformers have made the more persuasive arguments, as measured in terms of effective action. Consolidation efforts in Nebraska began with an 1869 law that authorized the merging of two or more contiguous districts having more than 150 children. The real turning point, however, came with legislation eighty years later. The Reorganization Act of 1949 created two new agencies to assist in school redistricting—the State Committee for the Reorganization of

2. Nebraska Department of Education, *The Great Plains School District Organization Project; Guidelines for School District Organization* (Lincoln: Nebraska Department of Education, July 1966), p. 85.

School Districts and a parallel committee for each county. The act encouraged voluntary consolidation and set up the mechanisms for state approval of redistricting plans. Proposals for consolidation could be initiated by either the voters in the affected districts or by the county committees. Regardless of how initiated, the county committees had to act on the proposal before sending it to the state committee. Once requirements for public hearings were met, county superintendents were empowered to create and take jurisdiction over the new districts. Through this mechanism, much progress in consolidation has been achieved, although not without resistance along the way.

Before passage of the 1949 law, there were 6,734 school districts. By 1966, the number was 2,400; in 1972 it was 1,461, and at this writing there are 1,044 school districts. Such progress should have pleased the reformers, but there are still a rather large number of school districts for a state with as small a population as Nebraska. In 1972, for example, Nebraska contained 8.4 percent of the nation's school districts but less than one percent of the nation's population. Of the remaining school districts, 388 are one-teacher operations, which, educators argue, cannot possibly offer students all the advantages of larger schools. Some districts have no students at all and, at latest count, fifty-two districts are not operating. In the absence of students, according to state law, the tax liability for schools remains for at least one year, after which students must enroll or the schools close.

Because they see the job as incomplete, the reformers have been in favor of greater state involvement in the consolidation process. The 1949 action was relatively harmless, as far as local government advocates were concerned, since it was based on voluntary action by local officials. In 1953, the legislature passed a bill that made mandatory the closing of four-year high schools with fewer than fifteen students over three consecutive years and two-year high schools with fewer than ten pupils for three years if another school was within fifteen miles. This first step toward compulsory consolidation was also the last one. Resistance to more stringent limitation on local schools has stymied the efforts of reformers.

The opponents of school consolidation have their greatest source of strength in the legislature, where the representatives of the ''outstate'' areas (outside of the Omaha and Lincoln metropolitan areas) still maintain a majority. Rural residents tend to suspect state action, especially when generated by officials located in Lincoln. As Winter concluded in 1958: "Probably the groundwork of elementary opposition to the redistricting lies primarily in the suspicions the prototype rural-agricultural 'man' holds for almost all emanations from the urban industrial areas of the state. Thus, one can assume . . . that any proposal attributable to an Omaha or Lincoln source automatically will invoke a negative response from a large number of rural folk."[3] In a sense, then, the resistance to consolidation is more than a matter of educational techniques; it is seen as the last line of defense for the mythic ideal of the rural community.

Over the years, our vision of the participants in the struggle has become less clear. It is no longer so easy to see either dedicated reformers or virtuous rural yeomen. The educators, in particular, have come in for much criticism. The economists have begun to investigate questions about the real beneficiaries of consolidation and, in some instances, have concluded that, as in other bureaucracies, it is the teachers rather than the clients who reap the biggest rewards, largely in terms of higher salary and chances for advancement into administration.[4]

Another group of critics of consolidation have demanded to see evidence of improved educational outcomes because of larger schools. In a blast at the reformers, the sociologist Robert Cole stated, "Boys and girls in the rural sections of this country have been outrageously victimized by condescension, aloofness, and yes, the ignorance and callousness of arrogant bureaucracies."[5] And for what purpose, the critics ask? There is no conclusive proof, they say, beyond the theories of the education profession, that bigger makes for better education.

The reformers may in fact be conceding that point since in recent

3. A. B. Winter, "A Critique of School District Reorganization in Nebraska," *Nebraska Law Review* 37 (1958): 764.

4. Robert J. Staaf, "The Public Schools in Transition: Consolidation and Parental Choice," in T. Borcherding, ed., *Budgets and Bureaucrats: The Sources of Government Growth* (Durham, N.C.: Duke University Press, 1977).

5. Robert Cole, "Foreword," in Jonathan Sher, ed., *Education in Rural America: A Reassessment of Conventional Wisdom* (Boulder, Colo.: Westview Press, 1977), p. xv.

years their arguments have shifted from those of educational quality, which is hard to document, to matters of fiscal equity. Many critics of consolidations, it is asserted, are not defenders of the old homestead but rather rich farmers and ranchers interested in preserving a lucrative tax shelter. The tax levy for a one-room school will be less than that imposed for a large consolidated school. Even if parents in the small district have to pay tuition to send their children to secondary schools elsewhere, they will probably save on their total tax bill. According to one report, citizens with $50,000 worth of property in District 13 of Dawson County pay $155 in property tax for schools; if merged with the Cozad schools, they would pay $440.[6] In fact, the tax angle has become so important in the debate over consolidation that some rural senators are justifying the status quo as a form of tax relief for owners of agricultural property.

The main point here, however, is not the pros and cons of school reorganization. This is only one illustration of the painful adjustments that must be made in a number of areas as the movement towards greater centralization continues. The same mixture of noble motives and individual selfishness can be found in a number of areas where the reality of modern life is forcing the modernization of local government.

Substate Regionalism

A form of centralization of local government that stops short of the state level is substate regionalism. Although local governments had been engaged in a number of voluntary cooperative arrangements for their mutual benefit for a number of years, the real impetus came from the federal government in the 1960s. The continuing proliferation of state and federal agencies as well as an almost incomprehensible number of grant-in-aid programs were creating chaos at the local level. The duplication of efforts and the misuse of public funds were constant worries for administrators at all levels. In an attempt to increase intergovernmental coordination of efforts, the federal gov-

6. "School Consolidation Plan Stirs Rural Opposition," *Omaha World-Herald*, January 25, 1981.

ernment encouraged the states to develop mechanisms for the better delivery of public services.

Nebraska's response, in 1970, was the creation of twenty-six Planning and Development regions. Three of the regions were designed to be contiguous with the Nebraska portions of two Standard Metropolitan Statistical Areas (Omaha-Council Bluffs and Sioux City) and all of the third (Lincoln). The other districts were multicounty units designed by the staff of the former State Office of Planning and Programming (SOPP). As SOPP was quick to point out, the regions ''do not represent a new level of government. Rather they are a tool to be used by existing governments to increase governmental efficiency and facilitate solutions to problems that are regional in scope.''[7]

The most basic function of the regions is the coordination of the field operations of state and federal agencies. In particular, if all state agencies were to use the regional approach, several benefits would accrue: (1) a common geographic base would create a constituency for all the departments; (2) joint boundaries would facilitate the cooperation of state agencies at the local level; (3) data gathering and analysis could be done more efficiently; and (4) ''because of an obvious commonality of interests and frequency of contacts, closer working relationships among federal, state, and local agencies will develop within a region.''[8]

The success of the Planning and Development Regions was mixed. Some units of state government, such as the supreme court and the Public Service Commission, have the shape and number of their districts determined by the constitution, statutes, and judicial rulings on apportionment. Others, such as the natural resource districts and educational service units, are defined by statute. Still another large group of agencies, perhaps because of inertia, were slow to modify their preexisting regional field offices.

Throughout the 1970s, state and local officials expressed some dissatisfaction with the orginal regional setup and, in 1979, Governor Thone appointed a task force to review the matter. This group found

7. State Office of Planning and Programming, *Nebraska Regions* (Lincoln, Nebr.: State Office of Planning and Programming, 1974), p. i.

8. Ibid., p. 3.

that, despite the regions, "fragmentation and lack of overall coordination still existed in areas of the state."[9] Most problems stemmed from the smallness of the regions; state agencies rarely used single regions but instead combined several. In 1981, as a result of the task force recommendations, nine districts were superimposed on the regional structure, and one region was eliminated. The districts, it is anticipated, will facilitate more cooperation because of their larger scope.

By themselves, neither the substate regions nor the districts require any action on the part of local governments. The federal government, however, has done much to stimulate local governments to think along regional lines and thus give operational effect to regionalism. In Nebraska, this movement has been helped by the existence of the Interlocal Cooperation Act, passed in 1962. The act permits local governments to enter into cooperative agreements for the joint conduct of any activity within their legal jurisdictions. For example, two or more neighboring cities may sign a mutual assistance pact enabling one city's fire department to respond to major fires in another city. Or the sheriff may contract with cities in the county for the provision of certain public safety functions.

The major outcome of the Interlocal Cooperation Act was the growth of Councils of Government (COGS). COGS are, theoretically, voluntary associations of local governments—counties and municipalities—organized on a regional basis. Although there may be some question about the precise definition of what constitutes a COG, it is generally accepted that there are now fifteen within the state—thirteen of them staffed and operational and two unstaffed. The staff size varies, with MAPA (Metropolitan Area Planning Agency) in Omaha-Council Bluffs having the largest. Many of the rural COGS have only two staff members, usually a director and a secretary. The regional associations are governed by a board composed of elected officials from participating governments.

Since participation is voluntary, why do so many local governments participate? The answer probably lies in the A-95 review process discussed in chapter 6. As a condition for eligibility for many federal

9. Nebraska Department of Economic Development, *Nebraska Districts/Regions*. (Lincoln: Nebraska Department of Economic Development, 1981), p. 1.

Map 10.1: Nebraska Districts and Economic
Development Regions

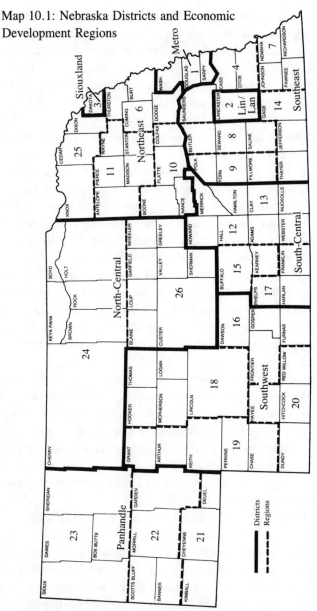

SOURCE: Department of Economic Development,
Nebraska Districts/Regions.

grants, local governments must have their applications reviewed by some regional planning body. In this process, local officials in a region are informed of a single government's plans for federal funds. This may have positive effects when, for example, two cities apply for money for a hospital or an airport in a region where only one facility is needed. COGS cannot deny or approve a grant application; their power is based on the A-95 requirement itself and any official comments that are attached to an application when it is forwarded to the state review agency or to Washington.

There is no way to tell what might happen if the federal government repealed its requirement for grant review. Some critics say the entire idea of regional cooperation would collapse. The friends of COGS, however, insist that there are so many advantages to such formal cooperation that they would survive because of the self-interest of member governments. COGS provide technical assistance, such as planning, for their members; serve as a forum for the discussion of common problems; and offer assistance to localities in the complicated business of preparing applications for federal grants. In this latter role, COGS have helped many smaller, rural governments compete more successfully with bigger entities in the contest for federal dollars.

Another especially useful function of the COGS in the more sparsely populated parts of the state is the provision of a circuit rider. This person is a member of the COG staff who gives management assistance to member governments. The visiting administrators can answer a variety of questions concerning management practices, federal guidelines, state mandates, and other technical matters. The small city then receives professional advice from an officer no single government could afford to maintain by itself.

While COGS in Nebraska appear to be doing a satisfactory job of serving regional needs, their efforts are mitigated somewhat by the proliferation of other regional arrangements. Instead of conforming to a single plan of regionalization, many federal programs have encouraged the creation of more specialized regions. For example, three health service areas are mandated for the state by the Department of Health and Human Services; twelve community action agencies, six area aging organizations, and nineteen regional crime commissions are also required by federal regulations. These and other specialized groups, as well as other district forms promoted by the state, detract from the centrality of the COGS.

COGS have come a long way in the past fifteen years, but they still have far to go before they become anything resembling a real unit of government. For one thing, they cannot levy taxes but instead depend on federal support and local contributions for their maintenance. They have no powers of enforcement and can use nothing stronger than persuasion in the implementation of regional plans. However, the continuing problems in intergovernmental relations may be a fertile ground for the future vitality of COGS. They serve as valuable coalitions of local government in relations with the state, and they also help to strengthen local governments by improving their capacity for gathering and better analyzing relevant data, an increasingly important weapon in the bureaucratic wars.

After some initial enthusiasm in the early 1970s, COGS were waning as the decade ended. Their advocates in state and local governments are now optimistic that forms of regional cooperation will be rejuvenated because of the district/region arrangement started in 1981. All that can be said with certainty right now is that their status is in flux. However, one can reasonably predict that COGS, or some form of regionalism, will continue to be an important dimension of intergovernmental relations in Nebraska, particularly because of the assistance they can provide to the smaller, less advantaged cities and counties.

State Revenue Sharing

Intergovernmental relations are often defined by the movement of money, and the relationships between the state of Nebraska and its political subdivisions are given shape by this critical transfer of resources. State activity since 1967 has intensified the fiscal side of state-local relations because the legislature has taken several actions to lessen the reliance of local governments on the property tax and, at the same time, has increased significantly the importance of shared state revenues. Nebraska follows the national pattern in increasing its shared revenues and also reflects the nationwide problem of setting the formulas by which money will be distributed to local governments. When dollars are at issue, politicians and citizens tend to become intense advocates of specialized interests.

The Advisory Commission on Intergovernmental Relations defines state-local revenue sharing "as money given to localities—primarily counties, townships, cities, and villages—to be spent on purposes determined by the localities themselves."[10] According to ACIR, most states find themselves sharing more revenue for these reasons: reduction in the extent of federal participation in certain programs; the greater financial strength of state sources through the use of income and general sales taxes; and compensation for state laws exempting various classes of property from local taxation. Nebraska's use of state revenue sharing results from all three reasons.

The ACIR study also found that the states most likely to establish programs of tax sharing are those with a high property tax burden, a high local share of state-local own-source revenues (the level of local financing of state and local services), and a high metropolitan fiscal disparity index (financial differences between central cities and the surrounding suburbs). Of all the states, Nebraska ranks eighth in property tax burden, third in local share of state-local own-source revenues, and forty-first in metropolitan disparities (a function, no doubt, of the state's fairly lenient annexation laws for larger cities). One would thus expect much pressure for state revenue sharing in Nebraska.

Local governments in Nebraska are demanding greater state shared revenue for two reasons. First, the expenses faced by many local governments continue to increase rapidly. And while expenses are increasing, the state has imposed a lid on the amount of locally raised money the governments can spend. Clearly, if there are to be no severe reductions in local services, other sources of revenues must be found. The second reason for demands for more revenue sharing is related to past state actions. During the past fifteen years, the state has exempted several categories of personal property, including household goods and intangible assets, farm equipment, business inventories, and

10. Advisory Commission on Intergovernmental Relations, *The State of State-Local Revenue Sharing* (Washington, D.C.: Government Printing Office, 1980), p. 2.

livestock, from the local property rolls. With these exemptions, the state did begin to share its revenue but, according to many local officials, at an insufficient level. The local officials assert that the gap between the value of exempted property and state relief precipitates property tax increases, a result inconsistent with the often expressed hope that the state would be able to reduce the property tax burden.

Small wonder then that local officials become nervous every time the legislature reconsiders the distribution formulas for allocating state shared revenues. A recent unpublished survey by the Governmental Research Institute at the University of Nebraska found that, among the 151 municipalities studied, the average city received 12 percent of its revenue from the federal government and 17 percent from the state. One municipality even claimed to receive 95 percent of its money from the state. At least nine of the cities received over half of their revenue from the state or federal governments. Any change in the way the state decides to allocate its dollars will have serious repercussions on local finance, which means that the issue is a perennial source of political controversy.

The legislature adopted a state sales and income tax in 1967. With these more productive sources of revenue at their disposal, legislators were confident in their ability to fund existing and new state programs as well as replace local revenue lost through exemptions of personal property. This capability was essential for further exemptions, since removing property from the rolls without concurrent revenue sharing would push the burden to real property owners. After the sales and income taxes were enacted, therefore, the state created funds to repay school districts, counties, and cities for the restricted tax base. Sentiment also began to build in the legislature for further exemptions of personal property, but such action had to await constitutional changes.

Constitutional authority was granted in 1970 with the approval of an amendment by the voters. The legislature now had the power to exempt other classes of personal property. In 1973, the legislature voted to remove from the tax rolls farm machinery, livestock, business inventories, grains and seeds, and agricultural inventories. These exemptions were to be added gradually over a number of years. Local governments were to be compensated on a dollar-for-dollar basis for all revenue lost because of the legislation. However, both political and

practical problems arose from the system adopted to reimburse localities for losses in revenue. In reality, the state could only be sure of the
value of lost property in the year it was removed from the assessor's
books, since in subsequent years there would be no means available to
assess the exempt property. The answer to this problem was the
adoption of Legislative Bill 518, which fixed the amount of money in
the funds for local governments at $70 million and allocated the same
proportion of the whole to individual governments every year.

Legal authorities were quick to see the problems with using a single
year as a basis for allocating shared revenues in all subsequent years.
Inasmuch as the future movement of exempted property could not be
known, the law created a "frozen class" of favored taxpayers, since
their jurisdictions might well receive an unjustifiable tax break in later
years. For example, a county ranking high in total business inventories in one year could receive a larger share of revenues in coming
years, even if its real share of business inventories should decline
drastically.

Everyone involved eventually conceded the questionable constitutional grounds of the 1977 legislation, so members of the legislature
were back at the drawing board during the 1980 session. The stated
purpose of changing the formula was to remove constitutional objections; however, the high stakes involved made this exercise the subject
of intense political debate. Its resolution was of central importance to
the structure of intergovernmental relations within the state. Beneficiaries of the 1977 formula saw the proposed changes as a threat to
the gains they had made, and others saw the debate as an opportunity
to regroup and have another try at gaining more revenue at the expense
of other governments.

The 1980 session approved a bill that retained the existing formula
for the first year and changed the allocations in subsequent years
according to the increases or decreases in total property taxes collected
in each county. The new formula was challenged by the attorney
general as still favoring a "frozen class" since it used an unconstitutional base as a starting point. The Nebraska Supreme Court agreed
and enjoined the state from distributing any of the $70 million. The
entry of the courts into the issue complicated matters without indicat-

ing an acceptable solution. The 1981 session found itself again with the issue, while the pressures from local governments for essential revenue continue to grow.

The deliberations included five major bills and a number of side issues, such as the repeal of city sales taxes, but the underlying source of contention came down to a basic urban-rural split. Urban senators wanted a thorough rewriting of the formula in order to increase the share of state funds sent to the cities. The rural senators saw the proposed changes as a threat to their existing advantages. The choices narrowed eventually to either a property valuation base or a population base for the formula. In either case, senators realized, the urban areas would stand to benefit, especially under the population-based formulas.

The legislature adjourned after passing a measure that would distribute the money in the first year under conditions favorable to rural areas and then shift to a permanent formula that would be based on each county's share of the total property valuations in the state. The provision for the first year was noncontroversial, especially since it guaranteed local governments their expected share of the $70 million. The decision to use property valuations, however, was seen as unconstitutional and the attorney general again took the issue to the supreme court.

The constitutionality of the 1981 formula became academic when the legislature in 1982 passed still another plan. The latest formula for distributing $78.7 million to local governments was seen as a victory for the Omaha and Lincoln senators, since the money will be divided primarily on the basis of population. As a measure of the high stakes involved, it is estimated that the city of Omaha will gain $6 million by the change. While urban senators were elated that they would now receive their "fair share," rural leaders deplored the "greed" of the big city folk. And so it goes, perhaps until next year, when the sides might be forced again to switch their rhetorical stances.

The tortured course of revenue sharing in Nebraska illustrates the central role of the legislature in the fiscal well-being of the local governments. Those governments were first penalized by actions of the legislature in exempting classes of personal property and then, despite earlier assurances, were never provided with an adequate source of replacement revenue. All that is certain is that local governments are even more dependent on the political machinations within the legislature, where urban and rural forces continue to work out their uneasy compromises. The independence promised by revenue sharing seems an illusion and one is reminded again of the "golden rule" of intergovernmental relations: Those with the gold do the ruling.

Conclusions

Intergovernmental relations in Nebraska are characterized by a number of administrative, political, and fiscal threats to the viability of the state's many local entities. While Nebraskans may remain loyal to ideas of small government, grassroots, and popular control, many of the very smallest units simply cannot respond to the challenges and larger governments have become ever more dependent on federal and state support. The move toward furthur centralization seems certain to continue.

The battle to consolidate school districts pits administrative reformers seeking increased efficiency and effectiveness against defenders of maximum local control over education. The latter have lost considerable ground over the past twenty years, but they have nevertheless succeeded in protecting over one thousand separate school districts. State legislative initiatives threatening the existence of the remaining small districts still prompt a great deal of political resistance.

The creation and continued existence of the Councils of Governments in Nebraska could have been seen as another threat to the powers of local government. However, COGs have instead become an aid to local governments wanting to remain fairly autonomous while enjoying the benefits of cooperation with other localities. They have also enhanced the power of separate cities and counties to confront the otherwise overwhelming power of the federal government. Being cooperative without being coopted is the secret of success for the COGs in Nebraska.

Finally, as the search for revenue becomes more intense, the state will play an ever growing role. As we have seen from the discussion of the politics of formula making, the legislature has become the most important arena for the localities. The very existence of some jurisdictions may be at stake as the legislators debate the precise wording of the distribution formula. Revenue sharing, while often an attractive alternative to desperate local officials, brings with it the possibility of a total reduction in local independence. Or worse, it may make local government the unwitting victim of wheeling and dealing within the capitol.

It may well be that some local governments in Nebraska will not be able to justify their continued existence, but then there is no such thing as a "right to life" for government. The push toward centralization may appear cruel to some, but as all these cases described here indicate, it takes place at a slow pace, with plenty of opportunities for opponents to resist. Reformers may regret that there is no master plan to guide this movement and the resisters may lament the loss of the good old days. But in a state as open to political participation as Nebraska, those for and against the movement may be able to shape its direction.

Nebraska Politics and Government: A Bibliography

This bibliography is not meant to be exhaustive; it does not deal with such historically important subjects as the Populist Party or personalities like William Jennings Bryan or George Norris. The emphasis is on the period since 1945, with some topics, especially the unicameral legislature, covered a little more thoroughly. We hope it will be helpful to readers interested in exploring further the politics and government of Nebraska in the postwar years.

A. Books, Documents, Articles

Aiken, David. "Nebraska Ground Water Law and Administration." *Nebraska Law Review* 59 (1980): 917–1000.

American Legislator's Association. *Unicameral Legislation*. Chicago: American Legislator's Association, January 31, 1935.

Anderson, Stanley, and John Moore, eds. *Establishing Ombudsman Offices: Recent Experience in the United States*. Berkeley: Institute of Governmental Studies, University of California, 1972.

Arthur D. Little, Inc. *Organization and Administration of Public Services: Report to the People of the City of Lincoln and the County of Lancaster*. San Francisco: Arthur D. Little, May 22, 1973.

Axelrod, Allan. "Home Rule." *Nebraska Law Review* 30 (1951): 224–38.

Aylsworth, Leon E. "Nebraska's Nonpartisan Unicameral Legislature." *National Municipal Review* 26 (1937): 77–81, 87.

———. "Nebraska's Unicameral Legislature Saves Money for Taxpayers." *National Municipal Review* 27 (1938): 490–93.

Bansal, Prem Lata. *Patterns of State-Regional Cooperation in Nebraska.* Lincoln, Nebr.: State Office of Planning and Programming, 1974.

———. *General Revenue Sharing: Promise, Performance, and Problems.* Lincoln, Nebr.: State Office of Planning and Programming, 1975.

Barnhart, J. D. "Rainfall and the Populist Party in Nebraska." *American Political Science Review* 19 (1925): 527–40.

Bigelow, Elizabeth, ed. *Essays on Unicameralism.* New York: National Municipal League, 1972.

Boots, Ralph S. "Our Legislative Mills." *National Municipal Review* 13 (1924): 111–19.

Bowman, James, and Susan Eisenhart. "Program Implementation in Nebraska: The Safe Streets Act." *Midwest Review of Public Administration* 6 (1972): 14–28.

Breckenridge, A. C. "The Mockery of Classification." *National Municipal Review* 36 (1947): 571–73.

———. "Nebraska." In Wager, Paul, ed. *County Government across the Nation.* Chapel Hill: University of North Carolina Press, 1950.

———. "Nebraska as a Pioneer in the Initiative and Referendum." *Nebraska History* 34 (1953): 215–23.

———. "Nebraska's Unicameral Legislature Threatened." *National Municipal Review* 42 (1953): 563–64.

———. "Nebraska County Government: 100 Years." *County Officer* 19 (1954): 80–88.

———. "Nebraska." In President's Commission on Intergovernmental Relations, *The Impact of Federal Grants-in-Aid on the Structure and Functions of State and Local Governments.* Washington, D.C.: Government Printing Office, 1955.

———. *One House for Two: Nebraska's Unicameral Legislature.* Washington, D.C.: Public Affairs Press, 1957.

———. "Innovation in State Government: Origin and Development of Nebraska's Nonpartisan Unicameral Legislature." *Nebraska History* 59 (1978): 31–46.

Brown, E. Phelps, and Raymond McConnell. *75 Years in the Prairie Capital.* Lincoln, Nebr.: Miller and Paine, 1975.

Brown, Vincent. *A Look at Your Unicameral.* Lincoln: Nebraska Legislature, 1973.

Burdette, Franklin. "Nebraska: A Business Corporation." *American Mercury* 34 (1935): 360–63.

———. "Nebraska Completes Unicameral Districting." *National Municipal Review* 24 (1935): 348–49.

————. "Conference Committees in the Nebraska Legislature." *American Political Science Review* 30 (1936): 1114–16.

————. "Legislative Conference Committees: Lessons from Nebraska's Bicameral Experience." *State Government* 11 (1938): 103–6.

Canaday, Ralph. "Laws Affecting Public Power Districts." *Nebraska Law Review* 42 (1963): 777–88.

Carter, Edward. "The Unicameral Legislative System." *Florida Law Journal* 21 (1947): 112–15.

Cass, Edward C. "Flood Control and the Corps of Engineers in the Missouri Valley, 1902–1973." *Nebraska History* 63 (1982): 108–22.

Cessna, R. "Nebraska: A One-House State." *Christian Science Monitor,* May 24, 1941.

Cherny, Robert W. *Populism, Progressivism, and the Transformation of Nebraska Politics, 1885–1915.* Lincoln: University of Nebraska Press, 1981.

Cochran, Robert L. "Unicameral Legislature." In *Proceedings of the National Governor's Conference,* 29th Session, 1937.

Coffey, Marilyn. *Executive Sessions in the Nebraska Legislature.* Lincoln: University of Nebraska, School of Journalism, n.d.

Comer, John C. "The Nebraska Nonpartisan Legislature: An Evaluation." *State and Local Government Review* 12 (September 1980): 98–102.

Comer, John C., and James B. Johnson, eds. *Nonpartisanship in the Legislative Process.* Washington, D.C.: University Press of America, 1978.

Comer, John C. "Street-Level Bureaucracy and Political Support: Some Findings on Mexican-Americans." *Urban Affairs Quarterly* 14 (1978): 207–27.

Condra, G. E. *Terminology Relating to the Occurrence, Behavior and Use of Water in Nebraska.* Lincoln: University of Nebraska, Conservation and Survey Division, 1944.

Copple, Neale. *Tower on the Plains: Lincoln's Centennial History, 1859–1959.* Lincoln, Nebr.: Lincoln Centennial Commission Publishers, 1959.

Cranford, Robert. *The Nebraska Press Coverage of the 1960 Presidential Campaign.* Lincoln: University of Nebraska, School of Journalism, 1964.

Council of State Governments. *Unicameral Legislation.* Lexington, Ky.: Council of State Governments, 1937.

Creigh, Dorothy Weyer. *Nebraska: A Bicentennial History.* New York: W. W. Norton, 1977.

Crosby, Robert. "Why I Want to Get Rid of My Job." *State Government* 20 (July 1947): 193–94.

Crowder, Farnsworth. "Tattle-Tale Gray on America's White Spot." *Survey*

Graphic 27 (1938): 495–501, 521, 523–25.

Cunningham, Andrew. *Nebraska Municipal Government in Action: A Comparison of Manager and Administrator Governments*. Lincoln, Nebr.: State Department of Economic Development, 1977.

D'Alemberte, Talbot, and Charles C. Fishburne. "Why a Second House?" *National Civic Review* 55 (1966): 431–37, 457.

Davies, Thomas. "The Nebraska Unicameral Legislature." *American Bar Association Journal* 38 (1952): 240–42.

Davis, Clarence. *Nebraska's Public Power Explained*. Lincoln, 1949.

Dobbins, Harry T. "A Unicameral Legislature." *Quarterly of the American Interprofessional Institute* 13 (Summer 1939): 15–19.

———. "Nebraska's One House Legislature—After Six Years." *National Municipal Review* 30 (1941): 511–14.

———. "Legislative Procedure under the Unicameral System." *University of Kansas City Law Review* 11 (1942): 31–37.

———. "Ten Year's Test of a One-House Legislature." *Greater Cleveland* 44, no. 25 (March 2, 1944): 1–2.

———. "Nebraska's Fifth Unicameral." *Nebraska History* 16 (1945): 49–52.

Dolan, Ronald J., and William B. Fenton. "The Justice of the Peace in Nebraska." *Nebraska Law Review* 48 (1969): 457–87.

Donavan, Archia. *County Government in Nebraska*. Lincoln: American Legion, Department of Nebraska, 1951.

Donovan, Ruth. "The Nebraska League of Women Voters." *Nebraska History* 52 (1971): 311–28.

Engel, B. S. "Nebraska's New Unicameral System." *Scholastic*, January 5, 1935, p. 15.

Ewing, Cortez. "Lobbying in Nebraska's Legislature." *Public Opinion Quarterly* 1 (1937): 102–4.

Firth, Robert. *Public Power in Nebraska: A Report on State Ownership*. Lincoln: University of Nebraska Press, 1962.

Fisher, Ralph; Richard Harnsberger; and Jarret Oeltjen. "Rights of Nebraska Streamflows: A Historical Overview with Recommendations." *Nebraska Law Review* 52 (1973): 313–76.

Fleming, Roscoe. "Senator Norris' Legislature: First Unicameral State Legislature." *Nation* 144 (1937): 43–44.

Frank, Bernard. "The Nebraska Public Counsel—The Ombudsman." *Cumberland-Samford Law Review* 5 (1974): 30–58.

Galliher, J. R. "Nebraska's Marijuana Law: A Case of Unexpected Legislative Innovation." *Law and Society Review* 8 (1974): 441–55.

Governor's Task Force for Government Improvement. *Summary of Findings and Recommendations*. Lincoln, Nebr.: Governor's Task Force for Government Improvement, 1980.

Gradwohl, John M. "Labor-Management Relations and Nebraska Constitutional Revision." *Nebraska Law Review* 40 (1961): 648–96.

Green, Charles. "Nebraska Launches Unicameral." *State Government* 10 (1937): 3–5.

————. "Nebraska's New Legislature Begins to Test a New Theory." *Congressional Digest* 16 (1937): 207–8.

Gubser, William. "The North Central Nebraska Resource Conservation and Development Area." In *Land Use: Tough Choices in Today's World*. Ankeny, Iowa: Soil Conservation Society of America, 1977.

Guss, M. "White Spot of the Nation: Unicameral Legislature in Nebraska." *Forum* 108 (1947): 141–44.

Haggart, Virgil. "The Case for the Nebraska Merit Plan." *Nebraska Law Review* 41 (1962): 723–45.

Hard, Anne. "Nebraska's Unicameral Plan." *Independent Woman* 14 (1935): 151.

Harder, Marvin. "Nonpartisan Elections: A Political Illusion?" In *Eagleton Institute Cases in Practical Politics*. New York: McGraw-Hill, 1960.

Harmon, Robert B. *Government and Politics in Nebraska: An Information Source Survey*. Monticello, Ill.: Vance Bibliographies, 1979.

Harnsberger, Richard. "Nebraska Ground Water Problems." *Nebraska Law Review* 42 (1963): 721–64.

————. "Eminent Domain and Water Law." *Nebraska Law Review* 48 (1969): 325–455.

Harnsberger, Richard; Jarret Oeltjen; and Ralph Fischer. "Ground Water: From Windmills to Comprehensive Public Management." *Nebraska Law Review* 50 (1972): 179–292.

Henzlik, F. E., and Leslie L. Chisholm. *Nebraska Looks at Her School Districts*. Lincoln: University of Nebraska Press, 1948.

Hopkins, Anne; George Rawson; and Russell Smith. *Individuals, Unionization, and Job Satisfaction: A Comparative Study*. Knoxville: Bureau of Public Administration, University of Tennessee, 1976.

Hutchinson, Duane. *Exon: Biography of a Governor*. Lincoln, Nebr.: Foundation Books, 1971.

Janney, Richard. "Home Rule Charters in Nebraska." *Creighton Law Review* 5 (1971): 98–116.

Janson, Donald. "The House Nebraska Built." *Harper's Magazine,* November, 1964, pp. 125–30.

Johnson, Alvin W. *The Unicameral Legislature.* Minneapolis: University of Minnesota Press, 1938.

———. "Unicameralism Marks Time," *State Government* 12 (1939): 101–3, 108.

Johnson, Forrest. "The Nebraska Constitution and Taxation." *Nebraska Law Review* 40 (1961): 733–39.

Johnson, William E. "Unicameralism Works." *State Government* 12 (1939): 197–98, 207.

Jones, Lonnie, and Larry Morgan. "Consumer Responses to Rural Public Service Problems in Great Plains States." In *National Conference on Nonmetropolitan Community Services Research.* Washington, D.C.: Government Printing Office, 1977.

King, Judson. "Nebraska, the Public Power State." *Public Utilities Fortnightly* 39 (1947): 483–88.

Kolasa, Bernard. "Lobbying in the Nonpartisan Environment: The Case of Nebraska." *Western Political Quarterly* 24 (1971): 65–78.

Lamphear, F. Charles, and Theodore Roesler. *Impact Analysis of Irrigated Agriculture on Nebraska's Economy, 1967–1970.* Lincoln: University of Nebraska, Bureau of Business Research, 1974.

Lancaster, Lane. "Nebraska Considers a One-House Legislature." *National Municipal Review* 23 (1934): 373–76, 382.

———. "Nebraska Adopts Single-Chambered Legislature." *National Municipal Review* 23 (1934): 695–96.

———. "Nebraska Prunes Her Legislature." *Current History* 41 (1935): 434–36.

———. "Nebraska's New Legislature." *Minnesota Law Review* 22 (1937): 60–76.

———. "Nebraska's Experience with a One-House Legislature." *University of Kansas City Law Review* 11 (1942): 24–30.

———. "Nebraska Adopts Merit System, School Retirement Plan." *National Municipal Review* 35 (1945): 339–40.

League of Women Voters of Lincoln–Lancaster County. *A Handbook of Government: Lincoln and Lancaster County, Nebraska.* Lincoln, Nebr.: League of Women Voters of Lincoln–Lancaster County, 1978.

League of Women Voters of Nebraska. *Nebraska State Government.* 3d rev. ed. Lincoln: League of Women Voters of Nebraska, 1972.

———. *The Planning Process for Use of Land in Nebraska.* Lincon: League of Women Voters of Nebraska, n.d.

Lindeen, James. "Intra-State Sectionalism: Nebraska Presidential Election Behavior, 1916–1968." *Western Political Quarterly* 24 (1971): 540–48.

————. "Sectionalism and Nebraska Presidential Politics." *Nebraska History* 54 (1973): 647–55.

Luebke, Frederick. *Immigrants and Politics: The Germans of Nebraska, 1880–1900*. Lincoln: University of Nebraska Press, 1969.

McKibbin, Carroll. "Politics of Public Higher Education: Nebraska." *AAUP Bulletin* 59 (1973): 293–98.

McKibbin, Carroll, and Peter Shocket. *County Officials of Central Nebraska: Attitudes and Attributes*. Lincoln, Nebr.: State Department of Economic Development, 1974.

McPartland, Edward. *Measuring and Developing Methods of Attitude and Motivational Change in Implementing the Big Blue River Basin Water Plan*. Crete, Nebr.: Doane College, 1973.

Marsh, William. "The Rights of a Public Employee in Nebraska." *Nebraska Law Review* 46 (1967): 884–901.

Marvel, Richard. "The Nonpartisan Nebraska Unicameral." In Samuel Patterson, ed. *Midwest Legislative Politics*. Iowa City: Institute of Public Affairs, University of Iowa, 1967.

————. "A Member Looks at the Nebraska Unicameral." *State Government* 42 (1969): 147–55.

Marvel, Richard; Robert Parsons; Winn Sanderson; and N. Dale Wright. "Legislative Intent and Oversight: Nebraska's Experience in Higher Education." *State Government* 49 (1976): 39–42.

Mertens, Marilyn. *Analysis of Cooperation between the University of Nebraska–Lincoln and Nebraska State Government*. Lincoln: Bureau of Business Research, University of Nebraska, 1975.

Meyer, Clarence. "State Taxation in Nebraska." *Nebraska Law Review* 343 (1954): 332–65.

Miewald, Robert. "Special District Government: The Case in Rural Nebraska." *Midwest Review of Public Administration* 8 (1974): 231–40.

Miewald, Robert, and John C. Comer. "The Nebraska Ombudsman: An American Pioneer," in Gerald Caiden, ed. *The Ombudsman: An International Handbook*. Westport, Conn.: Greenwood Press, 1983.

Miller, C. S. *Nebraska State Finances*. Chicago: Council of State Governments, 1950.

Moreland, Willis. *Guide to Nebraska County Government*. Lincoln, Nebr.: Department of Economic Development, 1978.

Morgan, Robert. "A New Voice in Government: The Watershed District." *State Government* 26 (1953): 288–90.

Morrison, Frank, and Richard Shugrue. "Streamlining the Executive in Nebraska." *Nebraska Law Review* 40 (1961): 634–47.

Moschos, Demitrios, and David Katsky. "Unicameralism and Bicameralism: History and Tradition." *Boston University Law Review* 45 (1965): 250–70.

Nebraska Blue Book. Lincoln: Nebraska Legislative Council, published biennially.

Nebraska Citizens Council. *The General Administration of Nebraska County Government*. Lincoln: Nebraska Citizens Council, 1956.

Nebraska Constitutional Revision Commission. *Report*. Lincoln: Nebraska Constitutional Revision Commission, September 1970.

———. *Minutes*. 3 vols. Lincoln: Nebraska Constitutional Revision Commission, 1970.

Nebraska Management Analysis Study Committee. *Nebraska Survey and Recommendations*. Lincoln: Nebraska Management Analysis Study Committee, 1968.

Nebraska Soil and Water Conservation Commission. *Modernization of Resource District Legislation*. Lincoln: Nebraska Soil and Water Conservation Commission, 1969.

"Nebraska's Unicameral Adjourns: The Session in Retrospect." *State Government* 10 (1937): 131–34.

Nemeth, Sharon. *An Idea Becomes Law in Nebraska*. Lincoln, Nebr.: League of Women Voters, 1977.

Norris, George. "One Branch Legislature for States Would Improve Results." *New York Times,* January 28, 1923, sect. 8, p. 1.

———. "The Model Legislature." *Congressional Record,* February 27, 1934, vol. 78, pt. 3, 3276–80.

———. "Nebraska's One-House Legislative System." *Congressional Record,* February 7, 1935, vol. 79, pt. 2, 1635–37.

———. "Only One House." *State Government* 7 (1934): 209–10.

———. "One-House Legislature for More Efficient Legislation." *Literary Digest,* October 13, 1934, p. 8.

———. "The One-House Legislature." *Annals of the American Academy of Political and Social Science* 181 (1935): 50–58.

———. "The One-House Legislature." *National Municipal Review* 24 (1935): 87–89, 99.

Oeltjen, Jarret; Richard Harnsberger; and Ralph Fischer. "Interbasin Transfer: Nebraska Law and Legend." *Nebraska Law Review* 51 (1971): 87–146.

Office of Planning and Programming. *A Guide to Nebraska Land Develop-*

ment Law. Lincoln, Nebr.: Office of Planning and Programming, 1973.

————. *A Guide to Survey of Planning Activities in Nebraska Communities*. Lincoln, Nebr.: Office of Planning and Programming, 1973.

————. *Nebraska Regions*. Lincoln, Nebr.: Office of Planning and Programming, 1974.

Olson, James C. *History of Nebraska*. Lincoln: University of Nebraska Press, 1966.

"The One-House Legislature." *Greater Cleveland* 17 (1937): 49–52.

Orfield, Lester B. "The Unicameral Legislature in Nebraska." *Michigan Law Review* 343 (1935): 26–36.

Ottoson, Howard; Eleanor Birch; Philip Henderson; and A. H. Anderson. *Land and People in the Northern Plains Transition Area*. Lincoln: University of Nebraska Press, 1966.

Paul, Justus. "Isolationism versus Internationalism? The Republican Senatorial Primary in Nebraska, 1946." *Nebraska History* 56 (1975): 145–56.

————. "Butler, Griswold, Wherry: The Struggle for Domination of Nebraska Republicanism: 1941–1946." *North Dakota Quarterly* 43 (1975): 5–25.

————. *Senator Hugh Butler and Nebraska Republicanism*. Lincoln: Nebraska State Historical Society, 1976.

Pedersen, James, and Kenneth D. Wald. *Shall the People Rule? A History of the Democratic Party in Nebraska Politics, 1854–1972*. Lincoln, Nebr.: J. North, 1973.

Peirce, Neal. "Nebraska." In *The Great Plains States of America: People, Politics, and Power in the Nine Great Plains States*. New York: W. W. Norton, 1973.

Penstone, Giles. "Public Power Districts and Cooperatives: The Contribution to Rural Electrification." *Nebraska Law Review* 30 (1951): 442–67.

Peterson, Everett; Jack Timmons; and Fred Olson. *Nebraska Taxes*. Lincoln: University of Nebraska Extension Service, 1962.

Peterson, C. Petrus. "The Legislature and the Press." *State Government* 27 (1954): 223–25.

Powers, Mary. "The Right to Privacy in Nebraska." *Creighton Law Review* 13 (1980): 935–53.

Reichley, James. "Nebraska: Sons of the Pioneers." In Reichley, *States in Crisis: Politics in Ten American States*. Chapel Hill: University of North Carolina Press, 1964.

Riley, William. "Nonpartisan Unicameral—Benefits, Defects, Re-examined."

Nebraska Law Review 52 (1973): 377–403.

Rodgers, Jack W. "One House for 20 Years." *National Municipal Review* 46 (1957): 338–42, 347.

Rodine, Floyd. "The County Agent and the Nebraska Farm Bureau." *Nebraska History* 36 (1955): 205–12.

Sample, Steven B., and Eugene P. Trani. "The Foreign Policy of Nebraska." *Washington Quarterly* 3 (Summer 1980): 60–71.

Schmidt, Benno. "The Nebraska Decision." *Columbia Journalism Review* 15 (November–December 1976): 51–53.

Schmidt, Edward B. *County Consolidation: Relation of Size of Counties to the Cost of County Government in Nebraska.* Lincoln: College of Business Administration, University of Nebraska, 1934.

Schmidt, Edward B. *An Appraisal of the Nebraska Tax System.* Lincoln: University of Nebraska, 1941.

Schroeder, William R. *Project Report for Nebraska.* Lincoln, Nebr.: Great Plains School District Organization Project, 1968.

Schudel, Paul and Marcia Strand. *Goals for Nebraska: Statewide Attitude Survey.* Lincoln, Nebr.: State Department of Economic Development, 1972.

Scott, David. *Understanding Nebraska Municipal Finance.* Lincoln, Nebr.: Department of Economic Development, 1975.

Senning, John P. "The One-House Legislature in Nebraska." *Nebraska Law Bulletin* 13 (1935): 341–50.

———. "Nebraska Provides for a One-House Legislature." *American Political Science Review* 29 (1935): 69–74.

———. *The One-House Legislature in Nebraska.* Lincoln, Nebr.: Legislative Reference Bureau, 1935.

———. *The One-House Legislature.* New York: McGraw-Hill, 1937.

———. "Nebraska's One-House Legislature." *Southwestern Social Science Quarterly* 18 (1937): 115–25.

———. "Nebraska's Experience in Setting Up a One-House Legislature." *New Mexico Business Review* 6 (1937): 12–20.

———. "Nebraska's First Unicameral Legislative Session." *Annals of the American Academy of Political and Social Science* 195 (1938): 159–67.

———. "One House, Two Sessions." *National Municipal Review* 28 (1939): 843–47.

———. "Constitutional Essentials for a Unicameral Legislature." *University of Kansas City Law Review* 11 (1942): 10–15.

———. "Unicameralism Passes Test." *National Municipal Review* 33 (1944): 60–65.

Sheldon, A. E. "Unicameral Legislature." *Nebraska History* 19 (1938): 246–47.

———. *Nebraska Civil Government.* Lincoln, Nebr.: University Publishing Company, 1946.

Shocket, Peter. *Some Systemic Influences on Rural Regional Consolidation: A Case Study of Two Planning and Development Regions in Central Nebraska.* Lincoln, Nebr.: State Department of Economic Development, 1974.

Shocket, Peter, and Barbara Leigh Smith. *Regional Integration: A Guide for Community Development Specialists.* Lincoln, Nebr.: State Department of Economic Development, 1975.

Shumate, Roger V. *Local Government in Nebraska.* Lincoln: Nebraska Legislative Council, 1939.

———. "The Nebraska Unicameral Legislature." *Western Political Quarterly* 5 (1952): 504–12.

Simmons, Ray. "A Constitutional Convention Is Neither Needed nor Desirable." *Nebraska Law Review* 40 (1961): 604–20.

"The Single House Legislature: Nebraska Adopts the Unicameral Principle by Big Majority." *Greater Cleveland* 10 (1934): 41–42.

Sittig, Robert F. "Unicameralism in Nebraska, 1936–1966." *State Government* 40 (1967): 38–41.

———. "The Governmental Sector of the Economy." In Richard Lonsdale, ed. *Economic Atlas of Nebraska.* Lincoln: University of Nebraska Press, 1976.

———. "Presidential Primary Reform: The 1948 Nebraska 'All-Star' Primary." *Nebraska History* 60 (1979): 499–519.

———. "Unicameralism and the Nebraska Experience." *Parliamentary Journal* 21 (October 1980): 38–43.

———. "Legislative Apportionment in Nebraska." In Hardy, Leroy; Alan Heslop; and Stuart Anderson, eds. *Reapportionment Politics: The History of Redistricting in the 50 States.* Beverly Hills, Calif.: Sage, 1981.

Sobel, Robert, and John Raimo, eds. *Biographical Directory of Governors of the United States, 1789–1978.* 4 vols. Westport, Conn.: Meckler Books, 1978, 3:889–918.

Spencer, Richard C. "Unicameralism: Milepost—Not Destination." *University of Kansas City Law Review* 11 (1942): 16–23.

———. "Nebraska Idea Is 15 Years Old." *National Municipal Review* 39 (1950): 83–96.

———. "Highest Score Sheet." *National Municipal Review* 46 (1957): 502–5, 510.

———. "Nebraska Unicameral Operates Smoothly." *National Civic Review* 50 (1961): 424–25.

Srb, Hugo F. *Brief Comparison of the Bicameral and Unicameral Legislative Systems and Rules and Laws Governing Their Operation in Nebraska.* Lincoln: Nebraska Legislature, 1959.

———. "The Unicameral Legislature—A Successful Innovation." *Nebraska Law Review* 40 (1961): 626–33.

Steinman, Michael. "Low-Income and Minority Group Participation in Administrative Processes." *Urban Affairs Quarterly* 11 (1976): 523–44.

Stephen, Kenneth, and Richard Wegener. "Financing Public Education: Recent Developments and the Outlook for Nebraska." *Nebraska Law Review* 52 (1972): 77–157.

Stoner, John E. *Interlocal Governmental Cooperation: A Study of Five States.* Agricultural Economic Report No. 118. Washington, D.C.: U.S. Department of Agriculture, 1967.

Strand, Marcia, and Paul Schudel. *Goals for Nebraska: Analysis of State Plans.* Lincoln, Nebr.: Department of Economic Development, 1972.

Stromer, Marvin E. *The Making of a Political Leader: Kenneth S. Wherry and the United States Senate.* Lincoln: University of Nebraska Press, 1969.

Summers, Harrison. *Unicameralism in Practice: The Nebraska Legislative System.* New York: H. W. Wilson, 1937.

———, comp. *Unicameral Legislatures.* New York: H. W. Wilson, 1937.

Sweet, Fred. "School District Reorganization: Nebraska's Continuing Problem." *Nebraska Law Review* 46 (1967): 844–61.

Talcott, Stanley. "Amending the Nebraska Constitution in the 1971 Legislature." *Nebraska Law Review* 50 (1971): 676–91.

Thone, Charles. "A Constitutional Convention: The Best Step for Nebraska." *Nebraska Law Review* 40 (1961): 596–603.

Turner, George. "History and Commentary on the Judicial Article." *Nebraska Law Review* 40 (1961): 621–25.

"Unicameral Nebraska." *Economist* 214 (1965): 892–94.

"The Unicameral System of Legislation." *Congressional Digest* 16 (1937): 193–224.

University of Nebraska, Department of Political Science. *A Citizen's Guide to Running for Political Office.* Lincoln: University of Nebraska, Political Science Department, 1974.

University of Nebraska, School of Journalism. *Nebraska's Unicameral.* Rev. ed. Lincoln: University of Nebraska, School of Journalism, 1970.

———. *Prairie Paradox: Nebraska, Its Politics.* Lincoln: University of Nebraska, School of Journalism, 1966.

Wagaman, David. "The Evolution of Some Legal-Economic Aspects of Collective Bargaining by Public Employees in Nebraska since 1919." *Nebraska History* 58 (1977): 475–89.

Welch, Susan. "Identity with the Ethnic Political Community and Political Behavior: A Research Note on Some Mexican-Americans." *Ethnicity* 4 (1977): 216–25.

Welch, Susan, and James Bowman. "The Nonpartisan Legislature: Does It Affect Political Careers?" *National Civic Review* 61 (1972), 451–56.

Welch, Susan, and Eric Carlson. "The Public and the Campus: A View from Two Communities." *Social Science Quarterly* 53 (1972): 544–56.

Welch, Susan. "Impact of Party on Voting Behavior in a Nonpartisan Legislature." *American Political Science Review* 67 (1973): 854–67.

Welch, Susan, and John C. Comer. "Neb. Legislature Not Well Known." *National Civic Review* 68 (1979): 488–89.

Wesser, Robert. "George W. Norris: The Unicameral Legislature and the Progressive Ideal." *Nebraska History* 45 (1965): 309–21.

Willborn, Steven A. "A Time for Change: A Critical Analysis of the Nebraska Administrative Procedure Act." *Nebraska Law Review* 60 (1981): 1–34.

Winter, A. B. "Municipal Home Rule: A Progress Report?" *Nebraska Law Review* 36 (1957): 447–471.

———. "Home Rule Neglected," *National Municipal Review* 47 (1958): 451–56.

———. "A Critique of School District Reorganization in Nebraska." *Nebraska Law Review* 37 (1958): 736–80.

———. "Constitutional Revision in Nebraska: A Brief History and Commentary" *Nebraska Law Review* 40 (1961): 580–95.

———. *The Holdrege Story: A Case Study of Interlocal Governmental Cooperation*. Lincoln: League of Nebraska Municipalities, 1965.

———. "Nebraska's 'Truth in Politics' Law: A Short-Lived Experiment in Curbing Campaign Calumny." *Journal of Constitutional and Parliamentary Studies* 7 (1973): 20–37.

———. *Understanding Nebraska Municipal Government*. Lincoln, Nebr.: State Department of Economic Development, 1975.

———. "Nebraska Home Rule: The Record and Some Recommendations." *Nebraska Law Review* 59 (1980): 601–30.

Wyner, Alan. *The Nebraska Ombudsman: Innovation in State Government*. Berkeley: University of California, Institute of Governmental Studies, 1974.

———. "Complaint Resolution: Citizens, Bureaucrats, and the Ombudsman."

Nebraska Law Review 54 (1975): 1–26.

Yeutter, Clayton. "A Legal-Economic Critique of Nebraska Watercourse Law." *Nebraska Law Review* 44 (1965): 11–62.

Zabel, Orville. *God and Caesar in Nebraska: A Study of the Legal Relationship of Church and State, 1854–1954.* University of Nebraska Studies, New Series, no. 14. Lincoln: University of Nebraska, 1955.

Zimring, Franklin. "Punishment and Deterrence: Bad Checks in Nebraska—A Study in Complex Threats." In Greenberg, David F., ed. *Corrections and Punishment.* Beverly Hills, Calif.: Sage, 1977.

B. NASIS Surveys

The Nebraska Annual Social Indicators Survey (NASIS) is sponsored by the Sociology Department of the University of Nebraska–Lincoln. Since 1977, annual statewide telephone surveys have been conducted in order to measure the attitudes of Nebraskans toward a variety of policy issues. Brief reports summarizing the findings are available from the Bureau of Sociological Research, University of Nebraska, Lincoln, Nebraska, 68588.

1977

No. 1. Booth, Alan. *Nebraska, the Good Life: A Comparison of the State and the Nation.*

No. 2. Johnson, David. *Who Enjoys the Good Life in Nebraska? Determinants of Perceived Quality of Life.*

No. 3. White, Lynn. *Fertility in Nebraska: Current Trends and Prospects.*

No. 4. Welch, Susan, and Alan Booth. *Nebraskans and Their Natural Environment.*

No. 6. Booth, Alan. *The Quality of Life of Nebraska's Elderly—A Paradox.*

No. 7. White, Lynn. *Marriage and Divorce in Nebraska.*

No. 8. Booth, Alan. *Tax Supported Income Supplements and Nebraska's Poor.*

No. 9. Whitt, Hugh. *The Religious Situation in Nebraska.*

No. 10. Whitt, Hugh. *Ethnic Identification in Nebraska.*

No. 11. Welch, Susan. *Nebraskans and Their Political Participation.*

1978

No. 1. Booth, Alan, and Susan Welch. *More for Less: Nebraskans and State Government Programs.*

No.2. Welch, Susan, and John Comer. *Nebraskans and Their Legislature: Part I—Information.*

No.3. Comer, John, and Susan Welch. *Nebraskans and Their Legislature: Part II—Evaluation.*

No.5. White, Lynn, and Alan Booth. *Rural-Urban Differences in Nebraska: Debunking a Myth.*

No.6. Booth, Alan, and David Johnson. *The State of the State in 1978: A Report from the Nebraska Annual Social Indicators Survey.*

No.7. White, Lynn. *Nebraskans on the Move.*

No.8. Williams, J. Allen. *Nebraska's Ethnic Heritage.*

No.9. White, Lynn. *Congressional District and Planning Region Databook for the State of Nebraska.*

No.10. Williams, Steve, and Lynn White. *Nebraska's Crime Victims.*

No.11. Booth, Alan, and Kathleen Foote. *Fun and Games—Nebraskans and the Great Outdoors.*

1979

No.2. Welch, Susan, and Alan Booth. *Taxes: Are They Fair?*

No.3. White, Lynn. *Nebraska's Children—Learning to Work.*

No.4. Booth, Alan, and Susan Welch. *Nebraskans' Evaluations of Their State Government.*

No.5. Welch, Susan, and Gordon Kissel. *Nebraskans and State Water Policy: Part I.*

No.6. White, Lynn, and Nikolai Rudakov. *Voluntary Household Conservation in Nebraska.*

No.7. Welch, Susan, and Gordon Kissel. *Nebraskans and State Water Policy: Part II.*

No.8. Beeson, Peter, and Alan Booth. *Nebraskans and Their Mental Health.*

No.9. Whitt, Hugh, and J. Allen Williams. *Nebraska's Multiple Melting Pot.*

No.10. Williams, J. Allen, and Alan Booth. *Employed Wives and Marital Adjustment.*

No.11. Sallee, David, and Alan Booth, *In Sickness and in Health.*

1980

No.2. Welch, Susan, and Alan Booth. *Status of Women in Nebraska.*

No.3. White, Lynn. *Congressional District and Planning Region Databook for the State of Nebraska.*

No.4. Welch, Susan, and Alan Booth. *Nebraskans and Their Local Government.*

No.5. White, Lynn. *Migration in Nebraska: Movers and Stayers, 1977–79.*

No.6. Brinkerhoff, David, and Alan Booth. *Nebraskans and Their University.*

No.7. Moore, Helen. *Nebraskans and Educational Pluralism.*

No.8. Welch, Susan. *Nebraskans and State Water Policy: An Update.*

No.9. Welch, Susan. *Food for Thought: Nebraskans' Views on the Food Tax and Other State and Local Taxes.*

No.10. Booth, Alan, and Lynn White. *Nebraskans View the Recession.*

No.11. Eells, Laurie. *The Good Life: Smaller Is Better.*

No.12. White, Lynn. *Public Opinion and the Public Schools.*

1981

No.2. Welch, Susan. *Nebraskans' Interest in Government and Politics.*

No.3. White, Lynn, and David Brinkerhoff. *The Political Consequences of the "Age of Limits."*

No.4. Moore, Helen, and Miguel Carranza. *Nebraskans and Public Welfare.*

No.5. Booth, Alan. *Housing and Attitudes toward the Community.*

No.6. Booth, Alan. *Nebraskans and Their Natural Environment: Four Years Later.*

No.7. White, Lynn, and Peter Beeson, *The Mental Health Status of Nebraskans.*

No.8. Carranza, Miguel, and Helen Moore. *Independence and Institutions: Living Situations for Mentally Handicapped Citizens in Nebraska.*

No.9. Carranza, Miguel, and Helen Moore. *Juvenile Offenders: Public Attitudes toward Appropriate Placements.*

No. 11. Miewald, Robert, and John Comer. *Nebraska and the State Ombudsman.*

C. Theses and Dissertations

Appel, Stephen. "Substantive Due Process in Federal and State Courts: A Study in Contrasts." Master's thesis, University of Nebraska–Lincoln, Department of Political Science, 1970.

Arnot, Marie. "For Better or Worse? Nebraska's Demeanant Correctional System." Master's thesis, University of Nebraska–Lincoln, Department of Political Science, 1970.

Bain, Edgar. "A Study of the Principle of Bicameralism versus Unicameralism." Master's thesis, University of Illinois–Urbana, Department of Political Science, 1941.

Bennett, Gary. "A Study of Court-Ordered Desegregation in the School District of Omaha, Nebraska, 1972–1977." Ed. D. dissertation, University of Nebraska–Lincoln, Department of Educational Administration, 1979.

Bothun, Douglas. "Determinants of State Budgeting Change in Nebraska, 1955–1976." Ph.D. dissertation, University of Nebraska–Lincoln, Department of Political Science, 1978.

Capek, David. "Non-decision-making in Environmental Politics: A Case Study of Groundwater Politics in Nebraska." Ph.D. dissertation, University of Nebraska–Lincoln, Department of Political Science, 1977.

Cassel, Myrna. "An Analysis of Public Knowledge and Opinions of Locally Elected Boards of Education of Nebraska Public Schools and Technical Community College Areas." Ed. D. dissertation, University of Nebraska–Lincoln, Department of Educational Administration, 1979.

Carter, John. "The Role and Influence of the Republican National Party Organization in Mid-Term Elections, with Special Reference to Colorado and Nebraska." Master's thesis, University of Nebraska–Lincoln, Department of Political Science, 1963.

Chai, Yong-wha. "The Nebraska State Railway Commission, Its Organization and Administration." Master's thesis, University of Nebraska–Lincoln, Department of Political Science, 1962.

Clem, Alan. "Analysis of the 1958 Congressional Campaign in the Third District of Nebraska." Ph.D. dissertation, American University, Washington, D.C., 1960.

Cook, David. "User Charges in Nebraska." Master's thesis, University of Nebraska–Lincoln, Department of Political Science, 1980.

Decker, Louis. "Federal Grants-in-Aid in Nebraska." Master's thesis, University of Nebraska–Lincoln, Department of Political Science, 1946.

Despotovich, Sam. "The Merit System in the States with Special Reference to Nebraska." Master's thesis, University of Nebraska–Lincoln, Department of Political Science, 1951.

Dewey, Ellen. "The Procedural Revolution in the Lincoln Public Schools." Master's thesis, University of Nebraska–Lincoln, Department of Political Science, 1964.

Dobberstein, Arthur. "The Nebraska State Patrol." Master's thesis, University of Nebraska–Lincoln, Department of Political Science, 1971.

Donaldson, Sandy. "The Executive Removal Power in Regard to the Classified Civil Service." Master's thesis, University of Nebraska–Lincoln,

Department of Political Science, 1965.

Douglas, Louis. "The Development of Public Policies in Water Use in the West." Ph.D. dissertation, University of Nebraska–Lincoln, Department of Political Science, 1950.

Doyle, John. "Public Highway Administration in Nebraska." Master's thesis, University of Nebraska–Lincoln, Department of Political Science, 1951.

Henderson, Sidney. "A Post-War Political History of Nebraska: An Examination of the Voting Trends and the Underlying Explanations, 1946–1960." Master's thesis, George Washington University, Washington, D.C., Department of Political Science, 1964.

Hoffman, Kenneth. "The Role of the Administration in the Formulation and Implementation of Public Welfare Policy." Master's thesis, University of Nebraska–Lincoln, Department of Political Science, 1948.

Huntington, William. "An Analysis of Democratic Voter-Leakage in Douglas County." Master's thesis, University of Nebraska–Lincoln, Department of Political Science, 1972.

Jenkins, John. "Citizen's Complaints in the City of Lincoln." Master's thesis, University of Nebraska–Lincoln, Department of Political Science, 1970.

Johnson, James. "The Nebraska Legislative System: Legislative Roles in a Nonpartisan Setting." Ph.D. dissertation, Northwestern University, Evanston, Illinois, Department of Political Science, 1972.

Johnson, Virginia. "One Link in Civic Education." Master's thesis, University of Nebraska–Lincoln, Department of Political Science, 1967.

Kelley, William. "Extremist Politics in Nebraska: A Study of the John Birch Society, the Nebraska School Improvement Association, and George Wallace's American Party." Ph.D. dissertation, University of Nebraska–Lincoln, Department of Political Science, 1973.

Kolasa, Bernard. "The Nebraska Political System: A Study in Apartisan Politics." Ph.D. dissertation, University of Nebraska–Lincoln, Department of Political Science, 1968.

Larson, Gale. "An Assessment of Changing the Revenue Source for Nebraska Public Schools from Property Tax to Sales-Tax Income." Ed. D. dissertation, University of Northern Colorado, Greeley, Department of Education, 1980.

Layman, Marian. "A Case Study of the Citizen Participatory Groups in Lincoln–Lancaster County Governments." Master's thesis, University of Nebraska–Lincoln, Department of Political Science, 1976.

Lux, John. "Administrative Reorganization of the State Government of Nebraska." Master's thesis, University of Nebraska–Lincoln, Department of Political Science, 1951.

McClurg, Verne. "Political Influences upon Administrative Decision-Makers in Local Law Enforcement." Ph.D. dissertation, University of Nebraska–Lincoln, Department of Political Science, 1980.

McPartland, Edward. "A Study of Rural-Urban Conflict in the Nebraska Legislature." Ph.D. dissertation, University of Nebraska–Lincoln, Department of Political Science, 1970.

Marvel, Richard. "The Factor of Sex in Politics: A Case Study." Master's thesis, University of Nebraska–Lincoln, Department of Political Science, 1960.

Marvel, Richard. "Decision-Making in the Nebraska Unicameral Legislature for the 1959, 1961, and 1963 Sessions." Ph.D. dissertation, University of Nebraska–Lincoln, 1966.

Massey, Roger. "Effects of Non-Partisan Unicameral in the Seeking of a High Partisan Office: Case Study of State Senator Ross H. Rasmussen's Bid for Lieutenant Governor of Nebraska." Master's thesis, University of Nebraska–Lincoln, Department of Political Science, 1972.

Mertens, Marilyn. "New Federalism's Tool: Revenue Sharing in Nebraska Municipalities." Ph.D. dissertation, University of Nebraska–Lincoln, Department of Political Science, 1974.

Mitchell, Marion. "A Survey of the Nebraska Board of Control." Master's thesis, University of Nebraska–Lincoln, Department of Political Science, 1949.

Oberg, John. "Government Policies and Their Application in an American Indian Community." Master's thesis, University of Nebraska–Lincoln, Department of Political Science, 1966.

Olson, Harold. "Federal-State Cooperative Financing of Public Programs in Nebraska." Ph.D. dissertation, University of Nebraska–Lincoln, Department of Political Science, 1953.

Plummer, Dean. "The Development of State-Wide Law Enforcement in Nebraska: The Nebraska Safety Patrol." Master's thesis, University of Nebraska–Lincoln, Department of Political Science, 1955.

Reilly, Mary. "The Standing Committees in the Nebraska Legislature, 1929–1953." Master's thesis, Pennsylvania State University, University Park, Department of Political Science, 1962.

Scheele, Paul. "State Convention and State Primary." Master's thesis, University of Nebraska–Lincoln, Department of Political Science, 1962.

Scheele, Paul. "Regional Development Politics in the Missouri Basin." Ph.D. dissertation, University of Nebraska–Lincoln, Department of Political Science, 1969.

Shugrue, Richard. "Politics and Prayer: The Search for a National Consensus." Ph.D. dissertation, University of Nebraska–Lincoln, Department of Political Science, 1968.

Smith, Loran. "Advisory Opinions and the Nebraska Attorney General." Ph.D. dissertation, University of Nebraska–Lincoln, Department of Political Science, 1980.

Spicer, Belva. "State Administrative Supervision of County Government in Nebraska." Master's thesis, University of Nebraska–Lincoln, Department of Political Science, 1946.

Sternhell, Robert. "Negro Leadership in Omaha." Master's thesis, University of Nebraska–Lincoln, Department of Political Science, 1967.

Stone, David. "Politics and Elites in Nebraska, 1890–1895." Master's thesis, University of Nebraska–Lincoln, Department of Political Science, 1968.

Stromer, Marvin. "Congressional Redistricting in Nebraska, 1961." Master's thesis, University of Nebraska–Lincoln, Department of Political Science, 1962.

Stromer, Marvin. "The Making of a Political Leader: Kenneth S. Wherry and the United States Senate." Ph.D. dissertation, University of Nebraska–Lincoln, Department of Political Science, 1966.

Swartz, Frederick. "The Influence of Senator Norris in the Formation of the Public Power Idea." Master's thesis, University of Nebraska–Lincoln, Department of Political Science, 1961.

Timmons, Jackie. "The Nebraska Department of Aeronautics: Aviation Regulation and Promotion." Master's thesis, University of Nebraska–Lincoln, Department of Political Science, 1962.

Timmons, Jackie. "Development and Utilization of Multipurpose Watershed Districts." Ph.D. dissertation, University of Nebraska–Lincoln, Department of Political Science, 1972.

Wade, Harry. "Descriptive Analysis of Nebraska's Unicameral." Ph.D. dissertation, University of Kansas, Lawrence, Department of Political Science, 1969.

Wright, Mary. "Primary Election Laws in Nebraska." Master's thesis, University of Nebraska–Lincoln, Department of Political Science, 1967.

Zobin, Joseph. "Gag Orders and the First Amendment: The Legal Path to *Nebraska Press Association v. Stuart* (1970)." Ph.D. dissertation, University of Wisconsin–Madison, Department of Political Science, 1978.

Index